The One-State Condition

Stanford Studies in Middle Eastern and Islamic Societies and Cultures

The One-State Condition

OCCUPATION AND DEMOCRACY IN ISRAEL/PALESTINE

Ariella Azoulay and Adi Ophir

Translated by Tal Haran

Stanford University Press
Stanford, California

Stanford University Press
Stanford, California

A longer version of this work was originally published in Hebrew in 2008 under the title
Mishtar zeh she'eno ehad: kibush ve'demokratyah ben ha'yam la'nahar [This Regime That Is Not
One: Occupation and Democracy Between the Sea and the River] © 2008, Resling, Tel Aviv.

Financial support for the translation was provided by the Duke University Center for
International Studies.

Library of Congress Cataloging-in-Publication Data

Azoulay, Ariella, author.
  [Mishtar zeh she-eno ehad. English]
  The one-state condition : occupation and democracy in Israel/Palestine / Ariella Azoulay and
Adi Ophir ; translated by Tal Haran.
      pages cm.--(Stanford studies in Middle Eastern and Islamic societies and cultures)
  Abridged translation of: Mishtar zeh she-eno ehad : kibush ve-demokratyah ben ha-yam
la-nahar (1967-).
  Includes bibliographical references and index.
  ISBN 978-0-8047-7591-5 (cloth : alk. paper)--ISBN 978-0-8047-7592-2 (pbk. : alk. paper)
  1. Arab-Israeli conflict--1993---Influence. 2. Israel--Politics and government--1967-1993.
3. Israel--Politics and government--1993- 4. Palestinian Arabs--Government policy--Israel.
5. Democracy--Israel. 6. Military occupation--Social aspects--West Bank. 7. Military
occupation--Social aspects--Gaza Strip. 8. Israel-Arab War, 1967--Occupied territories.
I. Ophir, Adi, author. II. Title. III. Series: Stanford studies in Middle Eastern and Islamic
societies and cultures.
  DS119.76.A9813 2012
  956.95'3044--dc23   2012022025

Typeset by Bruce Lundquist in 10/14 Minion

CONTENTS

ACKNOWLEDGMENTS

This book has been co-authored in the fullest sense of the word. It is a product of living together through some of the history it describes and of many years of joint study, research, writing, and rewriting, which continued after the publication of the Hebrew edition in 2008.

Along the way, we have greatly benefited from other research projects: Ariella Azoulay's research for creating two photographic archives, "Act of State, 1967–2007" (first exhibited in Tel Aviv in June 2007) and "From Palestine to Israel, 1947–1950" (first exhibited in Tel Aviv in April 2009 as "Constituent Violence, 1947–1950"); the individual and collective research produced by members of The Politics of Humanitarianism in the Occupied Palestinian Territories, a research group directed by Michal Givoni under the auspices of the Van Leer Jerusalem Institute. Meetings with experts and officials working in the Occupied Territories, and the discussion and studies presented in the group's meetings, have left more traces in the present book than its notes could possibly reflect.

We wish to thank Sari Hanafi for friendly intellectual exchange that has prevailed through difficult time. Each of us drew inspiration and support from friends and colleagues. Ariella thanks Miki Kratzman for invaluable insights drawn from many years of photographing in the Occupied Territories, and Yosef Algazi for being the generous source of much knowledge about the early years of the Occupation. Adi thanks Hanan Hever and Yehuda Shenhav for many years of enriching, friendly conversations and for everything he has learnt from their writings on Israel's history, sociology, and culture.

The support of the Van Leer Jerusalem Institute and the Minerva Center for Human Rights at Tel Aviv University provided us with the research assistance of Liron Mor, Ariel Hendel, Udi Edelman, and Dikla Bytner (who was especially helpful in the translation process), and we extend our deepest thanks to them all. We also thank Shira Shmueli for verifying references to laws, regulations, and court rulings. Resling Publishing's trust and encouragement enabled the completion of this book and its publication in Hebrew. The trust and encouragement of Rebecca Stein and the editors of Stanford University Press's Stanford Studies in Middle Eastern and Islamic Societies and Cultures series launched work on the English edition, and Tal Haran's unusual commitment and professional dedication have been essential in bringing it to completion. Generous support from Rob Sikorski and the Center for International Studies at Duke University made this translation possible.

The English edition of this book consists of about one-third of the Hebrew version. Preparing the short version turned out to be as difficult as it was productive. To retain the main thrust of our argument, we had almost entirely to relinquish the account of our debt to and some disagreements with many authors on whose extensive research we nonetheless rely. Readers interested in this aspect of the book will have to consult the Hebrew edition. At the same time, preparing this shorter edition gave us an opportunity to clarify our position on two issues that gave rise to much misunderstanding and have become a center of debate: the continuity and break between 1948 and 1967, and Israel's democracy. As a result, sections of the Introduction and Conclusion, and much of Chapter 7 were not part of the Hebrew version of this book.

The One-State Condition

PROLOGUE

The First Year of the Occupation

On Wednesday evening, June 8, 1967, the Israeli army completed its occupation of the West Bank and Gaza Strip. Since then, Israel has ruled the entire area of historical mandatory Palestine. The apparatus to govern the roughly one million Palestinians who had become subject to Israeli rule was quickly created. In the nineteen years that had elapsed since the expulsion of the majority of the Palestinian population and the creation of the State of Israel in 1948, significant differences had emerged between the situation of Palestinian citizens of Israel and that of Palestinians living in the West Bank and Gaza Strip. The subjugation of the latter to Israeli rule intensified these differences by means of two separate ruling apparatuses—one for Israeli citizens (both Jews and Arabs) and the other for Palestinian noncitizens in the West Bank and Gaza Strip: two apparatuses in the service of one and the same regime.

The so-called Six-Day War took less than four days in the West Bank and Gaza Strip and sowed massive devastation. The Jordanian and Egyptian authorities in the West Bank and Gaza respectively were ousted. Infrastructure was ruined, the supply of food and water was disrupted, numerous houses were demolished by shelling, the border that had vanished left enormous minefields unmarked and unfenced, hundreds of wounded lay in hospitals, and myriads were homeless and had been deprived of their livelihoods.

At the end of the fighting, Israel immediately positioned itself as a merciful sovereign with the power, will, and authority to rescue the local inhabitants from the ravages of war and the distress in which they found themselves. This aid had an obvious price: acceptance of Israeli rule. In order to get life back on track, Arab leaders, mayors, and heads of local councils were forced to cooperate with the Occupation, which they regarded as temporary. "The City Council hereby announces that in conjunction with the Israeli administration it has managed to operate sanitation and water supply services in various parts of the city," Ruhi al-Khatib, mayor of Jerusalem under Jordanian rule, notified its residents on June 19, 1967. "The local electricity company has begun its operations in cooperation with the military administration."[1] But his city council did not last long. On June 28, following the annexation of East Jerusalem and several neighborhoods in and villages around the city,[2] the city council of Arab Jerusalem was dismantled and Israeli law was imposed on all parts of the city, from Qalandiya in the north to Beit Safafa in the south. In response, the president of the Jerusalem shari'a court called upon Palestinian public figures to convene and announce measures of resistance and protest, declaring that "the annexation of Arab Jerusalem is null and void and that the Occupation authorities have imposed it unilaterally, contrary to the will of the city residents."[3] Israel took severe measures against these signs of budding civil disobedience and hastened to penalize the participants, both leaders and private individuals. Four members of the Supreme Muslim Council, signatory to this public statement, were forced to leave Jerusalem and barred from political activity.

Israel's first census in the Territories showed 667,200 Palestinians living in the West Bank (71,300 of them in East Jerusalem) and 389,700 in the Gaza Strip in late 1967.[4] About one-tenth of the West Bank residents and nearly three-quarters of the Gaza Strip residents were refugees from areas of mandatory Palestine occupied by Jewish forces in 1948–49.[5] The entire population, except for those inhabitants of regions freshly annexed to Jerusalem, had now become subjects deprived of any kind of civil status. Residents of the annexed area were offered citizenship. Most of them declined, and they were then granted permanent resident status. Administration of civil life was handed over to military governors, and shortly thereafter, a military administration was set up throughout the Occupied Territories.

In the first days of the Occupation, Israel appeared to launch a new wave of ethnic cleansing and destruction. Demolition of three villages in the Latrun area, destruction of the Mughrabi neighborhood near the Wailing Wall in the Old City of Jerusalem, the depopulation of the refugee camps near Jericho, and preventing the return of most of the 250,000 Palestinians who had escaped the West Bank to Jordan and about 48,000 who had escaped the Gaza Strip to Egypt during the war were a familiar pattern.[6] Extensive actions of this kind ceased shortly thereafter, short of a second Palestinian Nakba, and eventually some tens of thousands of refugees were allowed to return.

However, other, less massive and demonstrative actions were taken to encourage Palestinian emigration. Homes of Palestinians suspected of being members of what were then defined as "hostile organizations," and of their relatives, were demolished;[7] those leaving voluntarily for Jordan were offered relocation grants;[8] free transport to Jordan from the Damascus Gate of the Old City of Jerusalem was offered daily to one and all, presented as a gesture in support of "family reunification" with relatives who had served in the Jordanian army; damage to the familiar fabric of life through closure of several institutions and crass interference in the management of others spread mistrust and alienation through parts of the local population.[9] Many Palestinians came to be suspected of resistance, whether violent or political, and were subjected to administrative detention, frequent interrogations, and torture.[10] All of these measures moved many to choose migration.

However, the issue, as it soon became clear, was not expelling the Palestinians, but ruling them. Various Israeli bodies had prepared themselves in advance for the task. There was a contingency plan for occupation of the Territories, drawn up a few years earlier by Meir Shamgar, then military advocate general, later president of the Israeli Supreme Court (1983–95). When standby was declared before actual warfare erupted, the military advocate general's office prepared itself accordingly, and the relevant blueprint can be seen implemented to this day, in spite of the many changes that have taken place in the legal corpus constituted by the edicts and regulations issued by the military government in the Occupied Territories.[11] Two years prior to the war, the General Security Service (GSS) began to consolidate action plans for a possible occupation of the West Bank and Gaza Strip, and trained its agents accordingly.[12] A series of courses was held at the Allenby army base in Jerusalem to practice the "lessons of administration learnt in Operation Kadesh" (also called the "Sinai Campaign," the occupation of the Sinai Peninsula in 1956), and especially in the occupation of the Gaza Strip. The courses were intended especially for reservists who had served in the military administration ruling Palestinian citizens inside Israel, as well as for GSS agents: "The purpose of this course was openly discussed: establishing military rule in occupied territories," David Ronen writes. "Practices included the immediate activation of local institutions and services, location of local leadership that would help return life to its normal course and handling possible religious strife."[13]

The early deployment of this administrative and legal apparatus calls into question the commonly held narrative presenting the Occupation as an event that took Israel by surprise, and describing Israel's hesitation in the first weeks and months as a search for the right way to handle the Occupied Territories and their inhabitants. The first months were indeed a time of anticipation of international pressure that would bring about an Israeli withdrawal, as had been the case following Operation Kadesh, but both preparations before the war and some of the actions taken immediately thereafter indicate that another possibility had also been considered: a long-term occupation requiring special deployment. The defense apparatus led by Defense Minister Moshe Dayan sought a model for ruling a civilian population that suited the time and Israel's international status. In an intuitive and haphazard move, various recent models for military and colonial occupation were studied—from World War II through French rule of Algeria to the American hold on Vietnam—and rejected.[14] Having no suitable model, the architects of the ruling apparatus first acted by way of elimination. Their first principle was not to replicate the military governing mechanisms that until December 1966 had ruled the Palestinian population within the "Green Line" of the 1949 Armistice Agreements between Israel and the neighboring Arab states.[15]

Throughout the years of its existence, this military government had aroused sharp criticism in wide circles of Israeli society.[16] The dismantling of this apparatus about half a year before the 1967 war was a show of confidence on the part of Israel's ruling bodies, the success—as it were—of eighteen years of efforts to segregate Palestinian citizens of Israel from the 1948 refugees outside the country and to turn them into loyal citizens of their new state. Palestinians inside Israel were expected to accept their new situation and actually to give up their claims and reparation demands related to damages they had suffered in 1948, along with their bonds with their Palestinian brothers and their dream of regaining their homes. Palestinian citizens of Israel were already enjoying civil rights—albeit partial—and especially freedom of movement—albeit incomplete; their assimilation into the Jewish economy, in public administration, and in Israeli political space was limited but growing gradually, monitored by the GSS, which was geared for early detection of any sign of resistance to the Israeli regime.

Dayan, one of the military government's staunchest critics in its later years, wished to differentiate between the new apparatus established in the Occupied Territories and the system that had previously controlled Palestinians within

the Green Line. He especially wished to avoid the severe restrictions on movement that had been the fate of Palestinian citizens of Israel. In the late summer, Dayan approved the "open bridges" policy, as well as the general permit
to exit the Territories into Israel—two measures that normalized everyday life
and had a decisive impact on the development of the Palestinian economy.
However, these measures soon created two arenas in which Palestinians were
exposed to the intervention and monitoring by the military administration,
making them all the more dependent upon its officials and officers. Free entry
into Israel, on the one hand, and passage to Jordan, on the other, took place
alongside detentions, inspections, searches, and humiliations at the crossings,
as well as frequent violations of freedom of movement within the Occupied
Territories themselves—especially by movement restrictions imposed on political activists and curfews imposed from time to time upon villages and neighborhoods where resistance was manifested.

Dayan wished to enable the rapid normalization of everyday life for Palestinians in the Occupied Territories without granting them citizenship or erasing their clear differentiation from Palestinian citizens of Israel. This policy
ascertained the contradiction between "enlightened" intentions and the means
necessary for their implementation. In order to gain favor with the new administration, Palestinians were now required to prove themselves loyal. Such imposed loyalty had to be coerced through familiar means by the GSS, which relied
upon the experience accumulated during eighteen years of military administration, as well as its short experience in military government of the Gaza Strip
in the Sinai campaign and on training practices held since 1965 foreseeing the
occupation of the West Bank and Jerusalem.[17] Since the subjects were not state
citizens, the organization could work in a less restrained manner. It exercised
a policy of divide and rule, implementing a whole system of prohibitions and
monitoring and policing measures to prevent the emergence of public space, or
violently suppressing such a space wherever it had been created. Interference in
the lives of subjects was common, creating numerous "points of dependence"
of the ruled upon the ruling power (for our use of the term "ruling power," see
Chapter 6 below), enabling ongoing surveillance. In extreme cases, the Occupation authorities expelled and exiled individuals, but the normalization of submission also meant recruiting Palestinians to low-ranking offices in the ruling
administration, forcing many into various forms of collaboration.

Parts of the organizational blueprint, administrative concepts, and control devices that had served the military administration imposed on Israel's

Arab citizens remained in force and were adjusted to the new policy, notwith-standing Dayan's intention to create a new ruling pattern. Political activity was monitored and suppressed, but labor and commerce were allowed a degree of freedom. Palestinian existence was reduced to bare everyday needs, the fulfill-ment of which was enabled and controlled by the Occupation regime. This was done, however, in a way that restricted development, required various forms of dependence upon Israeli rule and economy, and promoted the economic in-terests of government and private companies over Palestinian ones. This de-pendence hampered the building of infrastructure in the Occupied Territories, hindering industrialization and initiatives in the area of financial services, and tightly restricted developments in medicine and education.

This regime, whose architects called it an "enlightened" or "silent" Occupa-tion, was based first and foremost on the distinction between a private realm in which Palestinians could sense relief and certain improvements in their liv-ing conditions, and a public domain that became inaccessible for most of them and involved strict control and violent suppression.[18] The distinction between submissive Palestinians who had relinquished their public space and rebellious Palestinians who insisted on it was the basis for telling "moderates" from "ex-treme," "dangerous" Palestinians. The "moderates" were those who fully obeyed the rules and unreservedly accepted the rightless status the Occupation pre-scribed them, whereas the "bad guys" were those who took part in resisting it, did not recognize the legitimacy of its rule, and tried in various ways to tran-scend the place it allotted them.

Both government officials and critics used the carrot-and-stick formula to describe the Israeli regime's treatment of its new subjects.[19] The ruling appara-tus showed its "enlightened" face to the population who accepted its authority, but acted violently and resolutely against those who rebelled. It oppressed vast parts of the population with "insinuated" and "withheld" violence in order to deter them from forgetting their place and joining the rebels. The dual, "en-lightened" and oppressive faces of the regime have become a significant factor in justifying the ongoing harm to Palestinians. The ruling apparatus presented itself as enlightened and actually interested in improving Palestinians' living conditions, provided they showed moderation and maintained law and order. It usually avoided exposing its oppressive side to the Israeli public, which in any case showed no great interest in the details of ruling the Occupied Ter-ritories. When this side was occasionally uncovered by the media, it was in-variably presented within the permanent frame story whose protagonist, the "bad" Palestinian, forced the regime to act in order to thwart subversion and hostile intentions. In rarer cases, exposure of the oppressive side was an opportunity to condemn—almost never to punish—the rank-and-file soldier guilty of some "exceptional" conduct toward Palestinians, and publicly to declare an investigation of the matter.[20] At any rate, Palestinian resistance was stripped of its political dimension.

Thanks to the carrot-and-stick policy, only at the outbreak of the First Intifada did the inherent, ongoing harm and damage inflicted on Palestinians, which was not just a consequence of violent outbursts, appear to non-Palestinian eyes for what it really was: direct control of the population and a result of ongoing management of all details of life by means of edicts and decrees. Without the explicit approval of the military governor, lawyers were not allowed to photocopy legal documents, teachers could not hold meetings, students could not organize basketball and football matches, men and women could not gather at clubs and hold cultural events, journalists and writers could not publish their work, cooks were not allowed to pick thyme leaves, and gardeners could not plant azaleas. The institutions to which lawyers, teachers, or merchants belonged were subjected to constant surveillance, public services suffered budget cuts, decrees affecting daily life were kept secret, forms for registering the opening of businesses or the sale of property were not available for months on end, and their supply not renewed, libraries were closed or emptied of books, and books were censored. These and many other draconian decrees that had nothing to do with security, nor were a response to rebellious conduct on the part of the occupied or a focused punitive measure, became an integral part of the new fabric of life woven by the Occupation. The specific violation of fundamental rights represented by each of these edicts concealed the more basic harm done to the life of Palestinians as a result of the fact that they were exposed to such long-term withheld violence, enabling the regime to interfere in their lives and monitor every aspect of their world.[21]

The Occupation's "enlightened" face soon brought some benefits and certain improvements in various areas, such as health, agriculture, and livelihood, and per capita income increased considerably. Improvements were implemented sparingly, true to the carrot-and-stick method. The role of the stick here was both passive—denial of those improvements and benefits—and active—the deployment of a whole apparatus of military-spatial control devices throughout the West Bank and Gaza Strip in order to prevent and suppress any resistance to Occupation rule. Control technologies were activated against both identified individuals and the population at large. Under the auspices of the military governor and his administrative bureaus, which were the main agents of the carrot-and-stick policy, individuals were subjected to a permit policy from the very first days of the Occupation. While any permission to conduct normal everyday activities could be considered as the carrot, anything that could be associated with a "security risk" was likely to produce the stick immediately. The category of security risk included various political activities, such as commemoration rallies or hunger strikes, which were handled by the army and the GSS rather than by the civil administration.[22]

As soon as the war ended, the army carried out a series of operations to "cleanse" the Occupied Territories of "nests of Palestinian resistance." These actions targeted not only those suspected of violence but also leaders and public figures who expressly opposed various measures taken by the military administration or who disagreed with them, and these actions occasionally affected the population as a whole. Some of these operations were covert or carried out while removing Palestinians from the site of the action. Others were held as spectacles, in broad daylight, for the Palestinians to "take notice." Such, for example, was the operation carried out in Nablus in February 1968, when the Casbah (the densely populated old part of the city) was surrounded by hundreds of soldiers, who proceeded from house to house and arrested most men living in the city. After the men were transported to holding pens, they were forced to undergo an identification lineup in which detainees who had already been implicated in hostile terrorist activity were forced to identify their associates.[23]

In March 1968, responding to a rise in the military and ideological presence of the various resistance organizations of the Palestine Liberation Organization (PLO), Israel initiated an offensive against the village of Karame, in Jordan, then a PLO stronghold. Large forces crossed the Jordan River in order to "cleanse" the area of bases and members of the organized Palestinian resistance. The operation ended in Israeli defeat and numerous casualties on both sides. The next day, Dayan coined the precepts that have become the Occupation authorities' hallowed dogma to this day: "The IDF [Israeli Defense Force] operation was unavoidable—we have no choice but to fight back if we do not want our lives preyed upon and to forfeit our military and political achievements of the Six Day War. The question is not of a single battle but rather of a war—perhaps long-standing—to the very end."[24] This statement should be dwelt upon. According to Dayan, "our military and political achievements" had to be preserved at any price; they were fetishized to create a sense of "no choice" that precludes any rational planning or policy. How al-Fatah, then still a small guerrilla organization, had grown to pose an immediate threat to these achievements Dayan did not explain. If Israel's achievement was its defeat of the Egyptian, Syrian, and Jordanian armies in war, al-Fatah could not be relevant. It could hardly have been able to pose any threat to Israel's second achievement—the Occupation of the Palestinian territories—either. The direct threat posed by al-Fatah at the time was its incitement of the residents of these territories against the Occupation regime and emphasizing the oppressive aspect of the Occupation over its enlightened façade. However, behind this explicit threat perhaps lay a more severe threat, not spelled out by Dayan.

Al-Fatah, a secular national movement, founded in 1959, that became the major faction in the PLO, took up armed resistance in 1965. It was still fighting at the time against the transformation of Palestine into Israel. By its very existence, this organization invoked the Palestinian catastrophe and reawakened the ghosts of Palestinian existence in Israel proper, which the Israeli regime wished to erase. Even more than in its guerrilla and terrorist actions, Al-Fatah's discourse anchored the Palestinian struggle in the catastrophe of 1948. Its slogan "Return is the way to unity" openly and directly embodied something that Israel wished to continue forgetting, the denied moment of constituent violence—the violence that constituted the Israeli regime and almost entirely cleansed its body politic of Palestinians—and the refugees' claim to return to their homeland. Al-Fatah and its goals were the vanishing point in the perspective of the ruling apparatus established in the Occupied Territories: they were usually missing from its field of vision and action but determined its mode of operation and delineated its horizon.

INTRODUCTION

When we began writing this book in Hebrew, the Israeli occupation of the West Bank and the Gaza Strip was nearing the end of its fourth decade. We are now in the midst of its fifth decade: almost half a century of Israeli domination of a Palestinian population denied political status or political protection of any kind. Half a century is a very long time in modern history. One cannot possibly regard such a long-lasting political situation as a historical "accident" that happened to the State of Israel. Time enough has elapsed for the relations of dominance between the occupying force and the occupied population to institutionalize themselves in a regime structure with its own logic and dynamics.

The evolution of "the Occupation" from a temporary situation into a regime calls for a conceptual analysis of an entire structure of ruling and governance and a reexamination of the regime structure of the Israeli state, of which "the Occupation regime" and its unique ruling apparatus are a part. We offer such an analysis here, combining historical and structural reconstruction of Israel's rule in the Occupied Territories, and then go on to describe and analyze the Israeli regime that contains and enables this structure of domination. The discussion relies less upon new facts than on the reconceptualization of familiar ones in order to propose a new conceptual framework for narrating the history of the Occupation and reconstructing its structure.

This task requires a revised set of concepts—a new language, in fact. The most prevalent terms of the existing discourse, such as "occupation," "occupier" and "occupied," "violence," and "terrorism," should be problematized, because these terms and the political discourse of which they are part are in themselves part of the regime that we wish to describe. We use these terms with great care in order to present the Palestinians, not as a population belonging to "the other side," but rather as a distinct population governed together with us, Israeli Jews, by the same regime. Replacing some prevalent terms is, then, a part of our effort to give political expression to the Palestinians' place in the Israeli regime, as well as to their claim to take part in determining the regime under which they are or shall be governed. But above all, a new conceptual grid is necessary in order to explain *that* and *how* Israelis and Palestinians have been governed since 1967 by the same ruling power, within the bounds of the same regime.

.   .   .

Even now, after almost half a century of Israeli rule in the Occupied Territories, nearly everyone continues to speak—in everyday political discourse, as well as in legal and academic discourse—of this rule as one of a temporary control, a state of affairs incidental to the Israeli regime and not a structural element of it. Israel's willingness to end the Occupation is hardly disputed. Rather, the question is under what conditions it would be willing to do so. Most of those, on both the right and left of the political spectrum, who propose answers to this question assume and take as self-evident that the Occupation is temporary and bound to end someday. The ongoing control of the Occupied Territories is conceived of as incidental and, especially, external to the Israeli regime. Therefore one can quite easily refer to Israel as a democratic state, respect its citizens as enlightened people leading modern lives, and regard the Palestinians living in the Occupied Territories as an enemy threatening the regime from the outside. Hostility to Israel is perceived as an innate, generic feature of Palestinians, a second nature of sorts, of which the Occupation is a result rather than one of its main causes, and Palestinian resistance to the Occupation is misrepresented and misinterpreted.

The common view of the Occupation as temporary is based on separating the state founded in 1948—seen as a fait accompli—and the Territories it added to itself in 1967. From this follows a division of the Palestinians who lived in Palestine before May 1948, and their descendants, into three groups: those who were uprooted—by force or fear following the violence of the years 1947–50—and not allowed to return, most of whom have since then lived in refugee camps in Syria, Lebanon, or Jordan; those who remain in what became the State of Israel and were naturalized as its "Arab citizens"; and those living in the West Bank and the Gaza Strip, who became subject to Israeli rule in 1967. This separation of Palestinians into three groups has been "naturalized" and categorized accordingly. The three categories most often used to designate these groups are "refugees," "Israeli Arabs," and "Palestinians." The fact that the "refugees" are those whose return has been blocked since 1949, and that "Palestinians" are noncitizens of an occupied land, half of whom were made refugees in 1948, is repressed. In the same vein, the Palestinian identity of "Israeli Arabs" is repeatedly contested, and their sense of affiliation with the two other groups is questioned and delegitimized. These divisions and classifications have shaped the framework of public discourse in Israel and precluded problematization of the regime created in 1948 and of the basic power relations between Jews and Palestinians established at that time.

When the system of military government that had governed "Israeli Arabs" since 1948 was dismantled in December 1966, there was a moment of potential structural change. Until that point in time, Palestinians had systematically been excluded, whether as "refugees" considered complete foreigners or as second-class citizens subject to martial law. With the dismantling of the military government, the door to the inclusion of "Israeli Arabs" as equal citizens—able to share both political space and political power with their fellow Jewish citizens—was opened. Had this possibility been realized, the founding model of the Israeli regime would indeed have been transformed, and the question of the wrong associated with its foundation could have been openly addressed.

This potential was never realized, however, and there is no knowing whether it would have sufficed for creating a new regime: just six months later, the West Bank and the Gaza Strip were occupied, and their populations came under the rule of the Israeli state as noncitizens. The inclusion of over one million new Palestinians under Israeli governance ruled out the possibility of making the status of Palestinian citizens of the state equal to that of its Jewish citizens. Instead, the regime began to hone its ground principle—differential rule over populations of differing status—generating nuances to this principle in various areas of government. Thus, Palestinian citizens were accorded more rights, but they were not allowed to share power with the Jews and were not made equal citizens (let alone compensated after years of dispossession). Palestinians residing in the Occupied Territories were "naturalized" as noncitizens and not counted as part of the Israeli political system, despite their recruitment into the labor force and colonial expansion in their midst. The Occupied Territories have been ruled ever since as a temporary "exterior," whose inclusion has been denied, together with the duty stemming from that rule, and this denial itself was part of the externalization of what has been contained. We shall return to this configuration of relations later in this book, characterizing the Israeli regime that took shape after 1967 and distinguishing it from the one established in 1948.

Many Israeli Jews, on both the political right and left, agree that the Occupation constitutes a problem for Israeli democracy, but they will not admit that Israel is no democracy because of the Occupation, or that the nature of the regime during more than four decades of occupation, colonization, and ruling of noncitizens must be examined. The assumption that the Occupation is temporary and external is especially obvious in discussions of political programs that wish to "eliminate," "cut off," "cleanse," "terminate," "settle," "solve," or simply "make peace." Such programs rarely take into account the massive investment in infrastructure and its integration with infrastructure in "Israel proper" (within the 1949 Armistice lines), as well as the integration of the form of rule that has been established in the Occupied Territories into the governmental structure of the Israeli regime. Also ignored is the effect of the long, deceptive denial of 1948, the way in which "the Occupation" has reinforced the sweeping militarization of Israeli society, and several of its aspects have been presented as national projects, for the sake of which male and female Israeli Jews are conscripted from the cradle to the grave.

The false temporariness of "the Occupation" generates perceptual blindness that is at one and the same time caused by the ruling apparatus in the Territories and one of its active mechanisms. The widely accepted term "occupation" connotes this temporariness and implies a temporary, hence regrettable—yet still tolerable—state of oppression and violations of rights. "Occupation" has come to designate a black box that no one dares open. Often it insinuates a normative critique not followed by any practical consequences. Much of the common critical discourse about the Occupation screens out what is actually happening and, in fact, fails to realize that it is a distinct regime operating a productive ruling apparatus that shapes and transforms life in the Territories *and* in Israel. This perceptual blindness apparently contributes to the fact that Israeli scholars were reluctant for almost forty years to conceive of the Occupation as part of the Israeli regime and address it as a legitimate object of research.[1] They have accepted as given the lines of demarcation proposed and sanctified by all Israeli governments since 1967. But as an object of study, the Occupation regime cannot be conceived of in the way in which it has been officially framed by the spokespersons of all Israeli governments since 1967. We should rather examine how this framing—with its principles of separation and exclusion, and their enforcement—functions as a structural element of that regime.

Our interest in Israeli rule of the territories occupied in June 1967 is motivated by the question of its role in the construction and reproduction of the Israeli Occupation regime. We shall describe this rule and analyze both the active forms of domination and governance and their place in the regime that activates them. We assume that this form has its own history and logic, which cannot be exhausted by speaking of "the Occupation," and cannot be preconceived as a straightforward case of "colonization" or "apartheid."[2] All three terms, borrowed from commonly accepted legal-political discourse, are necessary but not sufficient. They indicate existing aspects of the form of Israeli rule in the Occupied Territories, but do not enable us to perceive other aspects; especially not the difference and link between the ways citizens and noncitizens are ruled by the same ruling power. Our working assumption was that the local case is unique, and that in order to understand it, one must suspend the use of the familiar categories and reconstruct the way in which occupier-occupied relations are maintained and have developed on both sides of the Green Line.

The phenomenology of power we propose below seeks to analyze colonization processes, to study the system of multiple separations of Jews and Palestinians that regulates—but also produces—frictions and exchange, and to deconstruct the mechanism through which the status of Palestinians as colonized subjects is reproduced and denied at the same time.

This phenomenology of power follows and articulates the systemic structure of Israeli control of the Occupied Territories, its unique historical dynamics, and the security, administrative, and political discourses into which it is woven, and through which it is conducted, represented, and justified. The phenomenological description follows its governmental technologies, under which familiar means of violence and biopolitical tools are activated in novel ways, and others are invented. We shall look closely at the ruling apparatus, that is, the specific technologies and modes of operation that the Israeli army, GSS (Shabak, or Shin Bet), legal system, and various government offices apply in the Occupied Territories, but also—and in matters related to their rule there—in Israel proper. By studying the ruling apparatus, we hope to reconstruct the main formations of the Occupation regime, that is, the general form of Israeli rule in the Occupied Territories. This form limits and enables the relations between the various mechanisms of the ruling apparatus and structures relations among all parties involved: Palestinians, soldiers, settlers, other

Israeli citizens, humanitarian, human rights, and political activists, UN agencies, and others.

The object of our research encompasses tools of control and strategies of resistance, forms of organizing and using space and time, labor, and other resources, alongside formal legal definitions, laws and regulations, political programs, images, points of view, and practices of observation. We also pay close attention to discursive mechanisms that provide and organize information, knowledge, and legitimacy, that create "foci of problematization," combine legal rhetoric and tools with the mechanisms of direct control of bodies and land—or allow their detachment, and that work to construct memory and forgetting, confer meaning upon the experiences of individuals, and represent the shared fate of entire communities.

This methodological approach—a phenomenology of the ruling apparatus and a reconstruction of the regime by which it is constrained and that it reproduces—precludes teleological explanations of the Occupation and suspends ready-made narratives such as the history of the Zionist movement, of the Jewish-Arab conflict, or of a "war of civilizations," in which the Occupation is a well-defined phase whose meaning is known in advance. We do not see the ruling apparatus as the result of planning by identifiable subjects (e.g., "the Israeli government," "the Zionist movement," or "the settlers"). Still, we think of these narratives as taking part in different fields of discourse that construct the experience of individuals who share the Occupation regime's ruling apparatus and are conscripted by it. We think of the Occupation regime as a web of relations and a state of affairs whose "grammar" could be described, analyzed, and understood in a way that cannot be reduced to the forces and agents that created them at certain identifiable points in the past and maintain them in the present. Naturally, these forces and agents will be taken into account, but this will always be done from the perspective of their systemic relations and accumulated effects, not solely of their motivations and intentions.

Making this kind of effort, one must remain skeptical about the categories that serve commonly accepted political discourse and its historical narratives, political agenda, and major questions. These narratives, categories, and questions cannot guide our scholarly effort or establish its frame of reference, for they are all part of what needs explaining when analyzing the Israeli Occupation regime, inasmuch as they themselves are an integral part of this regime or a series of its effects. They should be explained together with the programs and the visions proposing "solutions," while reiterating the categories and narrative through which the regime of occupation is perpetuated. We are interested in understanding the actual form of Israeli rule in the Occupied Territories, its effect on the Israeli regime as a whole, and the conditions that enabled the decades-long perception of that rule as a certain hump on the back of Israeli democracy, limited to the Occupied Territories. In other words, we wish to know how Israeli rule in the Occupied Territories works in order to understand in what kind of a state and under what kind of a regime we ourselves are living.

Positioning ourselves at a point that enables this question, trying to view the new horizon it opens for our thought and action, we must remember that we, too, cannot fully distance ourselves from the Occupation regime. Israeli citizens of Jewish descent take part in and are ruled by the regime of which "the Occupation" is one element; they contribute to its reproduction, not only as soldiers, settlers, or government officials, but also as its governed subjects, who tacitly accept its rules and perpetuate its legitimacy, mostly ignoring how it rules others, non-Jews and noncitizens, letting it be inscribed and reinscribed in the movements of their bodies, the wording of their language, and the limited horizon of their political imagination. The very meaning of Israeli citizenship is constructed through the active negation of Palestinian citizenship, which also determines the limits of Israel's democracy. This negation confronts Israeli citizens with the most crucial issue, the most serious matter that they have yet to decide, think about, and act upon, the matter over which so much time and so many lives have been wasted.

For the occupied Palestinians, at least as far as we can tell from our perspective as Israeli citizens, the Occupation regime is omnipresent. Most Israeli citizens, on the other hand, usually enjoy the privilege of suspending the Occupation's violent presence, distancing it from sight and heart and forgetting that it exists. But even as they do this, turning their backs on its action in the Occupied Territories, Israelis do so under its auspices and serve its interest in "normalizing" the ongoing rule of the State of Israel over millions of noncitizens, accepting the constant injury this subjection sows in all realms of life, not only to its direct victims, the Palestinians, but also to themselves; for "the Occupation" harms their emotional mind-set, education and culture, livelihood, employment, and housing, not to speak of their security. It is a systemic feature of this regime that so many individuals and groups are capable of bracketing off their participation in it, in effect, denying its presence in their lives. And, as we hope to show below, this denial—which creates the illusion that the ruling apparatus in the Occupied Territories is detached and separate from Israel proper—is crucial to the integration of the Occupation into the Israeli state and the transformation of its regime.

The representation of "the Territories" as an "exterior," outside the state's bounds, and ruling them as a state project will be interpreted here as a condition for conceiving "the Occupation" as temporary and the regime within "Israel proper" as democracy. Both will be presented as products of this regime's ideological apparatus. We shall assume that the occupation of the Territories is integral to the Israeli regime, not external to it. The Occupation regime and the ruling apparatus on which it is based cannot be conceived of as state projects, in the sense that the U.S. government's space program or occupation of Iraq are, or even the occupation of Chechnya by the Russian regime—the American or Russian regimes would not essentially change if they were to abstain from flying into space, withdraw from Iraq, or cease to "liberate" Chechnya. Not so in Israel-Palestine. The daily business of ruling the Occupied Territories is the *state of affairs* in which Israel's various branches of government and apparatuses have been active since 1967, and in relation to the constraints of which they organize even when dealing with very distant issues. Control of the Occupied Territories, which began as a major task added on to various others in 1967, has become part of the fundamental matrix in which Israel's various branches of government function.

The Occupied Territories are not an "exterior," like a distant continent or the beach in Thailand, something that one might forget altogether, no harm done, because there is no danger of its suddenly appearing in all its menacing proximity. They are an exterior the shadow of whose presence is internalized a priori, and an ongoing effort must be made to keep it from imposing its presence and breaking into one's consciousness as a sense of guilt and responsibility for deeds perpetrated in our name, with our tax money, for our children. To enable the normal daily life of a democratic society, the Occupied Territories are bracketed off, forgotten, and denied. This exterior must be denied in order to fancy that Israeli Jews belong to a free society, in order to maintain a rational public discussion of various issues at hand, in order to live at peace, not only with people at the opposite end of the political spectrum, but also with relatives and friends who happen to be soldiers and settlers. This effort to leave the Occupied Territories "outside" finds its ready expression in discourse and the familiar practices of everyday life. It is the precondition for an "Israeli normality" under one roof with "the Occupation."

We begin by rejecting this denial. Our basic assumption is that the Occupied Territories are an inseparable part of the Israeli regime, construed as an "outside" to that regime through a concerted, consistent, and continuous effort of the hegemonic political, legal, and academic discourses alongside many state apparatuses. Since the conquest of the West Bank and Gaza Strip, Israel-Palestine, the land between the sea and the river, has been ruled by one system of control, one set of state apparatuses, and two distinct systems of governance.

Following the Oslo Accords in 1993, some governmental functions in parts of the Territories have been outsourced to the semi-autonomous but entirely dependent Palestinian Authority, but Israel still has the final say and interferes with many aspects of daily governance. We shall try to show that even the disengagement from the Gaza Strip in August 2005 and the election of the Hamas government there in June 2007, despite all the changes they have introduced, have not altered this basic structure. Independent as Palestinian governmental bodies might be in some respects, they are severely monitored, controlled, and limited by the Israeli ruling apparatus.[3] Independent as the two systems of governance might be, they remain integrated into one system of control. The split and links between these two systems is articulated and maintained through a matrix of three distinct types of separation: of Jews from Arabs, of citizens from noncitizens, and multiple territorial separations that cannot be reduced to these binary separations. *Territorial separation* multiplies and redraws border lines and binary differences between "Israel proper" and the Occupied Territories; between the West Bank and Gaza; between Areas A, B, and C in the West Bank, as defined in the Oslo Accords; between East Jerusalem and the rest of the West Bank; between residential zones for Jews only and others for Arabs only in all of the "mixed" cities and towns within the 1949 borders; between closed military zones, including the seam zone along the separation wall, the security zone along the Jordan valley, and zones open to movement of civilians; and between various spatial cells created more or less temporarily by checkpoints and roadblocks.

The three types of separation do not form a coherent set; they are not derived from one another and cannot be reconciled as different points of one meta-principle. Some territorial separations follow the national principle, others follow the civic one, and some are derived from subdivisions within the national or civil separations. Some national and civil separation lines possess clear territorial aspects, others do not. In other words, separations are applied differentially through other separations; they have different meanings for different types of people and are applied differently for different purposes.

Here is a brief scheme of this matrix of separation: *Jews* can move freely in most areas (and are excluded from only a few others). In those areas, no restrictions keep them from buying land and merely a few restrictions are imposed on them for constructing houses. It matters little if they are *citizens* or not, and they can always become citizens if they so wish. Their place of birth matters even less, and they can become residents anywhere they wish, except for the Palestinian urban areas defined in the Oslo Accords as Area A. *Palestinians* can move freely in far fewer areas and suffer more or less severe restrictions on buying land, and even more so on the construction of houses. Whether they are Israeli *citizens or not* is of *extreme* importance. If they are not, the restrictions are much more severe: they are actually excluded from most areas and need special permits to enter others, they cannot buy land outside their built environment, and their habitat cannot expand to accommodate the growth of their population. Their birthplace is crucial and determines their freedom of movement and rights of residency. Formally, all Israeli *citizens* enjoy the same political rights, but *only Jews* can fully share in government and fancy the state to be "their own." *Jewish noncitizens* are governed like citizens, protected by law, and served by most state authorities; *Palestinian noncitizens* are forsaken by the law, hardly entitled to any of the services provided by the state. They are subject to military rule and are exposed to threats, arrests, violence, and dispossession, afflicted or justified after the fact by ever-changing decrees and regulations. When it comes to *citizens*, violence is generally regarded as a last resort when other means fail. Where *Palestinian citizens* are concerned, however, the authorities turn more quickly to violence and use it more freely. When *Palestinian noncitizens* are concerned, a whole economy of violence has taken the place of all other state apparatuses, most of which have ceased to function in the Occupied Territories.

Among all these dividing lines, the basic difference between citizens and noncitizens is the most rigid. From 1967 to the present, no Israeli government has offered any channel of naturalization to the noncitizens under its rule.[4] Although much of the ruling apparatus has withdrawn from the Occupied Territories since the Oslo Accords, no government has agreed to completely terminate its rule over Palestinian noncitizens.[5] Excluded from the political sphere and unwilling to be ruled as subjects with no rights by a power that presents and produces itself as foreign, the Palestinians in the Occupied Territories were left with no other choice but to resist "illegally," and some forms of their resistance have been violent. This resistance, whether actual or virtual, violent or not, has been used by the Israeli ruling apparatus in the Occupied Territories as a pretext for its own violence. Palestinians who have opted for violent resistance have joined groups of armed Palestinians, mostly refugees, who resorted to violence in the 1950s, following their expulsion from their land in 1948. Others joined the armed struggle later, when they realized that the regime created in the State of Israel was taking hold and its refusal to allow refugees to return to their homes proved permanent. Violent and nonviolent Palestinian resistance gave rise to and was used as a pretext for new forms of violence exerted by the ruling apparatus. To characterize the ruling apparatus in the Occupied Territories, tell its history, and understand its regime effects, it is necessary to account for the changing forms of Israeli violence in the Occupied Territories.

We have refrained from seeking to understand this violence instrumentally as a means to ends established by various state mechanisms. Instead, we have sought to follow the "inner grammar" of the whole economy of violence, and to describe it as a medium—like language, law, or economics—that constrains the actions of various groups and individuals, both "occupiers" and "occupied," participating in the web of power relations. Part 1 of this book develops this argument and reviews the emergence of various forms of violence since June 1967. Part 2, dedicated to the two most recent decades, attempts to reconstruct the "order of violence" that has crystallized since the collapse of the Oslo Accords and the outbreak of the Second Intifada, showing that the economy of violence functions as an arena of interrelations between the ruling apparatus and the ruled population. We argue that when violence is regarded as an arena with its own structural logic, one can understand, not only how "it" works ("it" meaning specifically the techniques and technologies of the ruling apparatus), but also how the general structure of the Occupation regime manifests itself in everyday control practices, how the "general principles" or the general matrix of control in the Occupied Territories are translated into details of operating the means of violence and governance, the performances of domination, subjugation, resistance, and persecution. We understand Israel's control of the Gaza Strip, even after the withdrawal of ground forces in August 2005, as a distinct constellation (described in chapter 5 in Part 2) that is inseparable from this general economy of violence. The grammar of separation and frictions and the technologies of power that inscribe it in the Occupied Territories articulate the main features of the Occupation regime and make visible its constitutive role as an integral component of the Israeli regime itself.

Parts 1 and 2 follow the transformations of the ruling apparatus in the Occupied Territories from its inception to the attack on Gaza in December 2008–January 2009), trying to reconstruct the regime formation of each stage.[6] The short description we offer here does not pretend to exhaust the history of the Occupation, nor does it propose a full historical explanation of the changes that took place between its various stages. These historical reconstructions are meant to provide the necessary background for delineating and analyzing the present form of the Occupation regime and its ruling apparatus. We do not pretend to explain why this regime took the form it did, but rather describe and analyze what has emerged and crystallized, singling out its unique features.

On the basis of this analysis, Part 3 (chapters 6, 7, and 8) asks pointedly: what is this Israeli regime of which the Occupation regime is a part? The matrix and grammar of separations sketched above is presented in detail, and some of the insights that have led us throughout this research are corroborated. Finally, in the book's Conclusion, we reflect on possible futures and ways to transform the Israeli regime.

**A SHORT HISTORY
OF THE OCCUPATION REGIME**

Part 1

1 THE FIRST DECADE

The apparatus for ruling Palestinian noncitizens in the West Bank and the Gaza Strip was not the only one created after the 1967 war. In the Sinai Peninsula and the Golan Heights, residents were ruled as noncitizens by separate apparatuses, which had separate histories. The apparatus in the Sinai existed for about fifteen years and was dismantled with Israel's total withdrawal from the peninsula in 1982 under the peace treaty with Egypt. Israel passed a law annexing the Golan Heights about half a year prior to completing its withdrawal from the Sinai, in December 1981, in a speedy legislative procedure that lasted a single day. The Druze inhabitants of the northern Golan Heights (about 13,000 living in four villages, not expelled in 1967) called a general strike, which ended only when they were explicitly promised that their legal status would not be changed. Shortly thereafter, however, this promise was broken. The authorities tried to impose Israeli IDs upon the Druze and implemented severe sanctions against those who refused to accept them. The strike was resumed, and the Druze escalated their struggle. After failing in its various coercive measures, including closure imposed upon the four villages, the government conceded. Except for several hundred Druze who did take up Israeli citizenship, all the others remained Syrian citizens, holding the status of permanent residents of Israel. In spite of the fact that they are not citizens, their situation is entirely different from that of Palestinian noncitizens, and in most respects, except for their formal status, their condition is closer to that of the Israeli state's Arab citizens. They are ruled and administered like other non-Jewish citizens, both directly by the various government ministries and covertly by the security services.

The ruling apparatus imposed upon Palestinian noncitizens in the West Bank and the Gaza Strip is different. We shall divide its history into four periods, relating mainly to the dominant ruling formations of each period. The periods themselves coincide more or less with the four decades of the Occupation. However, we deal in more detail with the first period, when some of the models and technologies of control that are in force to this very day were formed.

THE JUDICIAL SITUATION

The fundamental juridical features of the Occupation were laid out in a document prepared by Military Advocate General Meir Shamgar, a few years before the 1967 war broke out.[1] It consists of two basic principles: ruling Palestinians as noncitizens and separating the handling of the territories from that of their inhabitants.[2] An edict issued in June 1967 granted the military commander of the Territories vast legislative authority. Article 35 of the edict specified, however, that if legislation of any kind should conflict with compliance with the Fourth Geneva Convention, regulating the conduct of an occupying army, the Convention should take priority.[3] But in October that year, a further edict, no. 144, stated that the Geneva Convention had ceased to serve as a means of control and restraint of the ruling apparatus. From that point on, one can detect systematic and creative efforts by Israel to evade international law, whose language regarding occupation situations is clear and unequivocal, and is based first and foremost on the understanding that they are temporary.

In February 1968, Shamgar was appointed legal adviser to the government. In this capacity, he adopted the same judicial approach he had consolidated as military advocate general, giving it a civil-juridical stamp. He created a framework of rules and arguments under Israeli law that gave status to and made room for the judicial "creativity" implemented in the Occupied Territories during his tenure as military advocate general, reconciling the situation on the ground, Israeli law, Jordanian law, and international law. Shamgar defined the status of the Territories according to the prevailing "situation on the ground"—territories subject to Israeli rule—rather than by the type of action—military conquest—that had brought about this new status. The claim was that prior to the war, there had been no Palestinian sovereign power from whom the Territories had been taken by force: the powers that had ruled there de facto—Jordan in the West Bank and Egypt in the Gaza Strip—had held the Territories temporarily and without international agreement or recognition. Not having been taken from any sovereign power, they could thus not be claimed to be "occupied" in the strictly legal sense.[4] Precisely the fact that the Palestinians were stateless, and therefore more vulnerable and in need of protection by international law, enabled the Israeli government to claim that the Fourth Geneva Convention does not protect them.

The Territories were further detached from their inhabitants in February 1968, when the Israeli minister of the interior declared that they were no longer considered enemy territory; their inhabitants, however, were perceived as potential enemies and could be declared so at any moment. Aware of their vulnerability, Shamgar recommended to the government that it abide by the humanitarian articles of the Geneva Convention whenever possible as a matter of goodwill. In the first years of Occupation, the Israeli Supreme Court was careful not to contest the judicial approach and refused to regard this guideline as obligatory, but rather interpreted it as an administrative instruction and applied it only when it found that justice demanded it.[5] Thus Israel acknowledged its responsibility for the lives of the inhabitants of the Territories in matters of health, food, and personal safety, but separated their actual lives from their existence as political beings, and governing their lives from ruling their land.

The basic judicial form of the ruling apparatus was established, then, shortly after the occupation of the Palestinian territories. It is characterized by three features preserved ever since: subjecting the Palestinians in the Territories to a patchwork legal system that combines British mandatory, Jordanian, international, and martial law in an ad hoc, changeable manner; unraveling the territorial bounds of Israeli law in a way that has allowed it to "follow" Israeli settlers into the Occupied Territories;[6] and adding a special judiciary arm in the Occupied Territories in form of the military governor, who soon enough issued numerous rules and regulations. The legal system became heterogeneous regarding the origin of the law, the populations subjected to it, and its enforcement apparatuses. This heterogeneity enabled ruling the Territories under the guise of lawfulness without limiting the ruling power's predatory hold.

The Israeli government never explicitly recognized the validity of the Hague Convention of 1907, which governs the authority of an occupying power in international law. It did, however, accept the principle of the Convention that the occupying power is bound to preserve the law in force prior to the occupation. Israel declared its recognition of the local judicial system in force prior to June 1967 (Jordanian in the West Bank and Egyptian in the Gaza Strip), but observed it only to a limited extent, while violating mechanisms of judgment and enforcement. By means of special edicts, the military ruler annulled parts of the Jordanian law code, and on various occasions revived some of the Ottoman code, as well as the British mandatory "Defense (Emergency) Regulations" (authorizing administrative detention, censorship, prohibition of public gathering and association, movement restriction, etc.), which had been annulled by the Jordanian and Egyptian legal systems. These emergency regulations enabled Israel to promote land confiscation, change the designated use of land, and deploy various sanctions against Palestinians.[7]

Raja Shehadeh and Jonathan Kuttab, lawyers who had followed this process since its early phases, pointed out gradual changes that had already been introduced into the Jordanian legal system at the beginning of the Occupation.[8] In 1970, the ruling apparatus gave up the guise of preserving Jordanian law, and the military governors took the liberty of radically changing it. The principal change lay in crippling the independence of the local civilian legal system. This resulted in all the other changes: promulgating hundreds of edicts that remain unpublicized and thus not subject to the scrutiny of any public institution; the sparse distribution of such edicts to lawyers; preventing lawyers new at their profession from studying edicts issued before their time; keeping the legal corpus vague, so as to hinder both internal and international criticism; dismantling the Palestinian bar association; compromising the independence of judges; closing down the court of appeals; transferring the high court of justice from Jerusalem to Ramallah; introducing Israeli lawyers into courts in the Occupied Territories; and demanding permits for a variety of everyday activities not required under the Jordanian legal system for various kinds of movement and action.

Gradually detaching itself from Jordanian law, the ruling apparatus began to use each and every legal apparatus at its disposal, as well as their incongruities, to legitimize such actions as expulsion, administrative detention, and house demolition, in violation of international law regarding the duties and limitations of an occupying regime. Subsequent to these changes, Palestinian lawyers held a prolonged strike, which ended without result some years later. Numerous judges left the Occupied Territories without being replaced, and courts went into session with only an occasional junior official of the military administration presiding.[9] People soon lost faith in civilian courts, came to regard fellow Palestinians officiating in them as collaborators, and were left with no judicial institution they could trust.

The different legal systems inherited by the military administration were cobbled together by "security legislation," creating a new single judicial corpus. Security legislation granted the military commander authority to revoke or suspend any local law, rescind authorized, lawfully taken local resolutions, ignore international law, oust position holders, and act as legislator, adding rules and regulations and revoking them as often as he considered necessary for preserving order under Israeli rule. A parallel apparatus of military courts was set up to "judge any violation defined by security legislation." Soon "security legislation" actually covered every aspect of life and outlawed any expression of opposition to Israeli rule and anything that could be interpreted as a disturbance of public order. Palestinians were denied such fundamental rights as the freedom of assembly, speech, and the right to strike, and attempts to invoke these rights were treated as a disturbance of public order. The rule of law was replaced by a rule by decrees under a semblance of legality, articulating the changing interests of Israeli governments (or some factions within them) in the seemingly universal, neutral idiom of the law. Even rights that were granted in principle, such as the right to strike, were denied in practice, for example, by defining strikes as political.

About a month after war broke out, the authority of Israeli courts was extended to Israelis in the Occupied Territories, removing the authority of local courts to sit in judgment on Israeli citizens. This was the first manifestation of judicial segregation of Jews and Palestinians in the Territories.[10] Except for dependence upon the Knesset's approval, which has never been seriously doubted, and in spite of the fact that some formalities still differentiated Israeli citizens residing in the Occupied Territories from those living inside the Green Line, Jewish settlers were considered citizens subject to Israeli law like any others. The difference between settlers and Israelis living within Israel proper was not entirely erased, however, and it was invoked and amplified years later when the government decided to dismantle some Jewish settlements. These exceptional moments aside, and for most practical purposes, the difference did not lie in a different judicial status but in the existence of a separate system of law enforcement that consistently ignores the use of force against Palestinians, hardly deals with conflicts among Jews themselves, and has gradually come to grant immunity to Jews who commit crimes against Palestinians.[11]

On June 7, 1967, the first edict was issued regulating military administration in the Occupied Territories. Martial law applied to "every authority of governance, legislation, appointment, and administration of the area or of its inhabitants."[12] A government resolution of June 19, 1967, left intact the "military status" of the Occupied Territories, except for the annexed area in and around Jerusalem.[13] The territories that were not annexed were first called "seized," and soon "held" or "possessed,"[14] but never "occupied" de jure. The term "held territory" bridged an ideological rift between the Zionist Left, which insisted on using parts of the Occupied Territories at least as bargaining chips, and the political Right, which regarded them as "liberated land." The term became part of a common language and an ideological platform for the cooperation of the two political camps in the new phase of the colonization project. Although it reflected the situation ad hoc, even its temporariness, without establishing any future commitment, it could nonetheless be used for claiming the "held territory."

The polyvalent term reflected suspension—but not annulment—of a development that might have taken place in one of two opposing directions: complete withdrawal or full annexation. At the same time, it became more and more common to refer to specific regions within the Occupied Territories by Hebrew names that—when not ad hoc inventions (e.g., Merhav Shelomo [Solomon District], for southern Sinai)—certainly lack any clear geographical designation (e.g., Yehudah [Judea] for the southern part of the West Bank, and Shomron [Samaria] for its northern part). Hebraization of the map, as well as referring to the Territories in terms of "return" and "reclaim"—common even among nonreligious Israelis—along with the collective harnessing of a passion for an unknown land, sowed the seeds of eternity and messianic yearning in the language of legal temporariness. This ambivalence characterized the growing gap between the "situation on the ground" in the Occupied Territories and their judicial status, which the new legal dictionary was supposed to bridge: on the one hand, to give legal sanction to the physical, administrative, and demographic changes that Israel generated in the Occupied Territories; on the other hand, to postpone either legally redefining their status or putting an end to the Occupation regime. Caught in this gap were the occupied population, the vulnerable Palestinians who were governed as noncitizens in a land that was not recognized as theirs. The idea of their expulsion was contemplated by some but was rejected for political and moral reasons. Although they were not expelled en masse, as Palestinians had been in 1948, they could not "conceivably" become naturalized citizens either—naturalization was conceivable, of course, but only in order to reject the idea out of hand. Turning Palestinians into people whose status is yet to be determined and whose political rights have been temporarily revoked contributed to the legitimization of the de facto changes that began to take place on the ground at the time.

Acting in the Territories as though Israel were their recognized sovereign, although declaring them to be "held" and disputed (a diplomatic declaration of status as well as an internal political dispute), at least potentially created a loophole for legitimizing the colonial project. This undecidedness consistently enabled the Israeli Supreme Court to avoid ruling on the pertinence of the Fourth Geneva Convention—which forbids the transfer of population from the occupier state to the occupied territory—in the Occupied Territories. The court has never questioned the legality of the Jewish settlements, which clearly contradict the letter of the Convention. At the same time, however, the ambivalent status of the Occupied Territories, and the fact that Israeli law was not enforced in them, has made it relatively easy for the government of Israel to invoke the temporariness of the Occupation when it suits it. It has done so twice. Fifteen years after the settlement project in the Occupied Territories began, in spring 1982, following the peace treaty with Egypt, the government carried out a large-scale evacuation of settlements in the Sinai; twenty-three years later, in summer 2005, it dismantled the settlements in the Gaza Strip and a few in the northern West Bank. After the fact, the Israeli Supreme Court formulated the rule that had been in force from the outset when it declared that the military administration in the Territories is temporary, since "the nature of belligerent occupation is temporary in essence"; this has not changed since 1967, and even massive Jewish settlement in the Territories, which is "ideologically and religiously motivated in part," cannot change the juridical status of the area as "territory held temporarily under belligerent occupation."[15]

One month after the Territories were declared "held," Palestinian subjects were issued resident cards by the military administration, but their judicial status remained vague. Most of them had no citizenship that could be invalidated: Egypt had not claimed sovereignty over the Gaza Strip and had not granted the resident Palestinians there its citizenship, and Jordan, which did claim its sovereignty over the West Bank, gave citizenship merely to a small part of the resident Palestinian population. Israel, which along with most of the world's states did not recognize Jordanian sovereignty in the West Bank, did not have to regard the Palestinians as citizens of enemy states, simply because they had no such citizenship. However, although they were not declared citizens of an enemy state, they were not granted Israeli citizenship. In other words, the Palestinians were actually governed as *noncitizens* living in territory that was not annexed by Israel but remained an inseparable part of the area it ruled.

Ever since, Israel has been ruling the Palestinian noncitizens within the territory it occupies, but totally shirks any responsibility for them once they leave it. They are recognized as "residents," but this residency depends on their presence. Long absence is usually a pretext for denying this status, namely, total detachment from the habitat in which they were born and raised.[16] The military commander is vested with the absolute authority to permit or refuse the return of residents to the Occupied Territories, and the ruling apparatus has consistently granted such permission only in rare, special instances.[17] The law that enables Israel to rule Palestinians as subjects, allowing for the ruling power's interference with their lives, their political and social ties, their property and habitat, does not recognize them as its citizens.

The lives of these noncitizens are governed by military decrees. In the first three years of the Occupation, edicts were still publicized with introductions as a gesture of explanation. However, in 1970, instead of detailed explanations, the sweeping term "security considerations" appeared, doing away with the need to explain anything. Formally, decrees have been authorized by the highest-ranking military commanders, but they are in fact issued by middle-ranking officers and enforced by a host of low-ranking commanders positioned at semi-judicial junctions where all matters in the lives of Palestinians are decided. Understanding the problematic nature of this mode of governance, even before it was consolidated, and making one of the first gestures that would later constitute the "enlightened" face of the Occupation, Military Advocate General Meir Shamgar allowed a Palestinian subject to petition the High Court of Justice, which then recognized this subject's right to do so. Henceforth the right of appeal was granted to any Palestinian claiming that the military decrees or their implementation were illegal.[18] Palestinians were reluctant to use this right (during the first decade following the war, a mere few did). Appearing before the Israeli court was seen as implicit recognition of its authority in the Territories. In the eyes of the ruling apparatus, the very possibility of the appeal has made the Israeli legal system the only arena in and through which Palestinian resistance can legally be presented.[19]

The Israeli political system has consistently undone any initiative to implement Israeli law in the Occupied Territories. The ruling apparatus, for its part, has rejected various demands that it explicitly recognize customary international law and the Geneva Convention as binding. Hence, Palestinians in the Occupied Territories are not subject to Israeli law and are not protected by international law. Their limited access to the Israeli Supreme Court is one of the means of legally containing and excluding them at the same time. The Supreme Court, careful to relate to international law, later obliged the government to acknowledge the validity of the Hague Convention with respect to belligerent occupation (but not of the Geneva Convention), and ruled that the duties and privileges of the military commander of the Territories must conform with it.[20] In actual fact, however, its position could not change the situation of the Palestinian subjects, because in any matter of principle it interpreted international law in a way that was compatible with the government's deeds, usually without ruling specifically on the legal principle that had allowed it. "In its rulings pertaining to the Occupied Territories, the Supreme Court actually provided pretexts for all the controversial acts carried out by the Israeli authorities, especially those most problematic in view of the precepts of international law," according to the jurist David Kretzmer.[21]

While the Supreme Court has exercised its sovereignty and ruled on each case anew as to whether or not it should follow the letter of the customary international law, military commanders on the ground have exercised their sovereignty and ruled on each case anew as to whether or not they should follow the letter of the Supreme Court's verdicts. The result has been perfectly consistent: Palestinian claims have been rejected almost without exception, government actions have been granted legal sanction, and a permanent gap now lies between the judicial situation—both de jure and de facto—and a façade of legal discussion guiding and accompanying the acts of the government in the Occupied Territories.

As noncitizens, Palestinians were a priori denied access to the law itself and, naturally, to points of decision-making by the government, places where law is enacted, resources are allotted, and their objectives established.[22] Usually, in theory and in practice, Palestinians' access to Israeli law has been limited to petitions to the Supreme Court and to the military courts in the Territories. Some criminal cases were handled by courts that had previously served Jordanian rule, and the defendants were tried and sentenced according to Jordanian law. The majority (from infliction of bodily harm to murder) were tried in military courts, which also handled economic (bribery, forgery, and fraud), administrative, and traffic violations, "disturbers of the peace," political activists, and anyone suspected of violent resistance of any sort to Israeli rule.[23]

Within this half-covert framework, security legislation has provided the basis for legality, cobbling together shreds of Jordanian and British mandatory law. Jurists from the military administration, usually reservists, officiate as prosecutors and judges.[24] In judicial procedures dealing with "security violations," sessions are usually held behind closed doors, and most of the evidence is withheld from the defense (so as not to incriminate informants and so-called collaborators, among other reasons). Israeli military courts are not obliged to announce arrests, interrogations, or remands, or to make proceedings, charges, or verdicts public. Confessions extracted from the accused by force and torture have played a decisive role in court. Most convictions in which Palestinians were sentenced to long prison terms were obtained through plea bargaining, because the Palestinians lawyers usually feared a much worse outcome if a trial took place, and the military court system wanted to cut proceedings short.

Due process was rare, violent types of sanctions and punishments were imposed, and prolonged administrative detentions were decreed, as well as expulsions and house demolitions. The military commander could issue confinement and arrest orders if he found this to be "necessary or useful" for public safety, order, or the existence of the state, and only he could revoke them.[25] But in this case, too, a certain legal procedure was introduced early on: from November 1967 on, decrees concerning land confiscation, permits, and customs could have been appealed to an appeals committee, and in May 1970, special committees were established for dealing with administrative detentions.[26] Those committees were part of the military administration, however, and their conclusions were mere recommendations; they hardly ever revoked the rulings of the military. Still, the legal show was kept intact.[27]

Most of the numerous Palestinians who encountered Israeli law did so within this kind of show. In the military court, the legislating, prosecuting, and judging functions all belong to a single hierarchical, centralized authority—the army. Only the defense attorneys were not a part of this authority, and soon many of these were perceived by Palestinians as collaborators with the occupying power. The fact that most defense attorneys were Arabs, from Israel and the Territories, and that most of the prominent Jewish defense attorneys were and still are women, did not improve the lot of defense attorneys at military courts. Still, the presence of a defense attorney is necessary in court, because the show cannot take place without it. The role of the legal theater was neither to expose the truth nor even to monitor other branches of the ruling apparatus and restrict the damage they did. Nor was it meant to serve as an arena where the individual could press charges against the government. From the outset, the military court was one of the places in which the occupying power asserted its legality and crushed any resistance. Here, oppression was exposed to public gaze, received legal sanction, and acquired a rational image, ensuring its perpetuation. Still, however, since the very beginning, military courts have served as an arena of negotiation and a place of friction and fraternization between Jews and Palestinians, citizens and noncitizens.[28]

Legality resembled a closely perforated sieve. The holes had many shapes: the permit regime; state-of-emergency regulations imposed by the British Mandate in Palestine, which remained in force in the Occupied Territories and in Israel; the authority vested in the military commander to suspend the law, cancel existing rules, dismiss publicly elected officials, deny individuals and entire groups their rights by restricting movement and canceling travel permits, and order administrative detentions, expulsions, house demolitions, and the like; the absence of any possible public or political supervision of budgeting for government actions in the Territories; and the Supreme Court's sweeping readiness to adopt nearly verbatim any "security considerations" presented by security elements that would justify rights violations. These extrajudicial and semi-judicial techniques perforated the rule of law on a single pretext—security. Their multiplicity enabled and required decentralizing the sovereign authority to decide over life and death, bringing deliberation, negotiation, and protestation to an end. This authority was vested, not only in the minister of defense, the chief of staff, and their deputies, but also in military governors and their subordinates, junior officers of the military, and agents of the General Security Services. All swore by security. Soon enough, on grounds of security considerations, there was a whole government apparatus administering a subject population in quasi-colonial conditions.

Three components made up this apparatus: the Israeli government's firm decision to govern the Occupied Territories as if it were the legitimate sovereign power without changing their legal status, turning the inhabitants into noncitizens devoid of any rights, and undermining their sources of livelihood in the Territories, driving them to integrate into the Israeli economy as cheap exploitable labor. Security per se became an increasingly abstract and generalized term and permeated more and more realms of life. It turned into an object of faith shared by the political Right and Left and the steady basis for political partnership of Jews in Israel. Furthermore, it was what justified and in fact necessitated continued rule over the Occupied Territories and the ongoing refusal to recognize their inhabitants as citizens. The sanctity of security was the other side of excluding Palestinians from the fold of citizenship, and those claiming security as their expertise have become "experts" on "the Palestinian question." When the Likud government came to power in 1977, it received this constellation ready-made, and when its turn came to escalate the colonization process, hardly any changes were needed.

THE MANAGEMENT OF LIFE

The Palestinians were ruled as noncitizens but also as subjects whose activities had to be governed and their well-being cared for by the ruling apparatus, on condition that they respected it and gave up their existence as political beings. Shortly after the end of the war, the military administration took on responsibility for the Palestinians' lives in various realms, first and foremost, health and agriculture, as well as education, trade, communication, and welfare. The West Bank and Gaza Strip were divided into districts, each of which was assigned a military governor and staff officials for civil matters, divided into two areas: the economy and services.

In the first years following the war, there were quite a few political and economic elements in Israel who conceived of Israel's role in the Occupied Territories along the lines of the classic colonial model and wished to promote the development of infrastructures for services, administration, and economy, and to lean upon cooperative local leadership and a cadre of Palestinian administrators and professionals. Indeed, after recovering from the shock of the conquest, numerous Palestinians at various levels of local administration and politics did agree to cooperate with the Israeli government. Various systems in the realms of education, communication, and municipal government were left intact by the military administration. Thousands of teachers, clerks, and Palestinian heads of local and regional councils remained in the posts they had filled before the war. The salaries of these functionaries were paid in part by the Jordanian government, which wished to retain its influence in the West Bank and support all those who refrained from cooperating with the Occupation regime.[29] By decree of the military administration and under its supervision, animals and humans were vaccinated, information changed hands, and regulations were promulgated to prevent the spread of contagious disease. At the initiative of the military administration, women were encouraged to deliver their babies in hospitals, doctors, teachers, and clerks were trained, farmers were guided and aided in various ways, new varieties of crop were offered for cultivation in order to improve the level of nutrition in the Occupied Territories, professional schools were opened, and training courses were offered in many fields of employment.[30] Five years after the war, the military administration gave its permission to found a new university in the Occupied Territories—the Bir Zeit University—and enabled foreign staff to teach there alongside Palestinian lecturers. From the outset, however, the military administration was involved in the curriculum, banning courses that might nurture national consciousness and closing the university for long stretches of time following allegations of political activity on campus.

However, implementation of the classic colonial model was limited, partial, and short-lived. All plans to develop the Territories for the well-being of their Palestinian inhabitants proposed in the first years of the Occupation—whether in the hope of integrating the Territories into Israel or because the Israeli state was seen as the sovereign power that bears responsibility for the population there—were shelved one by one.[31] Rather than becoming a lever for development, the integration into Israeli systems of infrastructure in the Occupied Territories (water, electricity, communication, and traffic) shortly after their occupation became a double-edged sword, which soon created additional channels of domination. At first, this integration did improve infrastructure in the Occupied Territories. Later, however, it enabled Israel to control agricultural water quotas, impose a cultivation policy favorable to Israeli growers, allot mountain aquifer water to Jews on both sides of the Green Line, divert streams, create water shortages and even thirst in some Palestinian localities, and splinter the West Bank with a set of roads serving Jewish settlers. The administration left the responsibility for sanitation and garbage disposal to the Palestinian local authorities.[32] It minded the distribution and reallocation of resources and the maintenance of existing systems, but did not invest in development, and even prevented investments in this area. It protected Israeli farmers and traders from Palestinian competition and turned Palestinians in the Occupied Territories into captive consumers of Israeli goods through its control of import permits.[33]

The status of Palestinians as noncitizens was manifest in every sphere of life, vis-à-vis both the authorities and Israeli citizens in general. The first decade after the war saw a systematic effort on the part of the government to provide the Palestinians with their basic needs, provided that they submitted to it, thus eliminating resistance to and even collaborating with the colonizing project. The military administration began collecting data about the population, its circumstances and activities, growth, and development in various spheres. The conclusions of these surveys were translated into a list of needs, the provision of which the administration wished to monitor. It even met some of them itself: partial connection of villages to water supply systems, telecommunication services, bus lines, gas supply, professional training, postal services, replacing local money with Israeli currency, and supervision of religious shrines and holy sites. At the discretion of the local commanders, the provision of these services was occasionally withheld as a punitive measure—or improved as reward for collaboration.

Spending on such provision of services and infrastructure was largely financed by taxes levied by the military administration rather than from government ministries' budgets. The budget of the military administration was considered a "closed market," supported by its independent income from taxes and excise collected in its area. The inhabitants were taxed directly (income tax, municipal property tax, business tax, and rural property tax) and indirectly (import tax, excise on local products, value-added tax, excise on goods and fuel, stamp and transit permit taxes). Income tax money was transferred directly to the military administration, while property tax money was passed on to the municipalities.[34] The balance of payments of the West Bank and Gaza Strip shows an article headed "budget burden," detailing direct transfers by the Israeli government for covering deficits in the civil budget of the military administration earmarked for consumption and investment in the Palestinian sector not covered by taxes collected from the inhabitants. The "budget burden" imposed upon the Israeli taxpayer as a result of the activity of the military administration changed over time. At the end of the 1970s, the rate of net burden amounted to about US$10–15 million a year.[35] But growth of the number and income of Palestinians working in Israel reduced the budget burden respectively, and in the mid-1970s and early 1980s, taxes collected from Palestinians in the Occupied Territories were spent in Israel proper, benefiting Israeli citizens.

The new Occupation regime promised to improve the Palestinians' living conditions and rescue them—thus the Israeli speakers—from the backwardness to which the Jordanian and Egyptian regimes had subjected them. Egypt and Jordan were held responsible for having thwarted any development for refugees in the camps, while Israel's responsibility for the existence of a "refugee problem" in the first place was entirely suppressed.[36] After volunteering to make restitution to Palestinians for the immediate damage caused by the war, Israel offered various programs to improve housing, agriculture, health, and education in the Occupied Territories. All of these were offered from an occupier's lordly position, demanding—in return—peaceful acquiescence and unequivocal recognition of Israeli rule. Local leaders could negotiate the form in which such recognition would be manifested, but could not do away with the actual requirement. Leaders who did not cooperate were dismissed, persecuted, and exiled. In 1971, for example, the military governor dismissed the mayor of Gaza, Rajeb al-Alami, for having refused to condemn terror and opposed the connection of Gaza to the Israeli electricity grid. In 1972, another mayor of Gaza, Rashad al-Shawa, who had been appointed by the military governor, was dismissed for having refused to collaborate with the ruling apparatus's attempt to reduce the separation of the Shatti refugee camp from the city of Gaza.

The ruling apparatus succeeded in curbing civil resistance and prevented it from spreading throughout the Occupied Territories in any coordinated manner. The creation of stable local leadership was halted, affecting the ability of Palestinians to maintain a public political space and distancing the echoes of their protests from the "neighboring" Israeli political space—but not quenching resistance altogether. More likely, resistance was pushed out of the political sphere and into that of violence, which took on changing forms and sprouted new leaders and patterns of relations between the semi-secret political leadership and leaders of the clandestine resistance organizations.

The executive branch of the Israeli government was directly involved in governing the Occupied Territories through a "CEOs committee," consisting of the general directors of most government ministries, which has convened often and regularly since the end of June 1967.[37] The committee made detailed administrative decisions regarding the ongoing management of all realms and levels of everyday life in the Occupied Territories, from principal resolutions about land-appropriation procedures and restitution for their owners, for example, up to decisions touching upon the private affairs of individuals, such as granting someone a permit to open a business, build a gas station, or plant an orchard. Officially, the committee was answerable to various ministerial committees, but these changed depending on political circumstances, whereas the CEOs committee was consolidated as an institution of continuity with professional bureaucratic authority. At the same time, a "coordination committee" was set up in the Ministry of Defense, whose members were representatives of the military, the Security Services, the police, the Ministry of Foreign Affairs, the government adviser on Arab matters, the army general advocate, and some lower-ranking officials and officers. This committee was headed by a general directly answerable to the chief of staff, and in spite of its emphasis on security, it also handled civil matters.[38]

These two committees actually duplicated the structure of Israeli administration in a version tailored for the Occupied Territories. Through the CEOs committee, a body consisting of high-ranking civilian bureaucrats whose main responsibilities concerned the citizens and territory of Israel proper, the Territories became an inseparable part of Israel's space of governance, and not just of its space of domination and control. However, this committee's activity took place under the auspices of the military administration and the implementation of its resolutions was officially subject to the army's general staff, which according to international law was responsible for the occupied area. It functioned in conjunction with the Ministry of Defense's coordination committee and was subject to permission given, and restrictions enforced by the military commander and the GSS. This included not only Security Services agents and those forced to collaborate with them but army troops on policing and securing assignments, as well as in training bases, which were swiftly moved into the Occupied Territories shortly after the war. This was the first extensive project initiated by the government for creating "new facts on the ground." Its initiator and executor was Ariel Sharon, the general then in charge of the army's training branch.

One of the main devices of governance and control used by the military administration was the system of permits needed in all realms of life, inherited from Jordanian law and greatly expanded. Permits were needed for construction, opening businesses, moving one's dwelling place, working in Israel, travel abroad, studies abroad, appropriating land for agricultural purposes, and so on and so forth. The permit itself is a familiar bureaucratic device for government control, but it acquired a life and logic of its own in the Occupied Territories. The kind of activity that required a permit and how to obtain it were never transparent. The extended demand for permits—first and foremost permits to work in Israel proper—created whole areas of illegal existence where the Palestinians were even more exposed and vulnerable than usual, having to live with extortion and assaults by Israeli citizens, mostly employers, who exploited the special dependence and vulnerability of their Palestinian workers.[39] Thus, for instance, lacking permits to stay in Israel after nightfall, thousands of Palestinians had to spend the night in work camps inside Israel, where they were—"voluntarily," as it were—caged with fences, locks, and chains. Employers looking for cheap Palestinian labor often did so against the law, which set a quota of legal workers or forbade the employment of minors. Surprise inspections by officials of the Employment Bureau could drive workers who were afraid to be caught and arrested from their workplaces, and their imposed absence from work mostly resulted in the employer's shirking his responsibility for their illegal hiring and withholding their wages.[40]

Clearly, relations between workers and employers, having developed on parallel tracks, just like those between the collaborator and his control in the Security Services, cannot possibly be summed up only in terms of coercion or exploitation. Friendly ties often developed, many later resulting in tales of treachery or bravery. But even the most trustworthy friendship could not overcome the entrenched, structural hierarchy and subjection of any relations to the surveillance of the Security Services. The permit system served as a link and interface between the security and civil branches of the ruling apparatus. Any permit issued required the approval of the Security agents in any administrative office, and thus the most routine everyday functions became an area of friction, negotiation, extortion, and collaboration between the ruled and the rulers, and the most routine rules were sown with exceptions who were granted special permission. Basic rights—to leave, to return, to study, to open a business, to publish, or to assemble in public—became favors that the government could bestow, deny, or transform into more or less explicit threats.

In this way, thousands of Palestinians were compelled by the Security Forces to provide information and help incriminate others, thus hastening the erosion of trust and camaraderie within Palestinian society. In the Occupation's first decade, implementation of administrative decisions was left to officers of the Israeli military administration, aided by officials of the Jordanian administration that had previously ruled the West Bank or by the former Egyptian apparatus in the Gaza Strip, as well as by members of local councils and *mukhtars* (village elders).[41] The local Palestinian leaders whom the military administration wished to strengthen acted as mediators, handing out permits, while those whom the administration wished to weaken could not obtain permits for their residents. Both groups were central targets for information gathering, denunciations, interrogations, persecution, and expulsion. Still, in the first decade, as the Security Services institutionalized their grip on everyday life, exclusion was still the exception to the rule, aimed mostly at individuals and not the population as a whole, and functioned more as a threatening potential than as a regular disruption of life.

The omnipresent permit system made the Palestinians greatly dependent upon the military administration, a dependence that exceeded the activities for which permits were required. This system forced Palestinians to expand their encounters with the ruling apparatus to fulfill the needs of their everyday existence, but also created a dependence on local leadership and urban and rural administration apparatuses attached to the military administration. Many Palestinians—willing or forced, their agreement obtained through bribery, deception, and violence—filled various functions in this administration such as translation, coordination, information gathering, tax levying, interrogation, identification, or reporting. In December 1967, half a year after the start of the Occupation, 6,534 Palestinians were already working for the military administration in the West Bank (in contrast to only 329 Israelis, of whom 123 were tax and customs officials), and 2,860 Palestinians in Gaza (and only 125 Israelis).[42] Not all service providers received due payment, and many were met with hostility by the Palestinian public. The lives of more than a few were actually at risk,[43] and they were not always protected by the Israeli regime.

The role played by Palestinians in the hybrid regime set up in the Occupied Territories was minimized or denied altogether by the Israelis, who soon enough grew accustomed to seeing Palestinians as subjects from whom services could be obtained cheaply. Although for years the ruling apparatus needed Palestinian support to preserve its rule and maintain normal life in the Territories, that support was often presented as contemptible, proof of the treacherous or greedy Palestinian nature, well expressed by the derisive term "collaborator."[44] Representing the Palestinian share in the ruling apparatus as collaboration made a special contribution to constructing this apparatus as temporary and completely separate from the population it dominated. Seemingly detached from its governed population, the ruling apparatus was represented as if it could fold up and withdraw anytime, anywhere, without leaving a trace or costing anything for which anyone would be held accountable. Thus the permit system, from the start the main channel connecting the government and the ruled, served as a central device of interpellation shaping the Palestinian individual as a subject of the Israeli regime, and presented that regime as an entirely alien power, in which the Palestinian had no part.

As a rule, the form of administration and management of life instated by the ruling apparatus under military administration was relatively effective in bureaucratic terms, both because of the ongoing coordination between the various ministries and because of its relative detachment from the political, juridical, and civil system in Israel proper. The CEOs committee was officially subordinate to the committee of ministers on civil matters in the Territories, but this was devoted more to political wrestling than to policy-making. Incoherent political decisions and laws stemming from a prolonged legislative

process were replaced by administrative decrees, regulations, and ad hoc resolutions made to accommodate changing circumstances. Some of these governmental devices were concurrent; others replaced one another in productive
disorder, without ever being assembled into an orderly code. The civil system
was intertwined with the military one, as civil considerations were with those
of "security"—always meaning security of and for the Jews.

The Israeli democratic ethos created the impression that the two sets of
considerations could be differentiated, but the systems of government, the civil
and the military, have become increasingly deeply intertwined over the
years, and their separation is a mere illusion. Complete separation could never
be achieved, if only because a complete picture of civil and military activity
in the Occupied Territories could never be obtained. The various government
ministries' activities developing infrastructure and services for the army and
the settlers in the Territories were subject to political and legal supervision just
like any other government activity, but they were—and are—budgeted by type,
not by area. These expenditures were thus buried in the overall budget, making
it almost impossible for critics, whether internal or external, to expose the nature of the activities involved or break down their cost.

Immediately following the war, inhabitants of the West Bank of the Jordan River were disconnected from the East Bank, and inhabitants of the Gaza
Strip were not permitted to leave for Egypt. The Jordan River in the east and
the border between Egypt and Palestine/Israel in the west, dating from the British Mandate, became the new borders, which the Palestinians were forbidden
to cross. But in late July 1967, goods were already allowed to be transported
between the West Bank and Jordan, and by autumn, the bridges over the Jordan had been repaired and reopened to controlled passage.[45] Concurrently, the
Gaza Strip was declared a closed military zone under a decree that remained
in force until 1972, but workers were still permitted to travel into Israel. A general exit permit issued on November 30, 1967, enabled relatively free movement
between Gaza and the West Bank.[46] Palestinians who obtained exit permits to
travel abroad and laissez-passer documents (in the absence of passports) were
able to fly out of Ben Gurion International Airport or leave for Egypt through
the Rafah crossing and for Jordan over the Allenby Bridge (albeit under strict
supervision, in harsh conditions, involving prolonged waiting, humiliation,
and harassment).[47]

The Jordanian and Egyptian currencies were replaced by the Israeli one,
but the Jordanian dinar was recognized as legal currency. Palestinians were en-

couraged to export goods, especially farm produce, through Jordan, and family and current social ties were maintained among Palestinians on both sides of the Jordan River. Passage via the bridges was granted Palestinians as a privilege, which might be revoked at any time, depending on "security needs."[48] Denying individuals or the entire population their right of passage by temporary closure of the bridges soon turned into one of the common punitive measures exercised in response to unrest and resistance. The open bridges also enabled the authorities to use expulsion as a cheap, easily practicable form of punishment.[49]

In 1972, Palestinians were granted a sweeping exit permit into Israel, but military edict no. 5 forbade them to stay overnight in "pre-1967" areas without a special permit.[50] Lively streams of workers, goods, and buyers resulted on both sides of the Green Line. Within two years, a third of the Palestinian labor force was employed inside Israel. Working there and in Israeli settlements in the Occupied Territories brought Palestinians into close contact with every aspect of Israeli reality. Aside from the relatively few Palestinian subcontractors who recruited other Palestinians, they were hired as cheap labor for work that needed no special training and offered hardly any chance of promotion.

The Israeli economy benefited from the labor of Palestinian children as well. Thousands of minors from the age of ten up worked for especially low wages at service stations, snack stands, cleanup jobs, dish washing, and in plant nurseries. Work was sought at sites that emerged spontaneously every morning at the main crossroads and corners of cities, which Israelis called "slave markets" with little sense of guilt or shame. At these sites, Palestinian workers felt as though they were putting their bodies and work capacity on the block, like wares for sale.[51] Palestinian buying power, rapidly growing because of employment in Israel and in the Gulf states, was exploited unilaterally. In many areas the Palestinian market was "captive" to Israeli goods, enabling the rapid growth of Israeli industry and creating a growing gap between the two economies.[52]

While the movement of labor and export of agricultural products were relatively free and encouraged, various limitations were placed upon importing raw materials, machinery, and farming equipment, depending on the government's perception of the Israeli market's needs. With the permit policy, the ruling apparatus prevented imports and the construction of new industrial plants in most areas and allowed local entrepreneurship only in limited areas (such as producing food for local consumption or textiles under subcontract from Israeli producers), according to the interests of various sectors of the Israeli economy. By blocking industrial development in the Occupied Territories, opening them to Israeli products, encouraging the flow of labor into Israel proper, and prohibiting Palestinian workers from organizing and fighting for their rights, the ruling apparatus restructured the Israeli economy and made the Palestinian economy an integral yet inferior and exploited part of it.[53] Income and social security taxes and customs and excise duties were imposed on Palestinians without creating any mechanism to safeguard their interests when decisions were made about the use of this revenue—and naturally without allowing the Palestinians any kind of representation in this decision-making.

The Green Line ceased to be a border between two states and became a productive marker helping to constitute Palestinians as noncitizens, shaping the everyday vulnerability that characterizes this noncitizenship and the modes of action open to people of this status: as workers, they were unorganized, unprotected by a professional union, exploited more than any others; as landowners, their property was free for the military to take for its own uses and for the expansion of settlements; as entrepreneurs, they became mediators between Israeli employers and Palestinian labor; as civil servants, they became mediators between the military administration and Security Services officials and Palestinians in need of permits; as collaborators, they were directly and indirectly recruited by the Security Services; as intellectuals and political leaders, they had to go underground in order to do things that under normal circumstances are the heart and core of civil society; and as political activists, they often were forced to translate their resistance into an armed struggle against the Occupation.

The integration of the Palestinian market and labor into Israel's economy extricated the country from a recession and in those first years even considerably increased the product per capita in the Occupied Territories,[54] largely improving the Palestinians' capacity for agricultural production. However, it created a growing structural dependence of the Palestinian economy upon the Israeli economy and systematically held back the development of the Palestinian economy. Civil, judicial, and class separation soon became institutionalized as a form of integration that imposed a relationship of domination—at that time, it was also one of production—which soon came to seem self-evident and inevitable. Yet prior to the First Intifada, this form of integration was seldom publicly articulated and problematized, or even made visible, although the subordination, discrimination, and expropriation that were its condition and effects were present everywhere. The naturalness with which integrating separation was institutionalized, the meager civil opposition to

it inside Israel, and the isolation of Palestinian resistance by the ruling apparatus enabled Israelis to regard the Occupation as "enlightened" and even to
take pride in it.[55]

COLONIZATION

When the State of Israel was established, Zionist colonization became a state
project. At the end of July 1948, an administrator titled the "custodian of absentees' property" was appointed by the Israeli minister of the treasury to take
custody of the assets left behind by Palestinians who had fled or been expelled.
These displaced persons were designated "absentees," and their property was
declared to have been "abandoned." A series of ad hoc rules and regulations
authorized the government to take immediate possession of such "abandoned"
property without any legal process and authorized it to issue certificates that
would constitute incontestable evidence in any future judicial proceeding. In
1950, the Knesset passed the Absentee Property Law, ordering the confiscation
of the lands and homes of all those defined as "absent" on the day of the first
general census. Palestinians who managed to return to Israel and obtain citizenship by presence or through family reunification procedures were declared
by law "present absentees" and lost their confiscated property too. Thousands
of Palestinians citizens were thus deprived of their lands and property.[56]

The new wave of state colonization that followed the war in 1967 began
shortly after the war with the reintroduction of similar procedures to take over
the property of "absentees," and once again the custodian of absentees' property
played a key role. In September 1967, the State of Israel held a census in the West
Bank and Gaza Strip. Anyone present in the Territories at the time and taking
part in the census was registered and recognized by Israel as a "permanent resident." Residents who failed to register were declared absentees and their property
was declared abandoned. Officers were appointed by the regional military commander to take charge of this "abandoned" property and authorized to manage
it at their discretion, and to lease or rent it out as if they were its legal owners.[57]

Under Ottoman law embedded in the Jordanian code of law that Israel inherited in the West Bank, declaring land as abandoned and expropriating it to
become state land, reversed the normal onus of proof: instead of the state being
called upon to prove its claim or justify an act of confiscation, the Palestinians
had to prove that the expropriation of their land was illegal.[58] But even when
they did, the state could still hold the land if it could prove that its officials
had confiscated the land "innocently," mistakenly considering it to be aban-

doned.[59] Soon the state also suspended procedures regulating land registration and made any transfer of landownership subject to approval of the military commander.[60] The obstacles facing Palestinians wishing to retrieve their lands were nearly insurmountable.

In the first years of the Occupation, the civil administration registered about 430,000 dunam (one dunam = 1,000 square meters, or 10,764 sq. ft.) and 11,000 buildings as abandoned property.[61] Some of these lands were leased to relatives of the absentees, but a considerable part were not tended and thus could later be declared state land. Both state land and private—confiscated—property were soon allocated to military bases and the establishment of what were then termed "security settlements." However, lands were first taken over without any consolidated blueprint for Jewish settlement. In the early years of the Occupation, this was a matter of dispute between advocates of settlement that would ensure Israel's hold on all parts of the West Bank and those who "were ready for territorial compromise"—that is, withdrawal from *parts* of the Territories—and saw the settlements as a means to redraw Israel's borders. Within a few years about 430,000 dunam—7.5 percent of the West Bank—were identified and declared absentees' property. Property that had previously belonged to the Jordanian or Egyptian governments (in the West Bank and Gaza respectively), together with anything belonging to citizens of other enemy states or to economic bodies registered there, was also declared absentees' property and became state land as well. By the end of the first decade of the Occupation, Palestinians lost access to about one-fifth of their land in the West Bank and one third in the Gaza Strip (over 700,000 dunam of "abandoned property" in the West Bank became state land, over 100,000 dunam were declared nature reserves, and over 47,000 dunam were confiscated for "military use").[62]

Most land grabs in the first years of the Occupation were merely of an administrative-legal nature, and only a small portion of the land was put to use. Expropriation was considered temporary, and on principle most of that land could have been returned to its owners without much trouble.[63] The Israeli imprint on the Palestinian habitat was irreversible only in and around Jerusalem. Israeli law was enforced in the Jerusalem area within borders that were redrawn several times. Most Palestinians residing in the annexed area became permanent residents—not citizens—and some of their lands were expropriated. Jewish neighborhoods were quickly built to the north and south of the city, and within a very short time, the landscape changed drastically. Palestinians—if they had not left the city for too long and did not lose their right to return[64]—

found themselves living beside and among Jews, benefiting from an influx of Israeli and Jewish tourists, and from a slight improvement in governmental and municipal services. The relatively calm integration of Palestinian residents was part of the colonization process in an ever-expanding city. Among Jews, legitimization of construction around Jerusalem was sweeping. Tens of thousands of Israelis moved into the new neighborhoods, constituting about 70–80 percent of all Jewish settlers in the first decade of the Occupation. However, they were never regarded as settlers by most Jewish Israelis, and for many years, they were not even counted in the dispute over the settlement project.

Away from the neighborhoods built around Jerusalem, colonization proceeded rather slowly and to the tune of recurrent, ritualized conflict between the religious-nationalist Right and their supporters in the Labor government who were eager to accelerate Jewish settlement throughout the Territories, on the one hand, and their opponents in the government who advocated a more limited scale and restrained pace of colonization, on the other. Few members of the Zionist Left questioned the colonizing project itself; the main questions in dispute were its scope and methods. Lacking its own settlement plan, the Labor government repeatedly gave in to settler pressure.[65] Soon these disputes took on a ritual, repetitive nature, and clichéd arguments became elements in one's political identity. The acquiescence of the Left in faits accomplis presented to it by the Right became part of the ritual. Such clichés had the guise of polarity and blurred the fact that both parties to this quarrel agreed at least tacitly, if not explicitly, to plant Jewish settlements in the Occupied Territories (and not just around Jerusalem), cooperating through numerous channels.

In the first decade of the Occupation, under Labor governments, settlements were perceived by government officials as a means to perpetuate Israeli domination, and most of them were built in areas declared vitally important, from which no withdrawal would ever be considered, even in the eventuality of a peace treaty. But there was no agreement, even within the ranks of the Labor movement, on the definition of vital areas. More than anything else, the map and pace of colonization reflected the power relations between Moshe Dayan and Yigal Alon. The former wanted a settlement map that would make the occupied territory no longer partitionable, while the latter envisioned a new partition whereby the Palestinians would give up the Jordan Valley and the eastern slopes of the Judea and Samaria hills and areas adjacent to the Green Line and make do with control of most of their urban areas and the mountain areas in Judea and Samaria. The dispute, which was never settled, framed Israelis' relation to the territories in the years to come: an internal Jewish affair in which Palestinians had no voice and were merely obstacles on a map that needed to be redrawn to serve Israeli Interest. In the meantime, settlements proliferated and gradually crept into the heart of the Palestinian areas. Still, by the end of the first decade, Jewish settlers remained a small minority—slightly over 7,000 Jews were then living in thirty-eight settlements in the Occupied Territories, aside from the Jerusalem area, and prominent cases of Palestinian dispossession still triggered public protest.

Politically, the settlement issue quickly found itself center-stage. Arguments for and against the settlements were being ritualized and they overshadowed all other aspects of the ruling apparatus in the Occupied Territories. The latter became the axiomatic framework of both Israeli and Palestinian daily lives and political existence. It was perceived mainly as the mechanism that enabled the expansion of Jewish settlements and mostly ignored with respect to its own expansion into every sphere of Palestinian life. Behind the political polarization on the question of settlement was a basic agreement regarding the necessity of the ruling apparatus, which was systematically misconceived, inasmuch as it was overshadowed by, and interpreted mainly through, the ongoing debate on the settlements.

Both parties in the settlement debate made the same assumption—that it concerned only Jewish Israeli citizens. Palestinians, including Israeli citizens, had no voice in the debate. This takeover of political discourse in Israel by the settlement issue itself in fact amounted to ethnic cleansing. Civil discourse was reduced to internal national Jewish separatist discourse. This became especially evident once a new settlement actually "took its ground," and any attempt to impact it was interpreted as an attack on Jews—in fact, on the Jewish people as a whole. Long before determining the map of colonization, the Right succeeded in hallowing the settlements, turning their leaders into heroic pioneers who dedicated their lives to the nation. This weakened the opposition voices contesting the basic justification for creating settlements in the first place and their specific locations, which could still be heard within the ruling apparatus, including the army. The settlers were adept at manipulating their image and expanding their influence through a typical mix of hugs and slander, loud confrontation and behind-the-scenes lobbying, lawlessness and self-righteousness, pragmatism and self-sacrifice. This combination, which made its appearance as early as the struggle over the first settlements in Gush Etzyon and Hebron,[66] is still in evidence today.

During the first decade of the Occupation, the right-wing settlers and their supporters had not yet managed to change the general balance significantly, notwithstanding that the first government of Prime Minister Yitzhak Rabin (1974–77), surrendered—or yielded—to them on the settlement issue, leading to the founding of Ofra, near Ramallah, and Kedoumim, near Nablus. A relatively limited effort by the government was first directed at territories where Jews had lived until 1948 (the Jewish Quarter in the Old City of Jerusalem, Gush Etzyon, Hebron) and areas sparsely populated by Palestinians along the Jordan Valley, as well as the Occupied Sinai Peninsula (the Rafah plain in the northern Sinai, and along the Red Sea shore) and the Golan Heights. The Labor government was eventually responsible during its term in office for the actual construction of twenty-six settlements, and the planning and initial phases of another fifteen. Expansive land-grab operations created the infrastructure for far more extensive settlement, but did not suffice to block a political move in the opposite direction. The Zionist Left refused to be impressed by the obvious colonization process, believing in its own ability to shape it at will in the future, and was locked into the conception that the option still open at the end of the first decade of the Occupation would remain open even when the number of settlements grew fourfold and the number of settlers fivefold or more.

RESISTANCE, SUPPRESSION, AND COLLABORATION

In the latter half of the 1960s, before war broke out, armed Palestinian refugees had begun to gather on the Jordanian side of the Jordan Valley. From there, they infiltrated Israel—and after the war, the West Bank—to attack Israeli soldiers, settlers, and officials. For the Palestinians, this was a necessary phase in their struggle to eliminate the "Zionist entity," permitting them to return to their lands, and most Palestinians idolized the *fedayeen* (those who risk their lives) who carried out these actions. The Israelis, however, portrayed them as terrorists (*mekhablim*).

The Karame Operation in 1968, which resulted in numerous Israeli casualties and a sense of victory among Palestinians, made the Palestinian combatants all the more determined to fight the dual occupation—in the areas conquered both in 1948 and in 1967. Their actions dragged Israel and Jordan into a series of violent confrontations along the Jordan Valley, which Israeli public opinion perceived as part of the war of attrition flaring up at the same time along the Suez Canal.

In late summer 1970, however, the Hashemite Kingdom of Jordan decided to put an end, not only to guerrilla fighters using its territory as a base, but to any armed Palestinian presence in Jordan. Thousands of casualties resulted when the Palestinian resistance organizations were expelled from Jordan in what became known as "Black September." Armed infiltration into Israel from Jordan ceased, but the remaining Palestinian fighters moved with their political leaders to refugee camps in Lebanon. From there, they soon renewed violent resistance to the Occupation.

Soon after the war, the Israeli security forces collected most of the weapons abandoned by the Jordanian and Egyptian armies in the Occupied Territories. An extensive wave of arrests in the first days after the war targeted political activists and those suspected of organizing armed activity. Al-Fatah, the main Palestinian organization, having changed its strategy of fighting Israel after the Occupation, sent cells of combatants and weapons into the Occupied Territories and began to organize and train its men for popular warfare against the occupier.[67] Its leader, Yasser Arafat, entered the Occupied Territories himself and took part in this operation. A series of assaults on Israeli targets enabled the Israeli security forces, which had already acted vigorously inside the Occupied Territories, to spot most of the activists and eliminate the infrastructure that al-Fatah had prepared for months.[68] Within a short time, the Israeli security forces destroyed al-Fatah's headquarters, killed dozens of combatants, and arrested thousands, putting an end to armed popular warfare in the West Bank. This spectacular success overshadowed the fact that most of the resistance was not violent and originated in various local groups rather than the Palestinian liberation organizations. Members of these groups (who, like the combatants, were tagged as "squads" in military jargon) often set fire to tires, but they also organized strikes and smuggled money from Jordan to pay the wages due Palestinians employed by the military administration who did not show up for work. The city of Nablus led the resistance, but the threat of flare-up hovered over the entire West Bank.[69] During the first year of Occupation, over 1,000 political activists were prosecuted. In the West Bank, however, resistance and oppression were only one dimension of the interaction and struggle between Jews and Palestinians.

In the Gaza Strip, things were different. Hundreds of thousands of refugees who had been expelled or uprooted from Israel in 1948 and had lived in Gaza since then in ever-worsening poverty and neglect now had their chance to confront Israelis. Hundreds of Gazans, living mostly in refugee camps, joined the

PLO, then led by its first chairman, Ahmad Shukeiri. They managed to obtain weapons and chronic violent resistance to Israeli rule occurred on a vast scale. Moshe Dayan wavered between retaliating with massive military action and halting the administration in the Gaza Strip in order to turn Palestinians' lives into "a living hell."[70] The killing of four Israeli soldiers in 1970 tipped the scales, and the army began a large operation in the Strip, with massive incursions into houses, searches, and violent arrests. At the same time, efforts were made to defeat the local leader Ibrahim Abu Sitta, secretary to Ahmad Shukeiri. Under total curfew imposed on the refugee camps, the army demolished thousands of houses and widened main roads, aiming to better control the "wasps' nests," as the Israelis called the camps. The extensive violence used by the Israeli army at the time hardly resonated in the Israeli media, although there were a few stories—dismissed by the army—of extreme cruelty by soldiers.

No state commission of inquiry was set up at the time, and the public was satisfied with mere fragments of information. Our picture of Palestinian resistance suffers from the lack of historical research based on primary sources, especially regarding the first two decades of the Occupation, and we have only a few splinters of testimony. A letter by four Israeli soldiers describing the horror raging in Gaza was sent to various newspaper editors, and *Ha'aretz* sent its reporter Amos Eilon to investigate. Eilon collected horrifying testimony from Palestinians in the camps about acts of murder, rape, bodies thrown into the sea, people disappearing, looting, and the expulsion of families to transit camps in the southern Sinai. In the article he subsequently published, he presented as factual only those stories he could cross-check against information gathered from Israeli eyewitnesses, portraying testimony that had not been validated by Israelis he had met as "fictitious."[71] When members of the Israeli League for Human and Civil Rights tried to collect testimony about what had gone on in the Gaza Strip, they had to make do with accounts by soldiers and local Palestinians, but were prevented from gathering further information. In their report at the time, they wrote that "under Israeli military occupation, the Gaza Strip with all its 350,000 inhabitants has turned into a horror zone of constant war and killing, raging terrorism and the murder of women, the elderly and children."[72] A letter to the journalist and Israeli Communist party member Yosef Algazi from a soldier who had been in Gaza at the time was censored in its entirety and consequently appeared in Algazi's 1974 book *Dad, What Did You Do When They Demolished Nadder's House* as a large patch of white. All that remained of the original letter was its opening paragraph: "I read the column

"Not indifferently . . . " in *Zu Haderech* ["This Is the Way," a daily published by the Israeli Communist party] of December 22, 1971, [and] saw the many patches of white [left by censorship], and this troubled my conscience, because during my service in the Israeli army (I was discharged not long ago), I was posted in certain locations in the Occupied Territories and witnessed several things that would shock any person who is still human and possesses a human conscience." From there on, the white patch replaces the censored text of the letter.[73]

Concealment was not only the outcome of direct and strict military censorship, compartmentalizing information, and closing archives to the public. The army chose to conceal no more than what the public chose not to know. Official censorship of Israeli voices was hardly needed at the time of the events in Gaza, either in the early 1970s or later. Investigative journalists and academic researchers were not invested in documenting and understanding the Israeli mode of controlling the Occupied Territories, and nongovernmental organizations allocated no resources to information gathering. Nowadays, with the proliferation of new electronic communication and social media and the existence of numerous nongovernmental organizations dedicated to monitoring human rights violations and deteriorating humanitarian conditions in the Occupied Territories, it is much more difficult to censor reports of atrocities and keep them in the dark for long. But it is still no easier to arouse public interest in the accumulating information, to direct resources for research, or to get access to archives that hold information from the first years of the Occupation. Lacking this kind of information, we are left with a medium-resolution picture. It clearly indicates the existence of an especially violent policy of suppression alongside relentless Palestinian resistance, of which the events in Gaza in the early 1970s were paradigmatic; whether these events were also representative we cannot tell.

The Israeli military presence in the Territories soon drastically changed Palestinians' living environment. Armed soldiers patrolled the streets with clubs, there were house demolitions and internal displacements, and areas out of bounds to Palestinians were fenced off. Telecommunications and the electricity supply were frequently shut down to "punish" resistance and "disorder." In the fall of 1970 (during "Black September"), the Jordanian regime expelled Palestinian militias from its territories, and the infiltration across the Jordan River stopped. Violent resistance in Gaza was completely repressed in 1972.

The defeat of the Palestinians' armed struggle was accompanied by a new state of humiliation. It is uncertain whether Israel's political and military leadership set the tone or was swept along by the media and the hundreds of thousands of Israelis who streamed into the Territories immediately following the war. The fact is that within a very short time, colonial patterns appeared in the relations between the Israeli "masters" and the Palestinian "subjects." Quickly adjusting to the new conditions, "good" Palestinians offered cheap goods for sale in colorful markets, where they could be bargained for in an oriental atmosphere. The "bad" Palestinians who persisted in resisting were portrayed as "rioters," or "an incited mob"; anyone found in possession of a weapon was a "terrorist." Arab leaders treated as legitimate by the Israeli occupiers were invariably "local dignitaries"—which came to signify people who had surrendered to Israeli rule and would collaborate with it. The leaders of the Palestinian national movement were "heads of terrorist organizations." Political activists were "outlaws" with a "nationalist background." Women who took an active or indirect part in resistance by throwing stones, "being rude," cursing, crowding, blocking streets, organizing support of families of the victims of violence, or sheltering members of the resistance were stigmatized as sexually promiscuous. The pejorative *sharmuta* (whore) was often used to abuse women activists, potentially exposing them to violence given the patriarchal code of Palestinian society. When that code was triggered, the ruling apparatus could present the women as in need of protection and appear as their enlightened protector against their "backward society" with its traditional, retarded ideas of women's and family "honor."[74]

Israel used considerable force against armed militants and civilians alike. Actions against "local pockets of resistance" and leadership groups hurt wide circles of the population regarded as suspect. Retrospectively, these did not yet amount to total, ongoing intervention in everyday Palestinian life, which was yet to come, but at the time Palestinians experienced a massive increase in withheld and eruptive violence exercised by the ruling forces. The civil uprising in most of the West Bank cities and the violent uprising in the Gaza Strip may be seen as evidence of the life-disrupting presence of the occupier. Still, the lethal effect of clashes between the security forces and "rioters," "terrorists," and suspects was relatively small: according to Israeli sources, only 650 Palestinians were killed in the first two decades of the Occupation. In the early 1970s, it seemed that Israel had completed its takeover of the West Bank and Gaza Strip and reduced pockets of resistance, and that little use of military force would henceforth be needed to rule them. Total calm in the Occupied Territories during the Yom Kippur War (October 1973) added to the sense that the ruling apparatus was functioning well, and that the real security problem did not lie there, but rather in a dysfunctional military preparation system, exposed by the Israeli fiasco during the first days of that war.

The interlacing of the ruling apparatus with the fabric of Palestinian life created various channels of cooperation, without which normal life would have been impossible. In agriculture, education, finance, and medicine, for example, Palestinians worked under military administration officials, and to a certain extent alongside them as well. In 1975, over 9,000 local workers were employed by the ruling apparatus in the West Bank, and 5,000 in Gaza, while Israeli workers there numbered only a few hundreds.[75] The everyday activities of Palestinian employees of the military administration were necessarily, to some extent, participation in Israeli rule. From within the limitations of their inferior position as occupied noncitizens under an alien government, however, these employees even negotiated with the administration over the nature of their participation.

For many Palestinians, this integration of Palestinians into the ranks of the administration always seemed a form of collaboration.[76] Having found shelter in the refugee camps outside the Occupied Territories, the resistance organizations, with al-Fatah at the forefront, vehemently opposed any such form of cooperation and struggled to thwart it by all means possible. Their response to the relative normalization of the Occupation was the creation of local committees aiming to disrupt the ongoing civil functioning of the Israeli military administration. But the centrally organized administration of everyday life made it impossible for Palestinians to provide for their basic needs without the mediation and aid of the military administration, and the local committees did not inspire widespread popular resistance among the public. Still, acts of resistance persisted: trades, schools, transportation workers, and court systems engaged in strikes, there were petitions against the military administration, and various protest demonstrations took place. Palestinians refused to reduce their political life to municipal issues. The ruling apparatus tried to treat this resistance as a local matter, even a domestic or familial one, placing responsibility on the shoulders of local leadership. "The IDF will take care of al-Fatah, and you'll take care of misbehaving girls," Moshe Dayan told local leaders in Nablus following a mass demonstration of schoolgirls to protest house demolitions.[77] This remark, which contains a formula whose echoes are still heard today, is instructive of Israelis' patriarchal-colonial view of Palestinians politics: women and children are subordinate to their menfolk, who must control and harness them; traditional local leaders enforce the political limitations imposed by Israel and do what the Israeli administration tells them to do.

The question was how to control Palestinians and deny them a political existence without tyrannizing over them. The approach adopted did not stem from a clear idea of the Occupation or from any specific strategy. It came about, rather, by trial and error, as a result of coincidences and changing political circumstances, the level of resistance, the changing needs of the Israeli market, business opportunities opened up by integrating Palestinian workers, and pressure from those who wished to expand the settlements. Along the lines of Dayan's explicit policy, local government heads were promoted as "administrative leaders."[78] However, their authority was very restricted. First and foremost, they were denied the right to grant construction permits and alter land use—in the context of the land-grab scheme described above, this was a role strictly reserved to the Israeli military commander, who also had unlimited authority to dismiss any *mukhtar* (village leader), whether elected or appointed, "whom he found unsuitable, who had neglected his duties or abused them."[79]

Clandestine talks involving senior Israeli politicians and King Hussein of Jordan and his men had been held since 1963 but had not yielded any accords.[80] During "Black September," covert cooperation between Israel and Jordan took place under American mediation, whereby Israel deployed reserves forces to deter Syria from attacking Jordan in an attempt to rescue the Palestinians from the Jordanian assault. Even this collaboration did not bear any political fruit. Most Israeli politicians and generals assumed that negotiations over the future of the West Bank should and would be with Jordan, not with the PLO. Palestinian political existence was thus restricted to a small group of supporters of the Hashemite regime in Jordan, and even this was sparsely allowed, closely monitored, and usually clandestine.

In March 1972, Israel, now confident of its rule, allowed elections for mayors and local councils in the Occupied Territories. These were "free" under Jordanian law, that is, those eligible to vote were at liberty to choose their candidates, but the right to vote was limited to male property owners over the age of twenty-one who were not residents of refugee camps and had paid their taxes on time—a mere 5 percent of the population.[81] Opting to uphold Jordanian law in this, of all matters, Israel excluded Palestinian women—who had taken an active part in political life since the beginning of the twentieth century, and especially since the Nakba—from the restricted political space of the elections.[82] In the next elections, four years later, the ruling apparatus chose to grant women the vote, explaining that "this is necessary for proper rule and upholding the rights of the population."[83] Exclusion and integration were both practiced to serve Israeli interests, as were similar measures whereby the ruling apparatus interfered with the internal lines of division and strife in Palestinian society and manipulated tensions among the various groups. The enfranchisement of Palestinian women was immediately advanced as proof that "the enlightened Occupation" promoted women's liberation, contributing to the modernization of a backward, patriarchal society.[84]

Al-Fatah's leaders saw the 1972 elections as an attempt to exploit the weakening of resistance following the expulsion of the Palestinian leadership from Jordan a year earlier, and they called on Palestinians to boycott them. Meanwhile, the Occupation authorities used carrot-and-stick measures to pressure the local population to participate. The idea was to nurture collaboration with local leaders and position them to replace the PLO leadership, whose symbolic role as national representative of the Palestinians Israel refused to acknowledge. The aim was to overemphasize local leadership and encourage it to deal with matters of governance beyond the narrow municipal sphere, although still only regional, of course. The threat made by Israel that it would appoint mayors if the Palestinians did not elect their own candidates eventually led to elections whose results matched Israel's expectations: they neither produced significant change nor created a new leadership in the Occupied Territories, and Israel could boast of the democratic proceedings it had facilitated there.[85] The PLO, having failed to thwart the elections, consequently tried to increase its influence in the refugee camps in an attempt to replace the mayors with their own, alternative leadership. However, these attempts were suppressed by the Occupation authorities, which systematically worked to undermine any independent Palestinian attempt to create a united leadership that would represent the Palestinians in the Occupied Territories as a national community with which any decision regarding the future of the Territories and the nature of their rule must be negotiated.[86]

Four years later, in April 1976, elections were held again in an effort to flaunt the propriety and stability of the Occupation administration and even give it a certain dimension of local democracy. The PLO leadership accepted participation in these elections only when it realized that they could not be prevented, responding to the recent emergence of young cadres of local leadership. Given the suppression of Palestinian political organizations and the prohibition of any public political action in the Palestinian sphere, it was Palestinian workers' mobility in and out of Israel and the fact that numerous Palestinian youths had served long terms in Israeli prisons that helped create a vibrant political community and consolidate the cadre that generated the First Intifada.[87] This young leadership regarded the elections as an opportunity to push aside the pro-Jordanian elite, perceived as part of a "Zionist-Jordanian conspiracy" aiming to prolong the Occupation rather than resist it.[88] The members of this new cadre had grown up, mostly in Israeli workplaces and prisons, relatively independently of the Palestinian communities, either rural or urban, and the Occupation authorities had worked hard—but failed—to depoliticize them. Although some of the candidates in the local elections who were affiliated with Jordan were supported by the military administration, most of the elected leaders were identified with the Palestinian national struggle. They were especially supported by women, who were given the vote on the assumption that they would tend to support "moderate" candidates, but who chose to elect radical ones instead.[89]

Israel reacted by boycotting and disconnecting itself from the elected leaders, seeking to continue governing while bypassing the "radicals" (and eventually removing some of them in response to violent Palestinian resistance in the early 1980s).[90] At the same time, despite the formal prohibition of political activity and the persecution of its leaders, the Occupation authorities often tended to look the other way when such activity took place covertly under the auspices of "nonpolitical" organizations, such as charities or teachers' unions. The latter had functioned relatively freely since the struggle over commencing the first school year under Israeli rule. It was then that the limit of permissible activity was established: the military administration hardly interfered in setting the curriculum or in teaching that did not treat Palestinians as political subjects. The Security Services were nonetheless involved in monitoring schools, censoring textbooks, hiring and firing teachers, and taking responsibility for the administrative aspects of the school system.[91] This monitoring did not aim to nurture Palestinian education, but only to prevent public expression of the Palestinian national narrative and eliminate anything that might inspire a national struggle.

In the first decade of the Occupation, the ruling apparatus was engaged in governing Palestinians' lives and providing for their needs, but only if those lives were apolitical. Anyone who dared call for political struggle, whether armed or unarmed, was penalized. Those who refrained from political activity were usually able to enjoy the public services provided by the military administration, but a sharp, clear line separated receipt of social welfare from people's liberty to shape their own lives through political action and struggle. The ruling apparatus justified this separation in terms of the need to curb Palestinians' national aspirations—perceived as a threat to Israel's actual existence—but separation was itself a primary motivating force in the nationalization of resistance, pushing aside Jordanian influence and consolidating broad popular support for the PLO, the main force struggling against the Occupation. By the end of the first decade, however, that support had not yet ripened and translated into widespread popular resistance.

The relative calm of this period enabled the Occupation authorities to maintain the façade of an "enlightened occupation" that observed the letter of the law and promoted democratic institutions, growth, and improvements in various areas. However, Israel ruled by decree, and the ruling apparatus in the Occupied Territories gradually freed itself from most constraints. The entire judicial system—legislation, regulations, edicts, legal authorization to suspend rules and revoke existing arrangements, military courts, appeals committees on land appropriation, administrative detentions, petitions to the High Court of Justice—was subordinated to the ruling apparatus. As a result, it gradually became virtually indistinguishable from the executive branch. Not a single component of the legal system in the Territories, including the Supreme Court, served effectively to monitor and curb the Occupation authorities. To a great extent, that system merely lent the guise of legality to institutionalized penalization of Palestinian noncitizens, burgeoning forms of expropriation, denial of rights, and tyrannical intervention in the fabric of daily life. At first, only individuals and groups who insisted on overt political struggle felt the impact of this; gradually, however, even those who merely by existing disturbed colonial expansion were targeted.

2 THE SECOND DECADE

The second phase in the history of the Occupation opened with the accelerated and visible colonization of the late 1970s, when the Likud party rose to power, and lasted until the outbreak of the First Intifada in December 1987. The Alon More affair of 1979 marks that turning point more than Likud's actual victory. Alon More, a Jewish settlement near Nablus, was built on private Palestinian land expropriated by military edict. In October 1979, the High Court of Justice declared this expropriation illegal because the government had failed to prove that it was strictly justified for "military needs." The Occupation authorities responded by introducing a new model of land appropriation that facilitated colonization at a faster pace.

Instructed by Plia Albeck, senior deputy to the state attorney general, the government resorted in the Occupied Territories to a Jordanian property law (Ottoman legislation dating from 1858) stipulating that unregistered land (constituting about two-thirds of the area) that was not claimed with official documentation and was found untended could be declared state land. Originally, the rationale of this law had been to protect unregistered land from trespassers, but the law also stipulated that the sovereign government could change the land's prescribed usage. Shortly after the Alon More ruling, the government declared all unregistered and untended land in rural areas to be state land, regardless of the decades-old claims to it of thousands of Palestinians. The latter were allowed to contest this at a special appeals commission appointed by the military administration, but in order for their appeal to succeed, they needed to show a *kushan* (certificate of ownership), usually not something they possessed and never before demanded by the authorities. State agents often resorted to various tactics of deception in order to make it all the more difficult for contesters to prove their claims. As the prescribed usage of areas declared as state land could be changed, vast territories could now be designated for the construction of Jewish settlements.[1]

Attempts to delegitimize this novel legal-administrative procedure failed. All dams broke after Israel's High Court of Justice accepted the position of the state attorney general, which blatantly ignored the earlier intent of the Ottoman law.[2] By the end of 1980, 35 percent of the West Bank was already designated for Jewish (settlers') regional councils, and 6.9 percent was under Jewish municipal jurisdictions. In addition to expropriating land on security grounds—mainly for the construction of military bases and the paving of roads—and declaring land to be state land and changing its prescribed usage, the government used its interpretation of Ottoman and Jordanian law to take over "for public needs" land declared to be "absentees' property." The government of Prime Minister Menachem Begin eliminated the monopoly on trading in Arab land held by the Jewish National Fund, Keren Kayemet le'Israel, operating through its subsidiary Himnuta, and welcomed Jewish private enterprise into the real estate market in the Occupied Territories.[3] Land registration was changed by special security legislation that simplified procedures and removed any vestige of external monitoring. This made it easier for private entrepreneurs to participate in the government's efforts to take over Palestinian land. Easing land registration encouraged fruitful collaborations between Jewish entrepreneurs and Palestinian realtors, both legal and illegal, and created a wide platform for applying political and economic inducements to both administration officials involved in land registration and Palestinians involved in land sales. A few years later, it even led to several criminal indictments involving government officials and elected figures.[4]

The first Begin government (1977–81) spawned thirty-five settlements, mostly in populated areas, which the Labor government had purposely avoided. Massive colonization began only in 1982, however, after the peace treaty with Egypt was signed and the settlements in the Sinai were dismantled, and when the First Lebanon War broke out. At the time, about 22,000 Jewish settlers were living in the Occupied Territories in over seventy settlements, and about 58,500 in neighborhoods around Jerusalem.[5] The trend was obvious, but the moment that Meron Benvenisti would call "irreversible" had not yet arrived. In October 1982, trying to dissuade various political elements from proceeding with the colonization process, Benvenisti still referred to it being "five minutes to midnight."[6]

Five years later, when the First Intifada broke out, about 100,000 Israelis were already living in over one hundred settlements in the Occupied Territories and colonization was in full swing. Likud governments subsidized the settlements both directly and indirectly, and offered potential settlers significant economic incentives.[7] Due to topographic conditions and the way the settlements were spread out, especially in the hilly regions of the West Bank, the Palestinian area under de facto Israeli control was much larger than the area formally taken over by administrative and juridical means.[8] Moreover, the spread of settlements, army bases, and access roads to them created a dense grid of Jewish presence in the Territories, fragmenting Palestinian space into separate enclaves. By the 1990s, this had become a fait accompli.

Employing its characteristic blend of disobedience, self-righteousness, and gestures of self-sacrifice with effective political lobbying, the religious Right assailed right-wing governments whenever construction in the settlements was halted for political reasons, whether as a result of American pressure or of the economic recession of the mid-1980s and the formation of a "national-unity" government.[9] On these occasions, too, no political determination had actually consolidated to the contrary. By that time, however, officials unequivocally committed to colonization on ideological and political grounds, with ample authority and resources at their disposal, were already siding with the settlers. The rate of growth in settlement construction was determined by a combination of circumstances and causes: internal politics, control of particular government ministries, the economic situation, and the extent of the interest and reservations of the U.S. administration at the time. However, these constellations merely determined the pace. The direction remained unswerving: a steady growth in the number of settlers and dwellings, and of the expanse of land taken over—whether expropriated, purchased, or simply stolen—throughout the Territories.

Alongside the spectacular but localized settlement operations, grandiose plans were being drawn up in government ministries, at the Settlement Division of the World Zionist Organization, and by the Jewish Agency, formally two independent bodies, but in fact organizations functioning as an arm of the Israeli state. Even if these plans were never officially adopted by the government, they did set a new horizon for the colonization project.[10] In 1977, Ariel Sharon, minister of agriculture at the time, adopted Professor Abraham Wachman's "Double Ridge" idea and began to create the "Stars Plan" for suburban localities close to the Green Line. One year later, Matityahu Drobles, head of the

Settlement Division, presented a plan prepared by a team headed by Dr. Chaim Tzaban for the creation of sixty rural and urban settlements. A new plan drafted by Tzaban and presented by Drobles five years later (in 1983) aimed at "maximal distribution of a large Jewish population in Samaria and Judea, in areas that are significant for colonization . . . within a relatively short time." The idea was to settle 100,000 Jews in the West Bank within three years, but Jewish population of between 600,000 and 800,000 within thirty years was envisioned.[11] The plans included extensive development of water and power infrastructures for the Jewish and Palestinian populations, paving roads, and constructing industrial zones. They would necessitate and encouraged a vast land takeover. Indeed, by 1984, 40 percent of the West Bank was already either in private Israeli hands or claimed by the State of Israel,[12] and land for the construction of dozens of new settlements had been identified.

Earlier plans to include the Palestinian population in various development initiatives led by Israel—either through its mediation or by mere agreement—were abandoned altogether.[13] Plans for developing infrastructures in Palestinian localities were not realized. The only development in the Occupied Territories was that of Jewish settlements. In 1981, they were accorded separate municipal rule by local councils, operating for all practical purposes as Israeli municipal authorities, constituting an effective channel for special permanent budget subsidies to Jews living in the Territories. Amendments of the emergency regulations introduced in 1984 authorized the minister of justice to apply Israeli law in its entirety to Israeli citizens living in the Occupied Territories and Jews wishing to be naturalized in Israel. Thus the settlers' legal status was already made nearly equal to that of Israeli citizens living in Israel proper, and legal separation drew Jews and Palestinians further and more deeply apart.[14]

With the legal separation between the two population groups complete, various processes of integrating the Territories and Israel were now advancing in full force. On the judicial plane, procedures and technical terms in different realms were standardized and reconciled (the electric power grid and water-supply network, taxation, vehicle insurance and traffic accident coverage, weights and measures, cost-of-living increments for public service officials, etc.).[15] The integration of infrastructures and technical standards naturally did not reflect equal levels of service. The infrastructure in the Occupied Territories resembled that of a Third World country even after two decades of Occupation.[16] Meanwhile, Israel completed its takeover of water sources in the Territories. Responsibility for water supply was transferred from the military

THE SECOND DECADE 65

administration to Israel's national water company, Mekorot, in 1982, and severe restrictions were placed upon new water drilling in the Palestinian territories.[17]

The most pronounced change, however, was felt in the accelerating integration of the Palestinian economy into that of Israel. Tens of thousands of Palestinians were employed as workers and contractors in the construction business and various services in Israel proper and in the building of Jewish settlements, transforming the Palestinians' habitat and living conditions beyond recognition. The rise in their living standards, following their shift to employment in Israel, was tempered considerably in the second decade of the Occupation and did not substantially contribute to the development of the Palestinian economy. Most of the Palestinian workers were still employed by contractors, unorganized in any form of labor union. Many of them lodged close to their workplaces during the week in unbearable, crowded conditions—in basements, storehouses, and abandoned buildings—and they were frequently victimized by their employers and in police raids. Investments in the development of local employment sources were mostly blocked, turning Palestinian society into an exporter of labor to Israel and the Arab Persian Gulf states (Bahrain, Kuwait, Qatar, Saudi Arabia, and the United Arab Emirates) and making Palestinians dependent on the demand for labor in those countries.[18] Palestinian workers in Israel were the first fired at any firm or industrial plant, and they were naturally the first impacted by the severe economic recession of the 1980s.[19] Economic dependence, a consequence (not necessarily intended) of Israeli domination in the Occupied Territories, became one of its most effective devices.

The economic integration that had actually improved living standards in Palestinian society during the first decade of Occupation now enhanced its vulnerability.[20] It did not atone for the land grab but rather provided the conditions for its exacerbation. Thousands gave up their traditional farming and went to work in construction and services inside Israel. They abandoned their lands, some of which were declared "survey lands," their status unclear and their prescribed usage suspended, while others were invaded by Israeli settlers without authorization on grounds that they were untended.[21] Although improved living conditions during the first years of the Occupation apparently curbed resistance to it, economic integration eventually created the conditions for a conflagration. Those working in Israel, many of whom resided in the refugee camps, were the main source of growing support for the PLO. This transformed Palestinian resistance into a national struggle, demanding the creation of a Palestinian nation-state. Growing resistance was still fragmented and sporadic.[22] However, its national expression in Palestinian discourse was loud and clear, and perceived by the State of Israel as a threat that must be removed. New steps were taken to deepen surveillance in the Occupied Territories and curb the growing influence of the PLO on people's minds and daily lives.

A calculated step in this direction was the attempt to create a trustworthy system of Palestinian collaborators to counter supporters of the PLO and of Jordan on the level of local government. The key here was the opposition of the former Jordanian cabinet minister Mustafa Dudin's "village leagues," backed by Israel, to nationalizing the Palestinian struggle against the Occupation. The first "village league" was founded by Dudin in the Hebron area in 1978, with the approval and encouragement of the Israeli minister of defense at the time, Ezer Weizman. Additional such associations were subsequently founded in the Bethlehem, Ramallah, Tul Karm, Nablus, and Jenin districts, encouraged by the orientalist Menachem Milson, adviser on Arab affairs at the Israeli army's Judea and Samaria HQ and later head of the civil administration. They were meant to restore and empower traditional *hamulah* (clan) rule and enhance the differences among regions inhabited by different clans, as well as between villagers and city dwellers. These associations benefited from Israeli government funding and were granted municipal government authorities, including the authority to levy taxes and to use firearms against "outlaws" and opponents. Opposed not only by the PLO and Jordan but by the Palestinian urban middle class and women's associations, which were playing a growing part in the political struggle, the village leagues did not obtain popular legitimization. When Ariel Sharon was forced to resign as minister of defense in February 1983, they lost all hold in the Israeli establishment, and they were dismantled shortly thereafter.[23]

In creating the village leagues, the Occupation authorities tried to impose premodern models of social organization, without considering changes in the power relations within Palestinian society resulting from two processes. First, young Palestinians integrated into the Israeli labor force became their families' main breadwinners, learned the occupiers' language, and enhanced their status in society, weakening the traditional family hierarchy. Second, women gained both increased status and recognition by the male leadership for their role in the national struggle. Among these youngsters and women, a new elite emerged, which interpreted its situation in national terms and mostly chose to join the various forces supporting the PLO. The ruling apparatus's ideological policing prohibited any manifestation of nationalism, but juridical and economic separation, felt most severely by workers commuting to Israel, made nationality a common denominator and the natural framework for interpreting Palestinians' social experience of the Occupation.

The failure of the village leagues revealed the PLO's rising power in the Occupied Territories in particular, and the nationalization of resistance in general, and induced a strong counterreaction on the part of the Occupation authorities. The first political organization of PLO-supporting mayors in the Occupied Territories elected in the 1976 municipal elections—the National Palestinian Front, created in 1978—was outlawed in 1979. In May 1980, following the murder of six yeshivah students in Hebron, suppression and censorship of all public and intellectual activity intensified, and the elected mayors of Hebron and Halhul were exiled to Jordan, along with Hebron's Muslim judge (*qadi*). The Israeli authorities ceased to ignore quiet political activity outside the public sphere. As in the first days of the Occupation, intellectuals, labor union leaders, and party activists, especially left-wingers—already outlawed under Jordanian rule and skilled in clandestine activity—again became targets for interrogations, persecution, arrests, and expulsion. Sweeping censorship was imposed on publications of all kinds, including pictures and songs, to prevent the emergence of political discourse. Newspapers, periodicals, and books were confiscated. The public display of nationally symbolic images was not permitted, and Palestinian flags could no longer be flown. Strict supervision was applied to textbooks in all educational establishments, and any text even remotely associable with resistance was banned. Schools and institutions of higher learning were closely monitored, both in their curricula and as the focus of resistance and incitement against the Occupation.

In 1979, Israel signed a peace treaty with Egypt, and talks commenced on granting the Palestinians "autonomy" in the Occupied Territories. In the negotiations that had taken place prior to signing the treaty, Prime Minister Begin managed to postpone any significant discussion of the future of the Territories and avoided recognition of the Palestinian people's national delegation. The political horizon drawn by the treaty for Palestinians was an institutionalization of "enlightened occupation" and the creation of a limited political space for noncitizens who had accepted subjugation to Israeli rule, along with the colonization of the Occupied Territories and the structural inferiority of the Palestinian economy. An absolute majority of the Palestinians rejected this treaty outright. If even a sliver of a chance for real political negotiation had survived the autonomy talks, the official in charge of the Israeli delegation, Minister Joseph Burg, took care to stifle it.[24]

In view of the paralysis at the "autonomy talks," the civil administration of the Occupied Territories was created in 1981 as part of an overt unilateral attempt to promote "resident autonomy," which Israel promised the Palestinians in its peace treaty with Egypt. Formally and in keeping with the treaty, the civil administration institutionalized the separation of direct military action from the administrative control of Palestinian life. The head of the civil administration was authorized to issue new decrees and regulations, but the hub of authority of the civil administration remained the military commander, who also retained senior legislative authority.[25] The creation of the civil administration actually completed the transfer of administrative control from the Ministry of Defense into the hands of the Israeli army, a process that began after the resignation of Ezer Weizman in May 1980. The coordinator of government activities in the Territories was then subordinated to the army chief of staff instead of to the minister of defense, with growing involvement of military commanders in decisions regarding everyday life, at the expense of the military administration's professional officials.[26]

The jurisdiction of the military regional commands shifted in 1980: the Gaza Strip was placed under charge of the Southern Command, while the West Bank remained under the Central Command. The Occupied Territories were now governed as separate units, divided territorially into two military designated areas. Under the civil administration, the ruling apparatus continued to interfere in the lives of its Palestinian subjects with its permits, orders, and restrictions. Through close monitoring and surveillance, it tightened their dependence on the system, thickening its network of Palestinian informers and collaborators, who were pressured and blackmailed into aiding the Israeli security apparatus in return for permits to receive basic services. In this capacity, the administration began to create a comprehensive database of the population in the Occupied Territories that, beside the "usual" information on each and every subject, also included information about the person's unsettled debts to various authorities, past felonies or violations, and any other data that might make one suspected of "hostile" activity or a tendency thereto. This database, which became operational in 1987 and has been updated regularly ever since, serves as a basis for granting permits for work in Israel according to the policy implemented during the First Intifada.[27]

A second Palestinian mayors' organization, the National Steering Committee, was decreed illegal in 1982. That year, nine mayors in the West Bank and the mayor of Gaza City were dismissed by order of the civil administration and replaced by Israeli army officers. Army officials had already served as mayors in other towns in the Gaza Strip.[28] The limited "administrative autonomy" that the Palestinians had originally been promised became the limited autonomy of a single Israeli ruling entity—the civil administration—under another Israeli ruling entity—the army. The Occupation authorities could not accept the national politicization of the Palestinian struggle, but all measures taken only accelerated this process and eventually made the administration more militant and less civil. In summer 1982, it seemed that active suppression had succeeded, and that the struggle against the PLO—in fact, against the Palestinians' national existence[29]—had shifted from the Occupied Territories to Lebanon, where it was carried out violently and, to an unprecedented extent, in open warfare, nearly free of any legal or political reins.[30] In the Occupied Territories, a reasonable level of Palestinian cooperation was restabilized both by force and by choice, providing a few more years of seemingly normal existence, which the coordinator of government activities in the Territories termed "the invisible occupation rule."[31] Invisible it was, but—naturally—only to international and Israeli eyes that had also failed to see the efforts exerted in suppressing Palestinian resistance and in concealing and denying this suppression. For the occupied Palestinians, the Occupation was visible nearly everywhere, present in every corner of their lives, making them unbearable. Many Palestinians and a handful of Israelis had realized back in the early 1980s that the outbreak of a sweeping Palestinian uprising against this state of affairs was merely a question of time.[32]

In the mid-1980s, within this "normal" existence, Palestinian resistance grew and became routine in the Occupied Territories, alongside cooperation with the regime. Not a day went by without some "disturbances of public order," setting tires on fire, throwing stones, and—in rare instances—shooting, causing Israeli casualties.[33] It remained scattered, however, unorganized and lacking any political backing. Furthermore, it became popular and emerged from within the Territories, not from "terrorist bases" or "nests" in Jordan or Lebanon. In February 1987, Central Regional Commander General Ehud Barak explained that the character of the Palestinian enemy had changed: instead of trained infiltrators and terrorists, the army now faced students and schoolchildren, and instead of firearms, it had to deal with stones and graffiti.[34] Some military officials and politicians perceived this change but refused to understand it as widespread resistance to occupation. The few journalists who insisted on venturing into the Occupied Territories felt the growing hostility, but they, too, did not know what to make of it.[35] Still, the level of violent resistance was relatively low, and its political profile was vague. The ruling apparatus succeeded in quenching budding political and military organizations and in distancing the media from some of the more violent incidents. This relative success enabled a fairly sparse deployment of troops, who employed violence locally, avoiding a massive presence inside cities and on the roads, and not placing too great a burden upon the Israeli economy.

In those years, Palestinian resistance to the deepening processes of domination and dispossession was affected by close and ongoing contact with Israelis. There were meetings and talks between Palestinian activists—especially leftists in the PLO—and Jewish leftists. The latter began to document the "injustices of the Occupation" and criticize them, especially in terms of infringement on Palestinians' human rights. The question of contacts with PLO members outside the Territories became a bone of contention within the Zionist Left, and the official position totally excluding any such contacts was continuously eroded. Conceptualizing the damage to Palestinians in terms of "exceptional" violations of human rights made it impossible to understand the structural change that took place at the time. Some activists of the non-Zionist Left and a handful of intellectuals did offer an analysis of the colonization process and insisted that the Occupation could not remain external in the long run, and was perhaps already no longer external to Israeli rule.[36] But these voices were harshly criticized in mainstream Zionist Israel by both the Right and the Left, and remained lost in the wilderness.

The Palestinians were, of course, the first to perceive the change and realize that Israel was resolved to annex the Occupied Territories de facto and had launched a systematic, extensive process of land takeover, dispossession, and colonization. These actions, as well as ongoing oppression and humiliation by the ruling apparatus, resulted in Palestinians "voluntarily" leaving their lands. At the Arab summit meeting held in Baghdad in 1978, Arab heads of state decided to take direct action to put a halt to this phenomenon by creating funds and offering grants to those who would resist the pressure to leave and remain *tzamadeen*, adhere to their lands. One of the ways to manifest insistence was to resort to legalities. This was part of the new strategy of nonviolent resistance formulated immediately after Likud's rise to power. The juridical success of the Palestinian petitioners in the Alon More affair of 1979 encouraged Palestinians to appeal to the High Court of Justice, aided by Jewish and Palestinian lawyers. The discourse of rights developed and gradually became an accepted strategy of struggle against the Occupation. The courts, and especially the High Court of Justice, turned into an arena of contact and contestation, a place where the subjects could level their gaze at the regime, be recognized as speakers within their own rights and identity, and receive time and attention, regardless of the legal results of petitions filed.[37]

And indeed there was hardly any connection between the legal results and the nature of the Palestinian struggle. In the late 1970s, the High Court of Justice accepted the Israeli state's position regarding the construction of settlements as a security need. To this end, the court was even willing to overlook the contradiction embodied in the claim that the Israeli army was making *temporary* use of private property that had been taken over in order to establish a *permanent* civilian settlement.[38] Later, the court also accepted the new form of takeover of Palestinian lands by declaring them state lands. It sanctioned extensive takeover of lands for the paving of a whole network of swift east-west roads connecting the settlements to Israel across the Green Line, and evaded discussion of the legality of the irreversible changes introduced by the ruling apparatus in the West Bank. The court had sufficient arguments in its juridical arsenal to rule differently,[39] but it chose to reduce most of its interventions to one test—the question of whether the authorities' ruling was "reasonable." "Reasonableness" was nearly always measured by comparing "security needs" to the violation of the humanitarian principles of the Geneva Convention. The security in question was always that of Israelis on both sides of the Green Line, and in this, Palestinians had no say, no right to request information or to question. Their petitions were nearly always examined under the shadow of "security considerations." Only one side could fully take part in the juridical argumentation, and the court nearly always preferred the state's interpretation to "humanitarian considerations," justifying damage to individuals—Palestinians—for the sake of public—Jewish—well-being and welfare. The fate of the Palestinians' petitions, which essentially questioned this balance of "security" and "humanitarian" needs, was foreordained.

Appeal to the High Court of Justice was a possible channel to resist dispossession when the state or its institutions were involved either directly or indirectly. However, as *legislator*, the army commander was almost totally immune to juridical criticism, since he was vested with extensive authority to issue regulations and decrees or suspend existing rules and regulations, and as noted—the court rarely interfered with his judgment. Besides, a great part of the damage done to Palestinians, whether by the army, the settlers, or private entrepreneurs buying up Palestinian lands, took place in areas of administrative and legal vagueness. Real estate was traded in a twilight zone, even in terms of the legalities practiced in the Occupied Territories, through mediators and straw men operating in mafia modes, and seldom exposed to judicial scrutiny.[40] Discrepancies between army orders and instructions to soldiers on the ground, the division of responsibility between the army and the police regarding interrogation and remand, and the reluctance of the weak police forces to engage with the settlers undermined attempts at law enforcement and fostered Jewish impunity de facto (which later also applied to settlers' assaults on Palestinians' lives and property).[41] It is likely that Palestinians complained only about some of this damage; evidently, only some of their complaints led to actual investigation and a minute part of such inquiries resulted in charges; finally, hardly any charges led to indictment. In almost all cases where settlers have been prosecuted, their sentences have been notably light, and there is hardly a case in which a prison term imposed on a settler has not been reduced.[42]

Thus the juridical and para-juridical tools destined to legitimize the takeover of lands for Jewish colonization, refined since Likud rose to power, now became routine practice. They created a façade of legality for a colonizing project carried out through expropriation, takeover of land not officially claimed, forged registration of lands as state property,[43] the construction of dozens of new settlements, massive changes of the terrain through the building of an intricate system of bypass roads, bridges, tunnels, and fences, imposing harsh restrictions upon Palestinian construction, recurring demolition of existing homes of Palestinians under security and administrative pretexts, the uprooting of fruit trees and destruction of farmland, the erection of various spatial obstacles, and creation of a whole system of movement restrictions.

Nowhere did Palestinian resistance manage to halt Israeli expansion or change its modes during this period. Direct violent actions by the ruling apparatus were local and usually short-term, in accordance with the nature of Palestinian resistance. The essentially internal political and external diplomatic restrictions imposed by the government on the colonization project were removed by force of official political resolutions or bypassed through various administrative tactics meant to conceal its extent and blur its tracks, thus avoiding opposition in Israel and abroad until the "facts on the ground" could be presented as faits accomplis. These modes of taking over Palestinians' lands, integrating them into Israeli economy as cheap labor, ignoring them as political subjects, crushing their efforts to constitute themselves as a political community, and separating Palestinian subjects from Israeli citizens continued into the beginning of the third decade of Occupation, but they now encountered widespread, organized popular Palestinian resistance.

3 UPRISINGS, SEPARATIONS, AND SUBJUGATIONS

UPRISING

On December 9, 1987, a traffic accident in the Jabaliya refugee camp in the Gaza Strip in which four Palestinian workers were killed by an Israeli army jeep marked the start of the widespread popular Palestinian uprising that came to be called the Intifada (Arabic "Shaking Off").[1] Unlike any of the Palestinian protests against Israeli rule that preceded it, the Intifada broke out simultaneously in numerous places and succeeded in attracting the attention of local and international media. Men and women from all walks of life in Palestinian society took part. After the Likud government dashed hopes that Occupation was temporary, forceful resistance seemed the only course left open.[2] Resistance intensified first throughout the refugee camps in the West Bank and the Gaza Strip, spreading to towns and villages in early 1988.[3]

Soon the uprising transcended the frame in which Israel had managed until then to contain all acts of resistance. These were usually presented as "disturbance of public order" or "acts of terrorism" and attributed to "terrorist organizations"—that is, to this or that faction of the PLO that allegedly forced the entire population to suffer the consequences of its deplorable actions. This description did not fit a mass uprising of men and women, young and old, dwellers in refugee camps, towns, and villages. The Intifada expressed the democratization of the Palestinian struggle; it closed up the social and gender gaps that had divided Palestinian society and mobilized all sectors of the population in a new mode of struggle. Demonstrations, riots, and clashes with Israeli soldiers took place. Public order was disrupted by various tactics of civil disobedience. Barricades were set up. Stones and firebombs were thrown.

Fields, woods, tires, and vehicles were set alight. There were strikes in the public services. Trade came to a halt. Palestinians stayed away from work inside Israel and broke curfew. Policemen and clerks employed by the civil administration resigned. Israeli products were boycotted, creating a "domestic economy" to oppose the growing dependence of the Palestinian economy on Israel.[4]

At some point, the uprising also included active takeover of small areas by blocking access roads in relatively isolated rural areas. When the Israeli army refrained from entering these areas for a long time, they were declared "liberated zones." The use of firearms, grenades, and explosive charges was very limited.[5] The Palestinians sabotaged the functioning of the civil administration and gradually brought about the resignation of most of its Palestinian employees. By means of popular committees created as the uprising broke out and women's organizations, founded and active since the early 1980s, they reclaimed a certain measure of self-rule in the areas of education, health, welfare, and to a certain extent even internal policing.[6] A new local political leadership emerged in these committees and strongly bonded with them—underground in the Occupied Territories themselves and openly in Israeli prisons. This leadership regarded the PLO as its official representative and accepted its status unquestioningly, but did not necessarily act according to the exile organization's dictates, and it gradually transformed Palestinian politics as a whole.[7]

The Palestinian uprising penetrated the center of Israel's political arena and gave the Occupation—as a regime, as a situation, as a ruling apparatus, and as a relationship—unprecedented visibility in Israeli public space. It cracked the naturalness with which the exploitation of hundreds of thousands of Palestinian workers in Israel was perceived, as well as the silent Israeli acquiescence that had turned the "temporary" domination of another people into a permanent one. Public doubt ran rampant as to the possibility of an "enlightened occupation," "integrating" Palestinians into the Israeli economy, or "improving their situation compared to their brothers in the Arab states." The Palestinian uprising forced Israel to resort to clubs, water cannon, gravel-throwing vehicles (*hatzatzit*), rubber and plastic bullets, and, finally, live ammunition, always backed up by large armed forces—and forced public questioning of Israeli domination in the Occupied Territories, which has not stopped since.

The uprising brought the PLO back into the Occupied Territories and removed Jordanian power hubs in Palestinian society. In summer 1988, responding to Israeli Prime Minister Yitzhak Shamir's rejection of a peace plan proposed by his foreign minister, Shimon Peres, King Hussein's government, which was resigned to the loss of its influence in the Occupied Territories and feared that the Intifada would spread among the Palestinian population in the East Bank, backed off from any claim to Jordanian sovereignty in the West Bank, which was henceforth no longer a bone of contention between Israel and Jordan. The transfer of money from Jordan to the West Bank, which had, until then, proceeded under the supervision of a joint committee of Jordan and the PLO, ceased altogether, and some of the people on Jordan's payroll who lost their livelihood joined the resistance.[8] Egypt had never claimed sovereignty over the Gaza Strip, and the Jordanian declaration was, in fact, a redefinition of the Palestinians as a stateless people.

Israeli governments have consistently refused to admit that Palestinians are a nation deserving of a political existence and the right to self-determination, and insisted on regarding their political and national movement, the PLO, as a mere terrorist organization. But the Intifada altered the position of the PLO in the international arena. It became the only recognized representative of the Palestinian people in general and of the struggle against the Occupation in particular. Its leader, Yasser Arafat, was invited to address the UN General Assembly. Shortly after the Jordanian declaration was announced, the PLO took responsibility for filling the administrative void created by Jordan's withdrawal and began to pay the salaries of civil administration officials and teachers. A few months later, political pressure in the Territories led to a dramatic change in the PLO's political platform. On November 11, 1988, the Algiers conference of the National Palestinian Council confirmed a "Palestinian declaration of independence" calling for the creation of an independent Palestinian nation-state in a small part of historic Palestine, based on UN resolutions 181, 242, and 338. The document was vague, but the reference to resolutions 242 and 338 was interpreted as an implicit recognition of the existence of the State of Israel within the 1967 borders, which was made explicit in Arafat's speech at the United Nations. The formula of "a Palestinian state alongside the State of Israel," for which leaders of the uprising had called since it first broke out,[9] was implicitly adopted by the PLO, which helped it gain sweeping recognition, both Palestinian and international. The "two-state solution" became the political platform of a decisive majority of the Palestinian public.

For the first time, Palestinian resistance had a real impact on the Israeli ruling apparatus, generating a change in the forms of domination and control and significantly increasing the burden of "the Occupation" on the Israeli budget. It also forced a change in public discourse, epitomized by the adoption of the Arabic term *intifada* in colloquial Hebrew. Even when Palestinian resistance abated, control of the Territories was no longer practicable in the previous form, which had been relatively convenient for Israel. Israel could no longer unilaterally determine the nature of Jewish-Palestinian relations. At the end of the first year of the uprising, the U.S. government began to engage in an official, ongoing dialogue with representatives of the PLO, and Israel's boycotting of that organization seemed increasingly pathetic. More than ever before, it exposed Israeli diplomatic rhetoric as a tool for stalling any political change in the Occupied Territories and perpetuating the colonization project. The uprising also opened up vast possibilities for the entry of various foreign elements into the Territories. Foreign governments, international organizations, media channels, and Israeli and international human rights and humanitarian organizations set up delegations, created ties, documented and monitored the army's actions, offered human rights advocacy, and initiated development plans. A permanent international presence was consolidated in the Occupied Territories, which introduced its own agendas and imposed an ongoing confrontation with international law, global media, and critical Western public opinion on the Occupation authorities. This also brought into being a new kind of activism. Over time, both mainstream Palestinians and leftist Jews channeled their political struggles and personal aspirations into NGO's working in the Occupied Territories.[10]

The Palestinians attempted, as much as possible, to disrupt Israeli traffic by means of barricades and Molotov cocktails, creating a constant threat to passenger security and forcing the Israelis to change the nature of their rule on the ground, limit their movement, and change its patterns.[11] Numerous isolated settlements were compelled to become fortified bastions, and the Green Line took on new significance. The Intifada was a challenge to the ruling power, a reminder of its illegitimacy, contesting any kind of order it had wished to impose. Israelis who did not reside in the West Bank and Gaza stopped traveling or visiting there. Soon the Jewish presence in the Occupied Territories consisted only of settlers, members of the security forces, infrastructure technicians, and a few leftist activists.

In order to protect its rule, maintain its domination, and reaffirm its claim to sovereignty, the ruling apparatus had to employ brute force everywhere and defend itself violently, without, however, being able to reinstitute its authority. Ignoring the political significance of the Intifada—which was unarmed at its outset and nearly all along—the Israeli government responded to it with direct, expanding violence throughout the West Bank and Gaza Strip. The government avoided political contacts with the uprising leaders in the Territories, let alone with official Palestinian leaders outside. In spite of the decisive change in the visibility and acceptability of Palestinian national demands, the ruling apparatus insisted on seeing any form of organization, assembly, or political expression as a temporary disruption of order related to terrorist activity. From December 1987 until the signing of the Oslo Accords in 1994, the uprising was a permanent, unchanging given, imposing a new form of temporariness upon Israeli control in the Occupied Territories.

In order to quench the uprising, the ruling apparatus had to greatly increase the Israeli military presence and deploy forces throughout the inhabited area—the order of magnitude grew fivefold and came to include seven brigades. The Territories were reoccupied, as it were.[12] Tear gas, clubs, and rubber bullets were extensively used. Several original Israeli innovations were added (such as the *hatzatzit* armored halftrack, able to throw gravel up to a hundred meters), aimed at harming people, "breaking their bones" so as to neutralize them without killing them. Tens of thousands were arrested, indicted, and imprisoned, and about 14,000 were placed in administrative detention, usually for six months, but then reset again and again under British Mandate emergency regulations.[13] A prolonged curfew was imposed on densely populated areas; efforts to obtain information by various means became more aggressive and included frequent resort to torture; rubber bullets were used to deadly effect.[14] In 1988, a nighttime curfew was imposed on the Gaza Strip, which would be lifted only when the Oslo Accords were implemented in 1994. When the Intifada began, all schools and institutions of higher learning were closed, and most of them remained shuttered for many months. House demolitions and sealing were frequently carried out as punitive measures against people suspected of "terrorist activity," and hundreds of Palestinian families to whom no crime was attributed lost their homes in this way.[15]

Israel did not yet have at its disposal the crushing means of control it resorted to in the Second Intifada,[16] and it avoided the expansive violence against Palestinians that was used in 1948, the border clashes of the 1950s, and, in a different form, the attack on refugee camps and Palestinian neighborhoods during the First Lebanon War. The violence, humiliation, and brutality employed to suppress the uprising were severe in comparison to anything witnessed in the Occupied Territories before, or at least since the suppression of resistance in the Gaza Strip in 1970, but they were mild in comparison to the kind of violence that was involved in similar situations of colonial suppression elsewhere, like indiscriminate use of live fire, starvation, rape, or mass expulsion. The famous call of Yitzhak Rabin, then defense minister, to "break their bones" is emblematic in this respect, as it was a call to cause harm and avoid killing and resulted in much brutality. Israel did not totally shirk its responsibility for the Palestinians' lives, however, or give up the pretense of continuing to govern them. It treated them as rebellious subjects. Even in the worst days of the Intifada, the government insisted on presenting the suppression of the uprising as law enforcement and itself as a regime acting by law to maintain public order.[17]

Some of the means used to suppress the uprising took on a legal guise. The new reality whereby masses of Palestinians do not recognize the regime and do not obey it led to accelerated legislation to catch up with the events on the ground. The short time needed for legislation in the Occupied Territories,[18] and the lack of public mechanisms for monitoring and supervising it, turned the military commander's decrees into a tool no less important and effective than more familiar violent measures in suppressing rebellion and preserving Occupation rule.[19] Employing a series of edicts and instructions, the army forced the local population to obtain permits that had not previously been required, and thus to interact more frequently with the civil administration. These new army decrees expanded the civil administration's points of contact with the population, increased the areas of dependence and friction, and created an additional hold on the Palestinians' habitat. The aim was obvious: to quench the uprising more effectively by containing Israel's subjects, rather than by excluding them. The Occupation regime wished to return its rebellious subjects to its range of control and monitoring and to restore its authority.

The ruling apparatus sought in this way to strengthen its hold on Palestinian homes and intervene in the lives of Palestinian families. The edict regarding "custody of minors" (no. 1235 of 1988) made parents responsible for the actions of their children, the stone-throwers and tire burners, and imposed punitive sanctions on parents who did not prevent a minor child who had previously committed a criminal offense from committing another. The Israeli apparatus wished to harness parents and other family members to the effort of curbing young Palestinians' revolutionary zeal and commitment to the anti-Occupation struggle. Success was very partial and, in most cases, instead of causing a crack or rift within the families, these punitive measures generated greater commitment on the part of adults to their children's struggle.

The most severe impact upon the Palestinian family was a measure neither new nor proven to be an effective deterrent: demolishing the homes of "terrorists." Extended families often lived in houses targeted for demolition, and all their members were left homeless. The damage to a vast group of people who were not suspect of any hostile activity was not coincidental, but rather an explicit part of the method, counteracting the most basic principles of natural justice and international law. This procedure was put to the legal test in several petitions to the Israeli High Court of Justice, but the court did not flinch at the collective punishment of innocents and refused to condemn this measure, which was supposed both to punish and to deter and was perhaps the most drastic tactic used during the First Intifada. The High Court of Justice accepted the state's argument that house demolition was a vital preventive measure on security grounds.[20] In addition to demolitions, the ruling apparatus frequently resorted to collective punishment in other ways and impacted vast walks of Palestinian society regardless of their involvement in the uprising: shutting down institutions of learning, disconnecting water, electricity, and telephone grids, imposing restrictions on working inside Israel, curfews, and closures, and uprooting trees along thoroughfares.

As a rule, the emergency regulations dating from the British Mandate, which were part of Jordanian law but explicitly contradicted by international law, were condoned by Israel's High Court of Justice nearly every time petitions were made to contest their validity. The court listened to the legal discourse on rights—which began to resound loudly outside the court as well, courtesy both of the veteran Israeli League of Human Rights,[21] and of the new NGOs that joined it in the 1980s: the Information Center for Human Rights in the Occupied Territories (B'Tselem), the Center for the Protection of the Individual, and the Association of Physicians for Human Rights. But in the end the court chose almost exclusively to adopt the regime's "security" point of view. At times, it exerted restraint behind the scenes and during court sessions, persuading the representatives of the state to allow some procedure that was originally denied a suspect, pay reparations due some petitioners, or—in very rare cases—avoid a mode of action and choose another.[22] Both the court and the representatives of the security forces preferred negotiation to juridical intervention and ruling: not to impair the purity of the law. The third party to the discussion—the Palestinian petitioners—naturally had other interests, but these hardly concerned the court, which from the outset was party to a national struggle and not an arbiter between the regime and its subjects. The Palestinian, after all, was not a citizen, but considered a rebelling subject, and the High Court of Justice saw itself, rightly, as a part of the regime threatened by the uprising. To preserve a façade of legality, the Occupation authorities required that there be Palestinian petitioners but had no interest in meeting their demands.

Alongside violent measures, changes also took place in the nature of domination. New restrictions were imposed on Palestinian movement, and overnight stays inside Israel were no longer allowed. In 1988, a green identification card was issued to all Palestinians, without which entry into Israel was forbidden; a few months later, a magnetic pass card was added and became a condition for any certificate of entry and work permission, which was now granted sparingly. The card facilitated the identification of its holder in a database created by the civil administration and needed to be renewed from time to time. Every such renewal became an opportunity for extortion and further harassment of the applicant, and these became frequent, because the validity of the card, first limited to a year, was eventually set at three months.[23] The database was expanded to include tax payments, water and power bills, general data on the holder's personal status and the sociocultural group with which "the suspect" was affiliated, regardless of any actions. Details of one's daily life and civil conduct became part of one's security files, and security status determined one's position in everyday life. In the authorities' eyes, the Palestinian's whole existence was reduced to that of a walking "security threat."

The Palestinian is suspect until proven otherwise, and no incriminating proof is needed in order to deny him or her any of the permits required by the Occupation authorities. The data in the personal file of each and every Palestinian are subject to a truth regime under which there is no binary opposition between guilt and innocence, but rather a continuum between truth and falsehood, innocence and guilt. Any flimsy, unsubstantiated suspicion becomes part of one's guilt. The data are accumulated as a collection of evidence of "improper conduct" and improper ties (including family ties with anyone impacted by the security forces). Should these data cumulatively cross a threshold that is neither formulated nor preset, and that changes according to circumstances, the permit is denied. There is no need to explain this denial, nor is an explanation usually provided. None of the grounds for denial is sufficient in itself, and their combined effect is determined by ad hoc rules—if rules are applied at all—unknown to the person involved. Innocence can never be proven; at most it can be ascribed, and this may be withheld on the basis of administrative decisions.

Throughout that period, Israeli efforts to seize more land and settle more Jews beyond the Green Line never ceased. In 1988–91, about 500,000 dunam were expropriated, dozens of settlements expanded their area, and land was offered to settlers free of charge.[24] With massive aid of the government, settlements began to enjoy natural growth for the first time. The Yesha [Judea and Samaria] Council, the supreme regional authority of settlers in the Occupied Territories, created in the early 1980s as a public body, entitled to a permanent government budget, replaced the Gush Emunim [Bloc of the Faithful] movement and became the leading political factor in the colonizing project. The settlers' municipal institutions became state organs and authoritative bodies of control that administered the settlers' lives, while creating new tasks for the ruling apparatus.

Due to international pressure, the number of settlements created at the time did not grow significantly, but this was a merely formal guise of constraint placed upon the names of settlements, not the number of settlers. New settlements were defined as new neighborhoods in old settlements, and the distinction between a new settlement and a new neighborhood in an existing one turned into an international diplomatic issue, especially after the United States under President George H. W. Bush added its voice to the demand to freeze the settlement project. In the meantime, however, settler cities, towns, and smaller communities built close to the Green Line, or at a small distance from it, joined the ideological settlement map. This new form of settlement was made possible because the colonization process had become institutionalized and a government project par excellence. The government (primarily Ariel Sharon, then minister of housing) offered all Jewish citizens generous subsidized housing and support, with various public services. The new policy was aimed at Israelis who had no interest in the national-religious rightist settlers' ideological mission but wanted the economic benefit of living in inexpensive, not-too-distant suburbs. The Intifada somewhat slowed down the pace of inhabiting these new settlements, while the promises of benefits became all the more tempting as the privatization of Israel's welfare services proceeded and deepened.[25]

As a consequence of the new permit policy, the number of Palestinian workers employed in Israel was greatly reduced, and the impact on the Palestinian economy was felt immediately. In 1991, an additional economic blow was dealt: tens of thousands of Palestinian migrant workers were expelled from the Persian Gulf states because of PLO's support of the Iraqi regime during the First Gulf War.[26] The combination of these two factors created a steep setback for the Palestinian economy. The movement of workers and goods between the Occupied Territories and Israel was frequently disrupted (but did not cease altogether), and the thousands who did manage to enter Israel, often with the cooperation of their employers, now became "illegal aliens." The two economies were still integrated, and living spaces were still contiguous, but the model of their separation was transformed. The permit policy revived the Green Line one way, from the Territories to Israel, while the six-week closure imposed on the Gaza Strip (and shorter periods of closure imposed on several areas in the West Bank) during the First Gulf War set a new model of spatial control, aspiring to establish a clear correspondence between the separation of populations and the separation of territories.

CLOSURE, SUSPENSION, AND SIMULATION

The Oslo Accords

The violent Israeli reaction and the political and economic changes resulting from the First Gulf War led to a relative lull in the Intifada as a popular struggle and the renewal of armed struggle by small underground groups and a few private individuals. Knives replaced stones and became a regular threat to everyday life in Israel's major cities. In spite of the gradual decrease in the number of violent incidents, the Jewish public was growing more aware of the limitations of Israeli power in the conflict and realized that it was facing a determined national movement, recognized and trusted by the majority of the Palestinian population. The Palestinian problem remained at the top of the political agenda, and Israel's insistence on boycotting the PLO (political contacts with its members were still considered a criminal offense) became all the more vociferous and absurd. Journalists covering the Palestinian uprising and leftist activists who maintained contacts with Palestinian leaders were attacked—violently at times—by right-wingers. At the right pole of the political spectrum, separation between Jews and Palestinians through "willful emigration" or forced transfer became a legitimate agenda, and the party that advocated it, Moledet [Homeland], gained seats in the Knesset.

In the meantime, however, the dismantling of the Soviet bloc and the First Gulf War changed the nature of American involvement in the Middle East. Shortly after the end of the war, the United States initiated a large international conference in Madrid to solve the Israel-Palestinian conflict. At this conference, the Likud government, for the first time since the Occupation of the Territories in 1967, agreed to the presence of Palestinian "observers" and wore away its own boycott on meetings with PLO members. But the Israeli government made every effort to empty the talks of any content and managed to preserve the status quo in the Occupied Territories until Likud's Yitzhak Shamir was replaced as prime minister by the Labor's Yitzhak Rabin in July 1992.

The political process underwent a substantial shift some months after the rise to power of the Labor party. A years-long tradition of clandestine, informal meetings of Israeli leftists with PLO members had created the framework and supplied the conceptual infrastructure for political negotiation—covert at first, carried out mostly in Oslo, and later overt—between the government of Israel and representatives of the PLO. In September 1993, an accord formally called the "Declaration of Principles on Interim Self-Government Arrangements" was signed in the White House in Washington, DC, the first in the series of agreements known as "the Oslo Accords." Perceived as interim agreements, they were meant to prepare the conditions for negotiations over the permanent status of relations between Israel and the Palestinian national movement.[27] Israeli supporters of the Accords envisioned them as a means to gradual, partial, and orderly transfer of control of both population and territory from Israel into the hands of a quasi-sovereign Palestinian Authority. The Occupied Territories were divided into several main districts of control, as well as some secondary enclaves. In May 1994, the Israeli security forces began their withdrawal from the Palestinian cities. The army withdrew from all major cities except for Hebron and turned over some restricted areas around them to the direct control of the Palestinian security apparatuses. These bodies, which the accords defined as policing apparatuses, were provided with arms, ammunition, and other operational equipment, and took upon themselves both the protection of the Palestinian leadership from opponents of the accords within Palestinian society and some of the routine security tasks that had previously been performed by the ruling apparatus: first and foremost, the prevention of attacks against Israeli targets.

The Palestinian Authority was now fully responsible for Area A, consisting at first of about 3 percent of the territory, and including most of the larger urban localities, home to about one-quarter of all Palestinians in the Occupied Territories. Area B, about one-quarter of the territory and inhabited by about 70 percent of the residents, was to be administered by the Palestinian Authority, but remained under Israeli "security responsibility." Israel remained fully in control of and responsible for Area C, about 72 percent of the territory, home to about 4 percent of the Palestinian population, along the "seam line" (a strip

of land along the eastern side of the Green Line) surrounding the Jewish settlements and in the entire area defined as under jurisdiction of the settlers' regional councils, including a wide swath along the Palestinian Jordan Valley and
the eastern slopes of the Judean desert.[28] No agreement was reached at the time
regarding the city of Hebron, where several thousand Jews lived in the heart of
a Palestinian urban area.[29]

Israel was now in direct control of vast parts of the West Bank (60 percent)
and Gaza Strip (20 percent), and the areas handed over to Palestinian control
had no territorial continuity, necessary for the constitution of an effective control system. The freedom given the Palestinians to develop self-rule mechanisms was limited even within Area A, because all of these areas were enclaves
inside Israeli-controlled space.[30] In January 1996, the Palestinians elected a parliament and a president and talks between the two sides were now conducted
by representatives of two elected authorities, simulating negotiations between
two states, but took place under conditions of near-total subjection of the Palestinian Authority (PA) to the Occupation's ruling apparatus. What was left of
the political space created by the popular committees during the First Intifada
was now taken over by government mechanisms that were outwardly weak and
inwardly strong, incapable of withstanding Israel's demands and pressure, but
equipped and ready to suppress Palestinian opposition. The empty spaces the
weak government was unable to fill were rapidly populated by NGOs that enjoyed generous support of the international community.[31]

In August 1993, the simulations of negotiation that leftist Israeli politicians
and activists had held with Palestinian leaders since the 1970s were replaced by
real negotiation, and lofty, empty talk of peace between the two nations was replaced by a simulation of peaceful relations.[32] In certain areas, Israelis and Palestinians behaved as though their peace treaty had already been signed. This
attitude was aided by the spectacle of diplomatic treaty-signing ceremonies,
negotiations heavily covered by the media in various venues, as well as by regulated cooperation in several realms of life, beginning with joint patrols of security forces and continuing with exchanges of youth and culture delegations.
Nearly every arena of cooperation or confrontation of Israelis and Palestinians
was associated with the "peace process" and gained significance in this context.
But none of these reflected the radical transformation of the ruling apparatus
on four separate but associated planes, presented in some detail below: yielding
responsibility for some governmental apparatuses to the Palestinian Authority and mutilated Palestinian sovereignty; reorganization of Palestinian space

under a new regime of movement; a new momentum of colonization; and a new regime of representation.

Mutilated Sovereignty and a New Map of Violence

The withdrawal of the Israeli army and civil administration from Area A and their reduced presence in Area B, alongside the newly established Palestinian Authority, based on its security mechanisms, armed by the Oslo Accords, and abundantly financed by donations from Europe, the United States, and Japan,[33] all created the guise of transition from one sovereign rule (Israeli) to another (Palestinian). In this context, one should keep in mind that after many years of pedantic administration of the life of a large population, Israeli rule in the Territories took place as an apparatus shared—willingly or not, by agreement or coercion—by Israelis and Palestinians. Although they had tired of Israeli rule, the Palestinians were forced to rely on it for their everyday lives, and although they were constant suspects, the Occupation authorities could not operate without their services (even prior to the Oslo Accords, and certainly afterward). This combination of Israelis and Palestinians in the apparatus of the Occupation was transformed after the First Intifada broke out, but it had never ceased to exist. Following the Oslo Accords, the combination took on a new form, inasmuch as the control and administration of everyday life in most Palestinian towns and certain areas in the West Bank and Gaza Strip (Area A) was taken over by the PA—now beginning to function in the autonomous area as a quasi-government.

The PA received limited authority in legislative and economic matters, but was deprived of any authority regarding the Jewish settlers. In numerous matters—armed patrols, supervision of movement between the different areas, and customs or "security coordination"—the Palestinian apparatus functioned as an arm of Israeli power, which continued to influence things from a distance, but was always near enough to intervene immediately. The PA functioned alongside local, Israeli, and international religious and civil organizations, which intervened in the administration of life through cooperation, competition, and confrontation. Widespread Palestinian governance also took place in Area B, where an Israeli military presence remained. The Palestinians living in Areas A and B were now subject to a Palestinian bureaucratic and security apparatus with more or less permanent coordination and friction points with the Israeli apparatus.[34] With the reorganization of rule, the authority to exert violence became the subject of ongoing negotiation and frequent violent clashes. Israel demanded that the PA either curb Palestinian resistance itself or let Israeli forces do so.

The accords signed in Paris in May 1994 (the Paris Protocol), vested the PA with budgetary, fiscal, and monetary authority. Palestinian farmers were promised that restrictions on export to Israel would gradually be lifted. The accords gave PA officials quasi-feudal economic authority to issue franchises and levy taxes or exempt people from taxes, and these created a severe dependence of the population on PA officials and enabled the latter to grab their own chunk of the money flowing into the Occupied Territories from Europe, the United States, and Japan. But such authorities had a glass ceiling set by the "customs shell" remaining under full Israeli control. The Palestinian economy was doubly burdened—by Israel and by the PA mechanisms. Israel not only controlled the Palestinians' customs money; by controlling the export and import of goods, it also preserved the structural inferiority of the Palestinian economy. Since this forced economic linkage now functioned under conditions of separation, exclusion of most Palestinian workers from the Israeli labor market, and increased monitoring of movement from and inside the Territories, the Palestinian economy fell captive to security decisions on full or partial opening of crossings, the imposition or lifting of closure. Economic damage to the population at large in the West Bank, Gaza, or both became a permanent dimension of security activity, both as a response to terrorist actions and as part of the effort to prevent them.

Since Israel was no longer responsible for everyday governance in Areas A and B, it was shielded from these repeated blows, and they became a part of the unbearable burden placed upon the weak, inflated mechanisms of the PA (which had by now become the largest employer in the Occupied Territories, employing 150,000 workers, eight times more than the number employed by the Israeli military administration). Although incapable of meeting its community's needs, the PA had enough policemen to quench the least sign of rebellion.[35]

Meanwhile, Israel increasingly shirked its responsibility to the occupied Palestinians, transferring limited authority to a weak Palestinian apparatus that could not fill the gap. This process, which preceded and foreshadowed disengagement from Gaza and peaked after it, marked a new form of separation: the division of control within the Occupied Territories themselves (and not just separation between the Territories and Israel), and separation between two kinds of Palestinians: those whom Israel controls indirectly, running their lives only by violent intervention in their movement and space and without providing them with any service that a government normally provides to its subjects, and those in Area C and in the territories annexed to Jerusalem, whom Israel continues to control in various degrees as an occupying government, still providing them with some administration services.

In the meantime, Palestinian resistance took new forms. In 1995, responding to a massacre committed by a Jewish settler in the Cave of the Fathers at Hebron, and imitating Hezbollah suicide bombings in southern Lebanon, Palestinian members of Hamas and Islamic Jihad started to use this deadly form of violence. "Separation," hitherto a tactical response, now became an object of desire as well as a political and ideological formula, which more and more Israelis were willing to adopt. In 1996, the acclaimed Israeli writer A. B. Yehoshua formulated the principle of separation as the basis of a new Israeli Jewish consensus: "The decisive majority of Israel's citizens want clear-cut separation from the Palestinians. A separation required for security, and beyond that—for defining identity."[36] Demographic anxiety and fears for security are entwined in Yehoshua's words, reflecting a common discourse in which demographic changes are presented as a security threat and security measures are justified in terms of the need to protect "identity." The combination of the two kinds of threat necessitates a new combination of unequivocal civil separation (Palestinian cannot be citizens) and clear spatial separation: "the erection of a definitive separation system" in Yehoshua's words, until borders are established through mutual agreement.[37] Such separation should be imposed by Israel unilaterally; the Palestinians' view of the matter is irrelevant.

Shortly thereafter, Dan Shiftan, a researcher at Haifa University's National Security Studies Center, spelled out a strategy of separation in response to a request made by an official at the Ministry of Foreign Affairs. At the time, Ariel Sharon had already been appointed minister of foreign affairs, and Binyamin Netanyahu was prime minister.[38] Shiftan's document was based on discussions with high-ranking officials in the political and military establishment. Shiftan surveyed and documented what Yehoshua had sensed, popular public longing for separation from the Palestinians disconnected from any political context, and laid it down as a "national strategy." He recommended unilateral separation along lines that would leave most of the settlements in the Occupied Territories under direct Israeli control (seeking "national consensus in the mainstream of Israeli society"),[39] and the total shirking of responsibility for the fate of Palestinians across the separation line. Setting separation as a strategic plan meant, in his opinion, that separation should become a goal rather than a means, and that the major issues at hand—permanent borders and the feasibility of Palestinian sovereignty—should be seen in light of their contribution to it.

The moment was ripe for separation ideology and strategy. The fiasco of the Camp David negotiations in summer 2000, a wave of suicide attacks by Palestinians in Israel proper in 2001–2, the growing number of Israeli victims, and the refusal to address the Palestinians' political claims, reducing their uprising to a security problem, made separation the only viable "solution." In April 2002, the growing support for constructing a physical barrier led the Sharon government to adopt the idea and budget money for the project. However, the government refrained from deciding on the location of the barrier, leaving the decision to negotiation between military experts, settlers, and those engaged in planning and constructing new settlements. Three years later, following the logic of unilateral separation to its radical conclusion, Sharon decided on withdrawal from the Gaza Strip ("the disengagement plan"), separating it without giving up Israeli control over it. Unilateral separation proliferated and became a new form of control that reorganized spatialization and temporalization patterns in the Occupied Territories.

The Regime of Movement

For Palestinians, separation meant unemployment, frequent closures, and movement restrictions. Changes as regards freedom of movement were already in the works during the First Gulf War. General permission to enter Israel from the Occupied Territories—in force since 1972—was revoked, and any Palestinian needing to enter Israel had to apply for a personal permit. During the First Gulf War, the Occupied Territories were under total closure for forty-one days.[40] This unusual measure weighed heavily upon the Palestinian population and was explained as usual on grounds of security, which no one dared question in wartime. It created a new control model, which became routine at the time of the Oslo Accords and was frequently enforced as a conditioned reflex to terrorist attack, as well as on Israeli and Jewish holidays.[41] During the Oslo years, closure became the main means of control in the Occupied Territories and one of the main symbols of the ruling apparatus.[42] As a mechanism of rule, it lasted longer than all the accords it accompanied. It served as a formula of sorts for a fragmentation of space that framed the visible and the thinkable and shaped control practices whose effectiveness and brutality peaked during the Second Intifada.[43]

The first concrete manifestation of the new order was the refurbishing after the outbreak of the Second Intifada of the electrified fence erected around the

Gaza Strip in the mid-1990s, which had not functioned for several years.[44] The urban area in the Strip was handed over to the PA, and army troops inside and bordering the Strip were redeployed. The fence surrounded the entire Strip, and Palestinians were forbidden to approach the "security zone" adjacent to it, a one-kilometer-wide swath along its entire length. The few crossings remained fully under Israeli control, and once the fence was complete, life in the Gaza Strip could be disrupted by the simple act of closing them. Normal life in the Strip came to depend on a full state of siege not being imposed.

Closure imposed on the Occupied Territories in 1991 made entering Israel from the West Bank a rare, exceptional privilege, bestowed on a select few. Henceforth, the question of whether, where, and for how long a given area in the Occupied Territories would be isolated from its surroundings, or redivided, partitioned, and administered as a grid of "area cells," was a matter of ad hoc decisions taken by military commanders. Decisions to impose long- or short-term closure, either full or partial, have become rather frequent.[45] Given the abundant supply of non-Palestinian workers, made ever cheaper by changes in the structure of global economy, this led many Israeli employers to prefer such foreign "transient labor," whose importation the government now encouraged. Closure has always been rationalized in terms of the need to "fight terrorism," but it always impacts the population at large, restricting Palestinians' movement, disrupting their activity, and unraveling the fabric of social relations in every sphere of life. When closure is declared, the flow of everything—capital, goods, information, people, weapons, and work—is blocked, delayed, or suspended, leading to speculation and smuggling.[46] Alternative channels soon developed, and the partial disruption of everyday life was compensated for in various ways, but at a steadily growing price. The quasi-autonomy transferred to the PA was severely curbed by a system that made everything depend on a simple decision by the ruling apparatus: to close or to leave open?

With the army's withdrawal from the Palestinian cities and redeployment, the Israeli government began to implement a contingency plan designed by Sharon in 1981—essentially the cantonization of the Occupied Territories.[47] All Jewish settlements were declared closed military zones, a system of bypass roads and tunnels was built to enable relatively free-flowing Jewish traffic, and a mechanism of checkpoints and barriers was created—which at its peak, in 2003, during the suppression of the Second Intifada, consisted of 735 sites[48]—to delay the movement of Palestinians or prevent it altogether. Palestinians were caged in isolated enclaves, at the mercy of a handful of soldiers manning the crossing points. After years of erosion of the spatial separation between the Occupied Territories and Israel, a ruling order based on spatial separation was now reimplemented. Now, however, the lines of separation proliferated within the Territories themselves, around the Jewish settlements, around the Palestinian cities, villages, and refugee camps, along the Palestinian Jordan Valley, along the "seam zone," and around Jerusalem.

Within the Occupied Territories, enclaves in the shape of separate area cells of Jews and Palestinians came into being. The Jewish area cells constantly expanded, and not just to accommodate the growing settlements, but also to answer "security needs," which grew in their turn with the expansion of the Jewish areas.[49] An elaborate system of tunnels and bypass roads connected the settlements among themselves in the Territories, and with Israel within the Green Line, in order to assure relatively continuous movement. Israelis and those entitled to Israeli citizenship by force of the "law of return"—laundered legal jargon for Jews, whether residing in settlements or not—were thus allowed to enter the Occupied Territories as long as they moved strictly and only between the Jewish enclaves. Israelis and Palestinians needed special permits to enter the area cells that were not designated for them, and the regulation of movement was changed from time to time, sometimes on a daily basis, quite arbitrarily and without informing travelers. Arbitrariness and lack of information are not faults in the system; they are in fact *the system itself*. Ambiguities and indecisiveness are systematic, and myriad incoherent tactical local decisions, incarnated in the checkpoint, replace clear policy. Still, separation was never complete. Until the very day when the Gaza "disengagement plan" was carried out, maintaining separation in the numerous enclaves necessitated axes of access and interaction points that enabled the controlled transport of certain goods and the ongoing employment of Palestinians in the Jewish settlements in the Strip. These movements and contacts blurred the separation, isolation, and closure from one another of these ethnic area cells. In the West Bank, they still do.

Colonization

In the Oslo years, fragmentation of Palestinian space and its blatant separation from Jewish space in the Occupied Territories had not yet exerted their full potential impact and served mainly as a spatial grid for more conventional control of the relatively free Palestinian movement that still took place. In some parts of Areas A, B, and C, the formal definition and separation rules did not coincide with actual practice: Palestinian villagers moved in Area C, and Jews in Area A.

But the organization of area cells was gradually enhanced through bypass roads and outposts. The intricate traffic infrastructure created for Jews in the Occupied Territories helped simulate a habitat "cleansed of Arabs." For Palestinians, a system of policing and self-administration was created, simulating an independent state. Not satisfied with the "clean" but limited space made for them, the Jewish settlers then began establishing "illegal outposts," in close cooperation with the ruling apparatus. Between 1995 and 2000, only three settlements were built and recognized by the Ministry of the Interior, but no fewer than one hundred "illegal outposts" were put up by Jewish settlers. The Occupation authorities have always been vague about their number and precise locations, but hundreds of kilometers of "bypass" roads have been paved by the government for the use of Jews alone, and the number of settlers has grown steadily.[50]

An outpost in this context is an "unrecognized" settlement, that is, a neighborhood or hamlet not officially authorized but tolerated by the ruling apparatus, and whose existence is seemingly pending, as it were, hanging on a decision either to make it permanent, to evacuate it, or to move it to a permanent location elsewhere. Still, the ruling apparatus has always seen itself as responsible for the settlers' security and basic well-being wherever they are, legally or not. Thus, "illegal" outposts were quickly connected to water and power grids, roads leading to more and more hilltops were paved, and health and education services were often provided as well.[51] Even those who insisted on the illegality of the outposts have not hastened to dismantle them, and when dismantlement was ordered, implementation never followed. As far as international law is concerned, such outposts are just as "illegal" as all the other settlements, and for all practical purposes, they are just as permanent or temporary as they are. Only behind the façade of legal Israeli occupation is it possible to maintain a distinction, sealed in the piles of files lying in government offices and the Supreme Court, and revived from time to time by desperate petitions and insolent rulings. Under the Rabin, Peres, Netanyahu, Barak, and Olmert governments, numerous army officers, government officials, and administrative bodies were involved in both the planning and implementation of this activity.[52]

Palestinian space was now discontinuous, perforated by the spread of Jewish presence.[53] Some of the outposts were built as new neighborhoods or satellite communities of existing Jewish settlements, but many have been erected at quite a distance from existing settlements. In this way, the colonizing momentum has been maintained, and quick, deep penetration into many areas where there was formerly no Jewish population has been enabled, decentralizing the Jewish presence in the Occupied Territories relatively cheaply with small groups of settlers. This has ensured that no area of the West Bank remains Jewless, and that there be no quiet moment unmarked by the inherent ambivalence of the "peace process." In addition, it has given a semblance of legality, not only to illegal outposts that the government has refused to recognize formally, but also to the settlements themselves, which can now be distinguished from the outposts as "permanent settlements"—notwithstanding that the shadow of dismantlement hovers over them as well. The bluff of the "outposts," bolstered by numerous government officials and army commanders, is not so much hiding their exact number and locations, but rather that they change the perception of the existing settlements and create the appearance of a distinction between legality and illegality in the colonizing project, which the Oslo Accords require.

In creating this simulated distinction between legality and illegality in colonization, the government simultaneously invokes the need for discretion—as to exact locations, number of soldiers, and funds allocated—and ignorance of what steps are actually taken, making it difficult to show what exactly it might be doing wrong. Not only the outposts but the various state organs that deal with them are involved in this simulated distinction, which is a function of the inherent duality in the government's approach to them. On the one hand, since the outposts *are recognized as illegal*, the government can shrug them off. The funds allocated to them are neither mentioned in nor authorized by the budget law, and they are not marked on accessible official maps. There are no explicit instructions on how to treat their residents, terrain, structures, and installations. On the other hand, since they *are acknowledged* by the army, and their locations are known at least to the officers and soldiers in charge of their protection, measures are taken to guard the illegal outposts, connect them to infrastructure, and escort their children to school.

This schizoid attitude is inherent in the Israeli government as a whole. The mere existence of support of the "illegal" outposts is often hidden, not only from the media but also from certain government agencies that do not possess the administrative means to bypass this illegality or ignore it. When the U.S. government asked for a detailed report on the outposts, for example, Israel's prime minister did not turn to his minister of defense, but rather to a private sector attorney, Talya Sason, who had to conduct a prolonged investigation, because government officials refused to cooperate with her. Among other sources, Sason used maps she received from the leftist movement Peace Now to access information that the minister of defense could have provided, assuming that the regional army command knows at any given moment precisely where its troops are deployed and whom they protect.[54] Sason, who wrote the outpost report at the height of the Second Intifada, not only exposed the mechanisms of deception that had become routine among government officials; her appointment and work reflected and replicated the inherent schizoid nature of these mechanisms. The government that commissioned her report and later adopted it was the very same government that ignored it and has done nothing to act on its findings to this very day.

The schizoid nature of the ruling apparatus is no novelty. It appeared for the first time when closure was imposed on the Occupied Territories during the First Gulf War, when the High Court of Justice interfered with the military commander's judgment and required him to enable the exit of ambulances from the closed areas and entry of medical teams into them. However, as in numerous cases thereafter, this juridical ruling did not bring about any change, either in regulations or on the ground. One would be mistaken to interpret the army's and the Ministry of Defense's ignoring court rulings as disrespect of the High Court of Justice. Exposed in this case is not a quest for legality as a "guise" concealing an in-depth structure of violations of the law, but rather two branches of the ruling apparatus playing their roles according to a well-defined principle of division of labor. Following the court's ruling, supposedly making a sharp distinction between the legal and the illegal, a whole gray area of implementation is opened up. The military commander can always suspend action and request more time from the court because of new conditions on the ground. Once the court grants postponement of implementation of its ruling, the legality or illegality of an act can no longer be determined: by refraining from authorizing the act and insisting on its future cancellation, the court declared it illegal; but at the same time, the court has suspended the cancellation of the illegal act, and by this very act has made the outpost legal, for the time being. Nor is it clear who bears responsibility for injuries and damages during that ever-temporary, never-ending suspension of implementation of the court's ruling. Whom can the victim of such postponement (an ailing patient delayed at the checkpoint, the owner of a fruit grove who cannot access his land) address, demanding justice and compensation? If the petitioners seeking aid from the High Court of Justice are "before the law" (in Kafka's sense of the term), then the authorities supposed to implement its ruling are "behind the law" or above it. Rather than its subjects, the law protects the authorities that abstain from executing it.

The government's mode of operation in the illegal outposts affair, beginning in the Oslo days and ongoing, is a typical example of simulation turned into nearly official political strategy—nearly official, because in simulation one can no longer clearly distinguish between the official and the unofficial, between up front and behind the scenes. The outposts were more than just the settlers' response to the Oslo process; they were the response of the Israeli regime itself. Every such outpost served to integrate the settlers' institutions and leadership further into the ruling apparatus. Simulation was not limited to the colonizing project either. In their talks with the Palestinians during the Oslo years, all Israeli governments simulated *peace* and the end of the Occupation through redeployment of their forces in the Occupied Territories, as well as in some other minor initiatives. The effect—if not the conscious intention—was simply the reorganization of the ruling apparatus, restructuring the Israeli regime as a whole.

The Regime of Representation

In the Oslo days, the entire ruling apparatus was reorganized in light of the *declaration* of transition from a state of occupation into a state of peace and the need to create conditions that would facilitate this transition. Israel admitted for the first time that the Palestinian Territories were occupied, and that occupation was a temporary state that had to be terminated. In other words, in Oslo, a de facto occupation was recognized de jure, and the *intention* to end the occupation de jure and de facto was declared.[55] This was a transition into conditions of transition. However, the dialectics of separation and integration governing the operation of the ruling apparatus in the Territories have so far turned every act of separation into the point of departure for a new mode of integration, and now pose insurmountable obstacles to any attempt to create a real transition. Thus, the "peace process" quickly turned into a simulation of both the end of occupation and a façade for its indefinite continuation. The transition period was a state of occupation as much as it was a state of ending the occupation.

The most important structural characteristic of the new situation was the blurring of differences in a long series of contrasts, formerly perceived as polarized and unequivocal: between the temporary and the permanent, between war and peace, occupation and liberation, friend and foe, exterior and interior, price and gain, victims of occupation and victims of peace, senseless victim and victim for a noble cause, and finally between the false and the true, fiction and fact. As a result, any act, statement, text, gesture, event, symbol, or object was perceived as evidence of the persistence of occupation, but also as proof of its imminent end. People were getting killed, of course, becoming im-poverished or rich, and new friendships were born or lost, but one could never tell whether the cause was one thing or its opposite, the perpetually ongoing occupation or the buds of reconciliation.

When simulation regiments representation, the more effective action is the one that uses or creates more power simulations. Attempts to break through the logic of simulation and reach the real that presumably lies beyond the simu-lacra, usually in the form of death and destruction, face the immediate response of various systems of action working to restore the simulative order by lending any event its contradictory meanings, protecting hybrid areas, redeclaring tem-porariness, undermining any border line just drawn, and blurring unequivocal distinctions. The settlers realized this and invented the outposts. The Left re-stored the simulation of peace talks (e.g., with the Nuseiba-Ayalon Principles or the "Geneva Initiative" drafted by unofficial Israeli and Palestinian teams led by Yasser Abed-Rabbo and Yossi Beilin) after many months of Intifada. The Palestinians, too, enhanced their representation strategies, adopting typical Is-raeli images and stereotypes and making them serve their own struggle, but still paid the full price for their participation in the simulation games.[56] Simulation in itself is not violent, even when it requires the presence of vast forces. Erup-tive violence, action assaulting the human body, is the consequence of disagree-ment or inability to accept simulation. Under such conditions, rebellion means rising against the simulative nature of reality. And indeed, when the simulation became the constituting law of political reality, and contradictory meanings ac-companied every event, many people sought to extricate one final meaning and force reality to reveal its true face once and for all. On both sides, people began to seek a way to tear the veil of simulation and reach the thing itself. Palestin-ians sought to prove that the Occupation is ongoing and that the Israelis have no real intention of terminating it, while Israelis sought to prove that terrorism continues and that the Palestinians have no real intention of halting it.[57]

The massacre of twenty-nine Palestinians praying in the Cave of the Patri-archs in Hebron in February 1994 by a Jewish terrorist, and the assassination of Prime Minister Yitzhak Rabin in November 1995, should be seen in this light. The Israeli and Palestinian responses to these events hopelessly dam-aged the structure of gradual progress on which the Oslo Accords had been based. In Hebron, the army refused to tolerate the Palestinians' rage over the massacre and resorted to extreme violence to curb protest demonstrations and riots, killing nine more Palestinians. At the very last minute, the Rabin government refrained from removing the settlers from the city of Hebron, a measure that could have proven Israel's determination to pursue the Oslo track. When Hamas responded with lethal attacks, most Israelis quickly forgot the massacred Palestinians and failed to recognize in these attacks the same passion to force a set of binary categories on a hybrid, inherently ambiguous reality. The retaliatory Palestinian violence was taken out of context and portrayed as monstrous, casting a heavy shadow over any further compromise.

Israel framed the Palestinian violence as "terrorism," responding with additional fragmentation of Palestinian space, a series of closures and encirclement of entire localities. The separation mechanism provided for by the Oslo Accords was used to tighten control of Palestinian movement between the various area cells. The talks were disrupted again and again, implementation of redeployment of troops or further transfer of authority that had been agreed upon was postponed, and further withdrawal now seemed inconceivable. After the Rabin assassination, afraid or unwilling to use a moment of grace in Israeli public opinion that had reacted to the assassination by becoming more sympathetic to "the Palestinian cause" and to gestures of "concessions" and "reconciliation," the Labor government led by Shimon Peres chose to stall any progress in the talks with the Palestinians. In April 1996, it initiated a large-scale military action (Operation "Grapes of Wrath") in Lebanon in retaliation for the firing of Katyusha rockets at Israeli communities in the north. In June 1996, a mere six months after Rabin's assassination, Binyamin Netanyahu was elected prime minister, and stalling had become his declared policy. He did not revoke the Oslo Accords but did his best to leave them in the virtual space into which his entire politics was drawn. In this space, it was no longer possible to distinguish between concrete fact and image, between withdrawal and advance, the start of a new war and the birth of peace.

This structural ambivalence was unbearable for many. When Ehud Barak was elected prime minster in May 1999, he tried to extricate himself from it through a new negotiation tactic, accompanied by preparations for a new wave of violent clashes. Barak sought to impose swift decision-making in all matters at hand—borders, the settlements, the status of Jerusalem, and the lingering question of the refugees included—on the Palestinians, and to turn their agreement, at a conference that was supposed to take place in summer 2000, into a litmus test for the achievement of peace. This policy was in tune with mainstream Israeli public opinion. The Right and the Left in Israel both passionately desired to stabilize a reality that was hopelessly conflictive and inter-twined. They wanted a once-and-for-all solution: if not defeating the enemy, at least overcoming the question of who exactly this enemy was and where exactly the border was to be drawn between "us" and "them."

After the Camp David talks failed, a new wave of Palestinian violence swept through the Occupied Territories. The Palestinians, so it seemed, refused to let Israel enjoy the ambivalence of "the peace talks" indefinitely, trying to force it to continue to pursue what the Palestinian leadership believed to be the aim of the Oslo process: the end of the Occupation in the establishment of a Pal-estinian state.

The fantasy of once and for all separating inside from outside, "security threats" from peaceful citizens, while nonetheless paradoxically containing and ruling the excluded, would produce the most expensive construction project Is-rael has ever carried out since its founding as a state: the separation wall.

SEPARATIONS AND SUBJUGATIONS

Israeli rule in the Occupied Territories is based on two fundamental and incon-gruent divisions: (a) *spatial separation* between the Occupied Territories and Israel proper; (b) basic *juridical and administrative separation* between citizens and noncitizens. The spatial separation is supposed to keep the two national groups apart without giving up their containment within a single control sys-tem. What is kept apart is considered "outside," and is included as such. "Inclu-sive exclusion" is a model of domination whose basic nonspatial manifestation is civil separation. This is expected to restrict the presence of noncitizens to their living zone, while reducing their hold on their own territory and prevent-ing their assimilation among citizens. The two kinds of separation coexist, side by side, empowering but also limiting each other, and they cannot converge. The difference between them is irreconcilable (unless either full annexation of or full withdrawal from all of the Occupied Territories takes place, two options that have, however, been excluded since the early days of the Occupation, gener-ating inherent contradictions and instability and creating a constant movement of reintegration that necessitates ever-new articulations of the dividing lines).

In the days immediately following the 1967 war, the outline of Israeli rule in the Palestinian territories was simple. The occupied area was placed under military rule and could at any time, in part or as a whole, be declared a "closed mili-tary zone." It was comprised of two separate territories, the West Bank and the Gaza Strip, the inhabitants of which were subject to military administration.

The power that joined the new space and population to the realm of Israeli rule is the power that kept them apart—as territories that were never annexed and subjects who were never naturalized. The separation of Israel proper from the Occupied Territories coincided with the separation between its citizens and its new subjects. When Israel annexed East Jerusalem and its environs following the war, this principle seemed obvious, and the Palestinian residents were offered citizenship. But soon after the war—in a matter of hours, days, or weeks, depending on the area—Israel took a series of measures that ignored the spatial separation of the Occupied Territories, undermining its correspondence with civil separation. Lively civil traffic began to flow in both directions throughout the territory that Israel had formerly declared and construed as "enemy territory." Contacts and exchange between Palestinians and Jews were strongly encouraged by the permission granted to most Palestinians to enter Israel for work purposes, to Israelis to visit the Occupied Territories both to exploit the cheap labor available there and to enjoy the local markets and other tourist attractions, and to a handful of Jews to settle in the West Bank. If only because it was linked to civil separation that remained stable and rigid, spatial separation was never abolished, however, and its outline changed according to the changes forced by the colonial project. The Palestinians in the Occupied territories were not naturalized, and they were thus de facto and de jure noncitizens of Israel. Separate infrastructures and administrations were developed for the two populations, within which the citizens discriminated against, dispossessed, and exploited the noncitizens. Subjugation of the noncitizens and ongoing intervention in their lives was necessary in order to maintain the two kinds of separation within one framework of control. This created numerous points of contact and friction between Israelis and Palestinians. Interaction increased, not only for military reasons, but also because of Israelis' desire to tour, trade, and settle in the Territories, and the more friction there was, the more spatial separation eroded, the more civil separation came to seem the only solid basis upon which to distinguish Israel from the Territories, and the principle upon which separation of infrastructure, education, and economic systems could be based. In order to stabilize civil separation, it was grounded in edicts, regulations, military practices, and activity that ensured subordination. One was under no circumstances to erode civil separation itself—Palestinian residents were not granted citizenship even in annexed Jerusalem. There were several reasons for this. Such erosion—"creeping naturalization" alongside "creeping annexation"—might have made the use of Palestinian resources much more expensive; and it might also have been interpreted as outright annexation of the Occupied Territories, which would be perceived even by many right-wingers as politically impossible; worst of all, it was seen as a direct threat to the Jewish majority in the State of Israel, endangering one of Zionism's fundamental values.

Civil separation and subjection were two sides of the same coin—both the reason for and the result of Israeli rule devoid of legitimacy and growing Palestinian resistance. Relations of submission and obedience invaded all realms of life. Even without the involvement of the Occupation authorities, every encounter between Jews and Palestinians suspended spatial separation, articulated civil separation, and was shaped by the Palestinians' inferior status and the potential use of subjugation measures. This was not merely subjection imposed by military government for "security reasons"; its aim was to ensure freedom of movement for Israelis in the Occupied Territories, where they could take advantage of cheap labor and new trading opportunities, occupy land, and settle beyond the Green Line. Subjection was also a way to divide Palestinians and prevent them from uniting against the occupier.

Authority had to be consolidated and force exercised in two opposing directions to maintain separation and to increase intervention and subjugation. A series of military decrees unilaterally defined arenas of permitted and prohibited relations, as well as the special dosages of separation and integration, cooperation and subordination. The new, separate legislative system that developed in the Occupied Territories empowered the separation of citizens from noncitizens, just as it provided the legal basis for fragmenting, subjugating, and inserting itself into countless dimensions of life. Convoluted legal jargon was recruited to express the two countermovements of power, overcome their contradictions, and re-create the world by decrees. Often the same acts—erecting a checkpoint or a fence, carrying out an arrest or expulsion—simultaneously produce separation and contact. Interaction takes place anyway, since spatial separation is never complete and the normal flow of life (in trade, work, communication and transportation, operation of infrastructure, etc.) generates it anew, even when it is forbidden. Contact takes place because the ruling apparatus wishes to govern, monitor, enforce, prevent and enable, take, and sometimes even give. Separation exists in order to ensure subjugation and limit interaction to patterns allowed by the Occupation authorities, preventing both the blurring of difference and disruptive mingling.

The functions and interaction of these two power formations have changed over the years, but the basic pattern and difference have remained unchanged.

Power that seeks to obtain something through contact, whether by persuasion or coercion, creates separation—for example, when Palestinian residents abandon a neighborhood because of frequent incursions by the Israeli security forces or intrusions by Jewish settlers. And the power whose rationale is separation necessarily creates contact and friction, as happens at every checkpoint.

From the outset, Palestinian resistance has been a primary by-product of these opposing forces—not entirely unexpected, but not really planned for or calculated. It has taken on various forms, civilian and armed, but could nearly always be seen as an effort either to reestablish separation where the Occupation authorities had erased it or to eliminate separation and impose contact and friction where the Occupation authorities sought to institutionalize separation.

The war fought by Israel in Lebanon in the 1980s against the Palestinian national movement was accompanied by waves of rebellion in the Occupied Territories. These were characterized by the effort to disrupt the two formations of power described above. By blocking roads with burning tires and hurling stones, Palestinians tried to resurrect spatial separation between them and the Occupation army, while others resisted by insisting on coming to work in Israel against all odds. The struggle to reshape spatial separation acquired new dimensions during the First Intifada, which was a continuation and escalation of these waves of rebellion and their consolidation into an organized struggle. Refugees in Gaza, and soon afterward in the West Bank, barricaded the entrances to their camps; crowds hurled stones; people used one another as shields; individuals performed symbolic acts of resistance, such as grabbing weapons from soldiers and breaking them; public spaces were covered with protest graffiti. In certain areas, the Palestinians forced the army to withdraw for a while and managed to reduce and compress their encounter with it along the lines of separation and confrontation, which they—for the first time outside the refugee camps—took part in establishing. The crowds that ventured into the streets first and foremost rejected subjection to Israel and the resulting interaction and friction with Jews. They refused to be ruled that way any longer.

The Palestinians struggled for their right to public spaces of their own; barricades, strikes, and demonstrations were ways of reclaiming and shaping such spaces. The Israeli army responded by declaring those reclaimed spaces "closed military zones," a decree Palestinians ignored time and again. At the same time, relations of subjection were disrupted: Palestinian administration officials resigned, residents refrained from paying their electricity bills, and lawyers began a prolonged strike. The combined effect was a certain transformation of power relations and the opening of public space for political action. An important component of this action was the ability to imagine the entire Palestinian territory anew as an object of collective struggle. The Palestinian leadership that emerged from the uprising overcame many of the regional and status divisions, both traditional ones and new ones dictated by the ruling apparatus. It represented the Occupied Territories as a continuous Palestinian space and imagined this space as the territory of its future state. When the Palestinian leadership subscribed to the principle of "two states for two peoples" that year, they were demanding that the congruence of spatial and civil separation be restored and institutionalized as two sovereign states. Even the disintegration of the Occupied Territories into hundreds of area cells along countless temporary borderlines during the Second Intifada could not undermine the imagined integrity of occupied Palestinian space and the Palestinian leadership's uncompromising claim to sovereignty in it. However, political imagination is the only place where both the integrity of the Palestinian space and the congruity of civic and spatial separations hold true. Still, the partition of Palestine is not considered the only possible option and the "one-state solution" has not been excluded.

In the third year of the Intifada, the ruling apparatus managed to reestablish its own separation lines. The Territories reopened to Israeli traffic, more or less freely, and Palestinian movement was restricted by temporary separation lines, in the form of curfews and closures, declared from time to time. As far as Palestinians were concerned, separation of the Occupied Territories from Israel was clear and explicit for the first time, after years of blurring, when general closure was imposed during the First Gulf War. At the same time a new series of friction points was imposed by administrative means. New taxes on vehicles were levied, the replacement of vehicle license plates was decreed, payment of taxes was made a requirement for the issue of licenses, and so on.[58] Soon thereafter, with the Oslo Accords, however, separations proliferated again (between the areas A, B, and C, and areas H-1 and H-2 of the city of Hebron [see chapter 3, n. 29]), including new separations between residents of the different areas.

During all that time, there was one limited sphere of interaction in which contact did not mean subjugation. Israelis and Palestinians met, supposedly as two symmetrical "sides," in formal and informal "peace talks," where the structural asymmetry of power relations was suspended while the parties struggled together to agree on new principles of separation. But no one who engaged in these talks forgot his or her role: as representative of a government that would never give up its right to have the last word, on the one hand, and as representative of a subjugated people in a liberation struggle against that power, on the other.

Only in the new domain of nongovernmental politics could Israelis and Palestinians come together and be separated as equals, in principle, if not in fact. Relatively few Palestinians had access to that sphere, and only short, discontinuous periods of time were spent there.[59] In most other realms, the asymmetrical relations between the government and its Palestinian subjects prevailed. The ruling apparatus enlarged the points of contact with these subjects inside their own territory without coordination or agreement and at the same time greatly reduced the possibilities of their crossing the constantly proliferating separation lines both inside the Territories and between them and Israel across the Green Line.

Thanks to the division of Palestinian territory into the areas determined by the Oslo Accords, a new form of control began to take shape. The network of bypass roads created contiguity among all the Jewish areas, while more and more Palestinian areas became enclaves.[60] In late 1994, following the first phase of implementation of the Oslo Accords, it gradually became clear that Israel was tightening its grip on the Palestinian population, while greatly reducing its own responsibility for providing it with services.[61] Palestinian workers became redundant when, helped by global economic changes that had made foreign labor cheaper and more accessible, the government encouraged Israeli employers to substitute foreign workers for them in response to the deadly Palestinian attacks of 1995–96.[62] As soon as movement restrictions imposed on Palestinians no longer seriously impacted life in Israel, these restrictions could be used freely at no cost to the Israeli economy. Restriction of movement now became a primary means of control, and the organization of space was now made to fit this means, to enable its effective and inexpensive operation.

When the Second Intifada broke out in late 2000, the two sides previously engaged in bilateral negotiations "toward peace" became two sides in a state of warfare, and all lines of separation became lines of friction, subordinated to "security" reasoning and the logic of military action. In October 2000, the Israeli government defined the confrontation with the Palestinians as a state of war. The entire Palestinian area became a military map, as it were, and the Israeli army was soon capable of reaching and "regulating," as army jargon put it, any group or individual within this space.[63] Through such "regulation," the Israeli regime sought to crush the Palestinian side, but without destroying it.

Fragmentation of space and the regime of movement became the main mechanisms for controlling and managing life in the Territories. They created new conditions for the use of force, and the new order of violence in turn required the reorganization of space and new restrictions on movement. This dialectical process has been maintained at least since the Oslo Accords and has peaked, so far, in the Israeli disengagement from the Gaza Strip and in the new way military force has been employed there ever since.

Since the eruption of the Second Intifada, contact and friction between the ruling apparatus and the Palestinian population in the Occupied Territories have mostly been restricted to warfare. The PA, UN aid agencies, international NGOs, and foreign governments had in any case already replaced the Israeli apparatus in most of the other kinds of interaction that had existed earlier. Under such circumstances, the challenge was to sustain bare life while most forms of political life were being destroyed. This yielded a new form of suspension—the suspension of catastrophe—which since late 2000 has hovered like a ghost over the Occupied Territories and dictated the limits of Israeli violence and the intensity of Palestinian resistance.

Al Sawahir Al Sharqiya, East Jerusalem: Israel's "separation wall." The photographer clearly sought to convey the effect of an isolated fortress on a hill. Most available images of the wall, whose construction continues, document multiple points and zones of friction and reflect the endless work of separation involved in creating and maintaining the inevitable, always regenerated mixtures of that which has to be separated. This photograph documents, not the wall, but the Israeli fantasy of the wall, and its own separation from a whole repertoire of control apparatuses. Photographer unknown.

Children in Ashkelon in 1978 en route to what Jewish Israelis casually called "the slave market." To get to the market within the Green Line by 7 A.M., these children had to wake up no later than 4 A.M. The immediate transformation of the Palestinians into a cheap and available labor force was one of the first signs that the occupation was not going to be temporary—and certainly not external to Israel. Within a few years, Palestinian children turned into day laborers. Palestinian child labor is even cheaper than adult labor, and hiring them on a daily basis helped create the false idea that "Palestinian children are accustomed to working." Employment is not promised or guaranteed in the slave market, just a chance to offer one's body for work. Photographer: Uzi Keren.

Ration day at the UNRWA outlet in Dheisheh refugee camp, south of Bethlehem in the West Bank, 1984. Each of the children leaves gripping a quarter of a small flat bread. Since 1948, a large number of Palestinian refugees, still living in camps and not allowed to regain their homes, have been in daily need of food support. After 1949, Israel did whatever it could to create the impression that Palestinian refugees were the concern of UNRWA or of the Arab states that refuse to naturalize them, denying its responsibility for creating and perpetuating "the problem." Photographer: Rina Castelnuovo.

Beit Ur al-Tahta, a Palestinian village in the West Bank, 2001. Before the erection of the separation wall, the Israeli army deployed concrete blocks like these in hundreds of "separation lines,"
which still crisscross the West Bank. After the separation wall was built, the blocks remained to
create "local separations," which actually function as friction zones. At these spots, the military
devised "back-to-back" transfers, a simple mechanism for supplying food and controlling its
provision: two trucks, the one laden with produce, the other empty, approach from the two
sides of the cement cubes for purposes of the transfer. Food is allocated so as to avoid famine,
but the allocation itself is strictly controlled. Photographer: Miki Kratsman.

Clause 112 of Israel's emergency regulations has authorized expulsion of Palestinians from the West Bank since 1967. Here, in 1988, Amal Labadi and Nahla Ayesh, whose husbands were expelled to Jordan, hold their children in their arms. The idea of a "voluntary transfer," first broached by Rehavam Zeevi, a former commander in the Occupied West Bank who was then a member of the Knesset, was overtly discussed in Israel after 1987: "It's true that they won't want to leave; at first there will be just a trickle, then a stream, and then finally they will all want to go." The fierce opposition to this idea at the time created the democratic atmosphere under the auspices of which "silent transfer" continued, often almost unnoticed. Photographer: Micha Kirshner.

Demonstration in front of the Knesset in Jerusalem in 1993 by the wives of 415 Palestinians expelled to Lebanon as suspected Hamas activists. The camera in the hands of the wife of a Hamas activist, held to her eye, is a buffer, even if only a symbolic one, against the violent gaze of Jewish Israelis. At that time, Palestinian women could still protest in the Israeli public sphere against their relatives' expulsion, although such protest was merely symbolic, never effective. In this case, the murder of a security guard, supposedly by a Hamas activist, was the pretext, and the expulsion was done clandestinely and swiftly so as to avoid any petition to the High Court of Justice. Some of the expelled were picked up at their homes, others were "administrative detainees" and were taken from detention installations, in both cases without prior notice or due process. Photographer: Uzi Keren.

Taxis arriving in Gaza in 1968. Any image from the Occupied Territories, since day one, is a mixture of normality and abnormality. This photo records taxis driving across open borders from Gaza to Jerusalem, Tel Aviv, and other destinations, on the one hand, and the abnormal situation of tolerated illegal child labor that compels Palestinian children to live in permanent fear and to hide when a camera approaches, on the other. The child at the center hides his face with a shopping bag, "already knowing" what a year later policemen will tell any foreign correspondent who arrives in town: "No photographing in Gaza." The boy walking in front of the taxi holding a box full of lighters or other small trinkets for sale is not happy to have his face documented either. He already knows how frequent searches, detentions, and arrests are, as though necessary to make the Israeli soldiers "feel at home" in this occupied city. Photographer: Ariela Shavid.

Arrest of "illegal aliens" at Lod, southeast of Tel Aviv, in 2002. To avoid delays at checkpoints and get to their jobs on time, these men have stayed within the Green Line overnight, sleeping in dire conditions in shanties and basements. A plainclothesman cuffs the hands of an elderly man whose presence in Israel, after years of working for his Israeli employer, has been declared illegal. Photographer: Nir Kafri.

Palestinians in Bethlehem watch fireworks over Israel on Independence Day, 1995. For the West Bank and Gaza, closure is routine every Israeli Independence Day. Palestinians are forbidden to enter Israel, but the sky doesn't count. For a brief moment, the beauty of the fireworks banishes thoughts of the twin contexts of this day: "Independence" for Jews and catastrophe—Nakba—for Palestinians. In Israel, the catastrophe is remembered—if it is not denied altogether—as a Palestinian "internal" event, as though Jews could obliterate it from their memories, bodies, and history books. Photographer: Eldad Rafaelie.

Gaza beach, 1988. The barbed-wire fence makes the beach off-limits to Gazans, but they are allowed to sit in this café a few feet away, enabling them at least to enjoy the view of the sea. This is only the tip of the iceberg of a range of oppressive techniques that have been left un-documented and unreported. Among the soldiers stationed there to keep the Gazans behind the barbed wire was a photographer for whom this sight was important enough to be recorded in the visual diary he kept during his military service. Photographer: Oded Yedaya.

Gazans signal to friends and relatives on the Egyptian side across the divide at Rafah in the southern Gaza Strip in 1991. The forced migration involved in the creation of the Israeli state tore apart families and communities. Gazans, separated from their brothers in Palestine in 1948, were now separated from their communities in Egypt as well. Yells, looks, and hand gestures connect those who live on the "Israeli" side and those on the Egyptian side. As can be clearly seen in the photo, the fence is not meant to create a clear-cut separation. Just as Israel had hoped that opening the Jordan bridges would encourage Palestinians to relocate in Jordan, it expected the fence here to be flexible enough to get Gazans to move to Egypt. Photographer: Rina Castelnuovo.

Schoolgirls in Gaza pass a lineup of men being searched by Israeli soldiers in 1986. Each of the six very young girls walking down the sidewalk on the way home from school in their dark frocks and white collars needs to work out for herself how she feels about what she sees on this daily walk. Perhaps at their age they do not yet find the appropriate words to articulate their instincts and choices but this is certainly not the first time they have encountered an intolerable sight like this, and each of them has already had occasion to shape the way in which she will process what she sees, memorize the sight or avoid it and prevent it from getting to her. Three of them cannot help looking at the humiliating search of the bodies of ten or so men arbitrarily detained following the stabbing of a Jew in the area. If these young Palestinians were really dangerous, two rifle-bearing soldiers would not be enough. We don't know how long the men were required to stand with their hands up. It seems, however, that detaining them this way has to do with lack of manpower and not with the probability of their involvement in a crime. One of the girls looks aside, and the braided one is determined not to see. Photographer: Jim Hollander.

A Palestinian stone-thrower is forced to the ground surrounded by soldiers in Nablus, 1988. Massive arrests and detentions were a daily routine, but the degree of violence involved varied. The majority of such cases were decided on the spot according to soldiers' judgment. Here, for example, the soldiers' watchful eyes have determined that the suspect's hands have held stones. The picture was taken after he was arrested and thrown to the ground, his hands restrained. Seven armed soldiers surround him, most of them pointing their guns at him. His gaze is startled. In spite of his cuffed hands, he tries to remain braced and protect himself, perhaps also to prove them wrong and get them to release him. The soldier at the middle of the frame uses his right hand to distance the others a bit, calm them down, and prevent them from pouncing on the suspect in the photographer's presence. Photographer: Miki Kratsman.

Two *mista'rvim*—Israeli soldiers disguised as Arabs—arrest a young Palestinian at a demonstration against the separation wall at A-Ram Junction in north Jerusalem in 2004. Until a
moment ago, the Palestinian youth thought that the area was clear, but everything changed in
a flash, and he was arrested. The soldiers let the two *mista'rvim* run the show. The activities of
undercover units like the *mista'rvim* stoked Palestinian suspicions about collaborators. Photographer: Anat Zakai.

A Palestinian woman facing the refrigerator from her demolished home in the Jordan Valley, 1999. Regime change, Ehud Barak replaces Binyamin Netanyahu, a right-wing government is replaced by a left-wing one, and home demolition, ongoing since 1948, continues. Who cared about her refrigerator or whether she and her family would have anything to eat that evening? Photographer: Miki Kratsman.

House commandeered as a "flying checkpoint" to control the Palestinian population at Luban a-Sharqiya, north of Ramallah, in 2003. In a familiar procedure, the occupants were put out on the street and told to make do. The house was then covered with camouflage netting. Barbed wire was laid around it, and an Israeli flag was hoisted on the roof. Photographer: Dafna Kaplan.

Refugees explore the ruins after the battle of Jenin in the northern West Bank in 2002. A few days after the destruction of hundreds of houses in the refugee camp and the withdrawal of the massive Israeli military force, the refugees and their children start to explore their new environment. What was once a building has become a tall mound of rubble, from which one can see the effects of the military operation. Someone points out places that no longer exist and calls out their names. Even though they seem to have positioned themselves for a group photo, it is doubtful whether these people have noticed the photographer. Photographer: Rina Castelnuovo.

The wall of a school incorporated into the separation wall at Anata, East Jerusalem, in 2005. Schools are no obstacles for erecting the wall. Since the school's outer wall was higher than the separation wall, there was no need to build this segment of it. Studies were interrupted while the separation wall was being built on the school grounds, and, predictably, the school was closed altogether soon afterward. Photographer: Dafna Kaplan.

A woman waits to be taken away by the GSS at Huwwara checkpoint, one of the exits from the city of Nablus in the northern West Bank, in 2005. She appears in their lists as "wanted." We do not know her name. She gives the soldiers a quiet, distant, piercing look, as if seeking to disconnect and protect herself from what is taking place. She has been detained here for over an hour now, waiting for the GSS man to come and take her away. In a few minutes, she will be blindfolded and dependent—hunched over, her head bent—on the soldier leading her, from whom she was trying to keep her distance until just a moment ago. After being pushed into the army jeep taking her to the GSS installation, she will be swallowed up in a sinister realm from which few verbal and fewer visual testimonies have as yet emerged. The photographer can record only the start of her arrest. Photographer: Liriet Livni Lahav.

RULING THE NONCITIZENS

Part 2

4 THE ORDER OF VIOLENCE

THE ECONOMY OF VIOLENCE

Until the outbreak of the First Intifada, Israel ruled the Occupied Territories with a semblance of order. The menace of withheld violence was usually sufficient to destroy political space, although violence erupted from time to time in response to attempts at political organization or acts of overt resistance, both civil and armed. In the first twenty years of the Occupation, about 650 Palestinians were killed in clashes with the Israeli security forces and colonists. During the First Intifada, a substantial rise was experienced in the level of violence, and during the five years of uprising, over 1,400 Palestinians were killed, and more than 10,000 wounded. Even when it responded to terrorist activity, resumed following the Hebron (Cave of the Patriarchs) massacre of March 1994, Israel did not escalate its eruptive violence in the Occupied Territories, where as a rule, until the late 1990s, it had remained relatively limited. In spite of the growing number of casualties, it was still low compared with that of the years of the Second Intifada—more than 660 Palestinians dead and more than 4,300 wounded every year. But even this number is still low compared with the number of victims in ethnic conflicts elsewhere, a fact that should be taken into account in considering the logic and structure of Israeli violence in the Occupied Territories.[1] Before the Second Intifada, eruptive violence was exerted in more or less distinct incidents: clashes with armed resistance fighters, dispersing demonstrators, torture, home demolitions, arresting suspects. The main change felt after the Oslo Accords was the deployment of withheld violence.

With the onset of the Second Intifada and the entrance of massive Israeli military forces into the West Bank and Gaza Strip, the ruling apparatus ceased to function as an administration of civilian life that maintained a semblance of distinction between the two types of violence and displayed potential violence or employed eruptive violence according to fixed, known, authorized codes. The map of violence became characterized by a wide, contiguous deployment of forces that enabled the tangible, powerful presence of withheld violence and intensified uncertainty as to how this violence would be deployed and how its subjects were expected to submit to it. The span of time needed to exert violence and the frequently changing rules of engagement made it difficult for Palestinians to anticipate eruptions of violence, often of unprecedented force. Israeli military forces were now deployed throughout the area, almost as in a state of war, but there was no war. *War itself was suspended.* There were "only" army operations, violent arrests, occasional incursions into residential neighborhoods, and targeted killings, with their "collateral damage" and the destruction of infrastructure and dwellings, whether as punitive measures or as a form of attack.

Following the diminishing frequency of deadly attacks on buses and the change in the political situation as the disengagement plan was about to be implemented in summer 2005, a certain reduction was felt in the force and frequency of such army activity, but it never stopped altogether, and it was renewed shortly after the Israeli army left the Gaza Strip.[2] Still, notwithstanding the tremendous increase in the direct use of violence in the Gaza Strip since disengagement, most of the soldiers in the Occupied Territories do not engage in combat of any sort, and in spite of the growing presence of their weapons, these usually stay locked. Eruptive violence remains suspended, withheld in the club, the rifle, and the armored vehicle, but also in the amplified voice announcing curfew, in the computer that issues magnetic pass cards, in the metal arm of the roadblock, and the concrete ID inspection booth—and this is precisely how this violence is exerted. It imposes its constraints upon the movement of the subjects of the Occupied Territories and upon their conduct wherever it is present and wherever it might show up. And it might show up— as we well know—anytime, anywhere.

The control and administration of movement have been crucial in turning withheld violence into a highly efficient mechanism of domination and subjugation. Since the signing of the Oslo Accords, means of demarcating and closing off area cells of varying sizes have become highly sophisticated and enhanced by architectural and military devices, surveillance equipment and practices, a new spatial language and quasi-legal regulations. All of these together help contain any given habitat, isolate and seal it off, and create near-complete control over all its entrance and exit points. To accommodate the ruling apparatus's changing needs, new techniques and terms such as "demarcation" and "fragmentation" have been introduced, joining the older "siege," "closure," and "curfew."[3] The Palestinian Territories have become a mosaic of semi-isolated spaces, which may be redivided and demarcated anew at any given moment by decree of local military commanders. By simple means and reduced military force, any area cell or group of cells can be disconnected at any time from the rest of Palestinian territory, and the movement of people and goods among them can be checked. The ability to seal off specific area cells turns the practice of isolation and separation into one of intervention, traffic control, initiated or random disruption of everyday life, a means of extortion, and an area of negotiation. Thus, at any point in time, Palestinians can be prevented from tilling their land, going to work, supplying, marketing and exporting goods, holding everyday routine meetings, assembling, or simply spending time together.

Meanwhile, closing off area cells has enabled Jews to move in relative security among Jewish enclaves, hardly ever encountering Palestinians. The greater the separation between Palestinian space and Jewish space, the stronger the continuity between Jewish space in the Occupied Territories and Israeli space within the Green Line. Most Israelis who now travel the thoroughfares connecting the settlements with Israel are unaware of crossing the Green Line when they do, even if indeed aware of its existence. However, on both sides, one can only imagine a homogeneous spatial continuity. For the Palestinians, only their isolated area cells are homogeneous. For the Jews, the Palestinians' mere insistence on "staying put"—carrying on with their lives, working, moving around despite the hardships—disrupts any attempt at stabilizing a homogeneous spatial picture.

Under such circumstances, separation is not a situation but rather a never-ending project. Separation has become the ideology of the mainstream in Israeli society, and various arms of government have presented practical plans whose political implications differ, which were at the center of a heated debate. When it became evident that Israel could not halt Palestinian terrorism, Prime Minister Ariel Sharon retracted his opposition to erecting a physical barrier between "us" and "them," and in April 2002, his cabinet passed a resolution to create a separation wall. In August of that year, the route of the barrier was ratified, mostly winding its way east of the Green Line, surrounding the whole West Bank, but also biting deeply into its area—and construction began. The wall was meant to block the movement of Palestinians from east to west, but not that of Jews in the opposite direction. Naturally, it aimed to reduce the amount of violent resistance, as well as most contact between Jews and Palestinians, without affecting the total penetrability of Palestinian space to the occupiers' intervention. Nor was it necessarily supposed to reduce the points of friction that the ruling apparatus imposed upon the Palestinian populace.

The years pass and the wall is still uncompleted.[4] This monumental structure, hundreds of kilometers long, creates a false guise of continuous separation between Israel and Palestine as two distinct entities, while in actual fact it conceals the internal fragmentation of the Occupied Territories, the disrupted space that exists in its shade, and Israel's acts therein. The wall is a sophisticated geostrategic architectural machine for administering movement on the Palestinian side, and for its distancing, exclusion, and abstraction on the Israeli side. It not only exacerbates destruction and devastation but also distances them from the Israeli gaze and helps the Israeli rulership shirk its responsibility for what happens throughout the West Bank.

The wall is a typical, if particularly blunt, expression of the spatial principle that has characterized the Jewish colonization project from its outset: Jewish penetration of the Palestinian environment, accompanied by acts of separation of Jews from Palestinians and the expulsion of Palestinians from areas where their presence was limited or prohibited. This usually resulted in Jewish expansion and Palestinian compression, reduction of Palestinians' sources of livelihood and exploitation of their labor power. The area cleansed of Palestinian presence, where only Palestinian workers with special permits can stay during working hours, is much larger than the area of the settlements themselves. The built-up area in the Jewish settlements amounts to a mere 3 percent of the West Bank, but the municipal reach of the settlements—populated by 250,000 Jews, about 9.5 percent of the West Bank's population—stretches over more than 40 percent of its total area.

The separation wall joins the ruling power's other means of cleansing Israeli space of Palestinian presence—such as the incessant hounding of illegals and amendments to the Israeli citizenship law that prevent the return of Palestinians to the Occupied Territories and Jerusalem. Thus the wall and the entire regime of movement in the Occupied Territories join similar apparatuses of regimenting movement and administering borders in various places in the world where "security considerations" and risk management also disguise an effort to guard one group against mixing with and being penetrated by another. However, this is one-way separation. Israel reserves the right and has the means to penetrate any spot in the Palestinian area at all times. Thus, the separation that the wall is supposed to ensure can never be quite whole, even if its construction is completed. Absolute separation is a central component of the Israeli political imagination, but not of military and political reality, where the mere existence of the Occupation regime requires constant reinvention of points of interaction between the two sides.

The location and nature of such points are dictated, among other things, by the spread of settlements to the east of the wall and the network of roads laid out among them, and between them and the area to the west of the Green Line, in order to ensure free movement for Israeli settlers and soldiers. They are also dictated by the need to sort the governed population into categories, which occasionally change, and to issue or deny permits of passage. The need to apply for such permits and get them renewed creates dozens of points of daily friction between Israelis and Palestinians, sites where subjects negotiate with representatives of the government, provoke it, require its assistance, submit to it, or resist it. Moreover, this means that separation is maintained, not necessarily or strictly between Israelis and Palestinians, but first and foremost between Palestinians and Palestinians: most systematically, consistently, and severely between Gaza and the West Bank,[5] as well as between the northern and southern parts of the West Bank, among Palestinian localities to the east of the wall and villages and farmlands to its west, and between Palestinian Jerusalem on the Israeli side of the wall and the West Bank—the list goes on and on.

For the sake of such separation, the ruling apparatus must plunge its claws deep into Palestinian habitat, but such penetration is meant to be "under the radar," or at least low-profile and off-camera. Since 2003, the Israeli army has acted to reduce the area and duration of soldier and settler contact with the governed Palestinian population at checkpoints as well, in an effort to minimize the forces needed and to improve the conditions under which Palestinians must cross them. Some of the checkpoints have taken on the guise of border-crossing terminals, where the separation of soldiers from Palestinians is nearly total. Both there and at the "pillbox" posts, fortified watchtowers placed at key spots, Palestinians who try to move from one place to another have to be delayed without any access to the soldiers or civilian guards who man them.[6]

Suspension of activities and long delays are among the main effects of withheld violence in the Occupied Territories. By blocking movement and forcing people to loiter in the wrong place at the wrong time, withheld violence encumbers, complicates, disrupts preferences, undermines plans, maddens, wounds, infests, generates disease, and kills. This is the tangible, immediate effect of the withheld presence of force. Withheld violence prevents the individuals at whom it is directed from doing whatever is needed to avoid its harm, which is very hard to ascribe to a specific cause. Detaining women in labor at checkpoints or refusing to grant passage to ailing patients are extreme instances that speak for themselves. But people in good health and in no need of special medical care are harmed as well. When withheld violence suspends life, it takes its toll without erupting and with no direct regard for the obedience of its subjects. Its outcome might prove no less disastrous—perhaps even more so—than that of eruptive violence. Actually, in areas and periods when suspension of movement and activity becomes all the more forceful (such as in the crammed pens at checkpoints, full to bursting), or in areas deprived of water, electric power, and other basic utilities, the formal difference between eruption and threat is entirely erased, and the body is incessantly vulnerable to all types of harm.[7] In fact, the Occupied Palestinian Territories have become a "zone of indistinction" between the two types of violence, which, under stable sovereign rule, are otherwise distinct.

The destructive effects of this economy of violence cannot be captured by counting violations of rights, denouncing eruptive, scandalous showcase violence, or assessing deteriorating standards of living. No humanitarian chart can account for the normalization of suspension and waiting, and no human rights report can measure the loss of time and the humiliation of innumerable people detained and left for hours waiting at the roadside or near checkpoints, disposed of, blindfolded, their hands cuffed in tight plastic strips—only to be released later, just as they were picked up, without any explanation. The dominant discourse, however, tends to focus on the more spectacular and lethal eruption of violence, detached from its role and place in the economy of violence, quantified through the tally of victims, assessed by its proportionality, examined in light of international and Israeli law, or the Israeli army's "code of ethics," and almost always justified in the name of security.

However, this representation of violence is misconstrued and it misses the role of violence as a mode of governance. Even at the height of the Second Intifada in the spring of 2002, during the Israeli operation called Defensive Shield, when the Israeli army "reconquered" most of the West Bank, once more making the local population feel its powerful presence, and changed the nature of its control in the Gaza Strip—even then, the power active in the Occupied Territories was more withheld and checked than eruptive. Even then, withheld violence had a greater impact upon the lives of Palestinians than eruptive violence. Withheld violence impinges on everyday life. Eruptive violence is short-lived.

Whether as an unexpected reaction or as a premeditated operation, the eruption of force is meant to end by reaffirming the presence of withheld violence, which at times—though not necessarily—happens through a new deployment of forces and a reorganization of the space, time, and living arrangements of the dominated. Usually, one chooses to obey, retreat, pass or refrain from passage, go out of one's way, work or refrain from working, strip, stand in front of the camera, wait in line, clam up, resign oneself to the verdict (without trial), behave in an orderly fashion, and either speak politely or keep quiet.

For the functionaries of the Occupation, such behavior on the part of subjects validates the ruling apparatus's basic principle—that resistance be checked without any eruption of violence. But such validation is only temporary, and proof must be produced again and again. This requires both the reintroduction of withheld violence and direct action through eruptive violence. Sporadic bursts of violence, random in space and time, bear witness to the continuous existence of the withheld presence, to its homogeneity in space and time. These eruptions have to take place more and more frequently as the threat contained in suspended force gradually erodes. The threat is not necessarily eroded because the threatening force has weakened or retreated. It is not only a result of the introduction of armed forces, but also of the way in which their withheld violence is perceived by the threatened party. The more violence is exerted against it, the less the threatened side has to lose. The less it has to lose, the greater the threat against it must become in order to achieve the same result: destroying its power and will to resist.

This logic helps explain the steep increase in the use of live ammunition in the suppression of the Second Intifada (2000–2003), as well as the destruction inflicted on the Gaza Strip in Operation Cast Lead in 2009. For example, in 1971, when the army razed dozens of homes in refugee camps in Gaza in order to prevent the sheltering of fighters and "air the camps out," inflicting relatively small damage on their residents, there was scant resistance. In 2002, however, when the army razed 140 homes in the Jenin refugee camp alone in Operation Defensive Shield, Palestinians showed great determination and inflicted numerous casualties on the IDF in fierce battles.

TWO KINDS OF VIOLENCE

Accepting Michel Foucault's analysis, we define power as a mode of "acting upon the actions of others,"[8] and understand violence as a kind of power. Although Foucault wished to distinguish force from power, the use of physical force is clearly one way to act upon the action of others. Violence is physical force that acts upon the actions of people, because it inflicts or threatens to inflict harm on their persons and possessions or on those of their dear ones.

Violence is the exertion of physical force to injure its object. It is invasive, disruptive, painful, or erosive. Disruption, penetration, erosion, and the like are forms of destruction. After the injury, the injured party has difficulty existing in the state that preceded the injury. Regard for the law, central to a critical discussion of violence,[9] will always be secondary to the power of destruction. The law might allow or prohibit destruction, limit or ignore it, enable, restrict, or reject claims to reparation; however, destruction itself does not result from the law or its regard, but from the actual or potential contact between the active force and its object: a body or property.

Acts of violence such as invasion, penetration, or demolition have a visible aspect par excellence—even in the absence of eyewitnesses, such as instances of violent robbery in a dark alley or a massacre in a remote forest—because they are always visible events, at least in the victim's eyes. But an act is also violent when the force is not eruptive and violence is *withheld*. Withheld violence is the presence of a violent force whose outbreak may be imminent, but is not yet manifest. It differs from violence insinuated by words, a flag, or other symbols in the immediacy of its potential manifestation and the rapidly diminishing interval in space and time between the presence of such force and its actual eruption. In withheld violence, threatening and deterring gestures replace direct contact with the exposed body, but these are gestures of overt presence on the part of the threatening force. The difference between withheld violence and insinuated violence is a matter of degree and continuity. At times, insinuations of violence act as threats, and their deterrent effect is no less powerful, even greater, than its overt presence. But in an ongoing conflict, insinuated threats lose their effectiveness, and the threatening power tends and needs to intensify them by displaying withheld violence. In any case, violence—whether insinuated or withheld—is effective even when there is no outburst of physical force. There is no visible bodily contact, and yet the traces of destruction are clear.

In this respect, insinuated or withheld violence does not differ from economic power, purchasing power, the rhetorical power of persuasion, and other such acts and representations in which people "act upon the actions of others" without exerting physical force. Potential power—money and possessions, political authority, physical fitness, courage, or an arsenal of arms—has meaning as an "action upon actions," or upon the behavior of others, only if something indicates it or signifies it—only if it shows its presence. Potential force acts through the discourse that represents it and through the imagination that simulates its action without necessarily being linked to the actual designated force. Potential force, like any "thing in itself," is applied merely through the mediation of whatever represents it, acting according to the effectiveness of such a representation according to the way in which it is designated, leaves traces, is expressed and symbolized, imagined, metaphorically molded, counted, and quantified. Purchasing power that has not been consummated, but is represented; knowledge that has not been demonstrated, but is signified; political authority that has not been exercised, but is declared; violence that has not been actually exerted, but leaves traces, are all significant in defining the possible field of action of power, its range of influence. Every such form of presence of potential power partakes of the actual productive game of power.

These distinctions are true of all sources of power—physical, economic, political-governmental, or cognitive-cultural.[10] In the present context, however, attempting to understand Israel's control mechanism in the Occupied Territories, as in other contexts where violence is practiced widely and systematically alongside other control mechanisms, it does not suffice to treat violence as equivalent to other sources of power. Violence in the Occupied Territories—and in this the region does not differ from many "emergency zones" throughout the world—is a comprehensive form of regulating and administering human life—people's interrelations, activities, and movement. Better understanding its functioning as a sui generis ruling system relatively independent of other power sources and ruling systems is necessary in order to fully comprehend the way in which it is incorporated into them.

One obvious difference between violence and other sources of power in modern society is the special weight intrinsic to the relation between the potential force and its manifest state. This difference is expressed in two aspects of the transition from potential to manifestation: the regulation of this transition and its frequency. The transition from political authority to political resolution, from purchasing power to actual purchase, and from covert to overt information is fluent, frequent, very partially regulated, and determined mainly or even exclusively by the enforcing party. It is restrained only within the limits of a specific activity: certain things may not be purchased, certain people are prohibited from purchasing certain things, certain things must not be known or revealed, and the like. The nature of the transition from insinuated violence to withheld violence to the eruption of violence is at the heart of state rule and at the base of social order. This varies from regime to regime.

The prevalence of such a transition is a function of the ruling power's legitimacy in the eyes of its subjects and of the stability of the political order. A stable, legitimate rule is one in which such transitions are rare and regulated by law, restricted in space and time, and generally accepted by the governed. The effectiveness of violence in a political system is affected by the gap between withholding force and its exertion, on the one hand, and the continuum between potential violence and its manifestation, on the other. "Proper" rule—especially political rule, but also the kind of rule in educational, industrial, or military institutions—works mainly by means of insinuated threats of violence, and not through actually applying violent force. When it is challenged, it usually chooses to deter and defeat its opponents through the display of withheld violence and would hesitate before instructing its armed forces to open fire. But the essential meaning of an insinuated threat is that it might be carried out at any moment—all the more so when withheld violence is overtly present.

When a government loses its legitimacy and stability, it tends to display withheld violence on a wide scale and exert overt violence on an irregular, ad hoc basis. In actual fact, these differences are blurred, of course, but on this continuum, it is important to maintain three distinct ideal types: proper rule under which withheld violence is an exception to the rule and its eruption a rare event; proper rule under which, in certain distinct areas, withheld violence is the rule; and unstable, illegitimate rule whose jurisdiction is typified by the daily occurrence of both forms of violence, withheld and eruptive. In spite of the differences between these three types of rule, as long as the government is concerned about its legitimacy both internally and externally, it will tend to maintain a guise of continuity and ordered transition between the two forms of violence and to present its violence as a legal response to severe legal transgressions and eruptions of violence on the part of the governed—both as part of the legal order and as a condition for its existence.

Obviously, the Occupation regime is not considered legitimate by the Palestinians in the Occupied Territories, but for the regime, only Israelis and sections of the First World public have a say in determining legitimacy. By using euphemistic language to describe "enlightened" checkpoints, "targeted eliminations," and "smart bombs," and the legal safety net beneath all of these, Israel seeks to diminish the extent to which direct violence is employed and to create the impression that whenever possible, its forces are mobilized only to deter.

State violence in the Occupied Territories cannot be regarded as based on law or convention. However, what is conceived of as the legitimate use of violence has changed quite dramatically since August 2005, following the Israeli disengagement from Gaza. At that time, two entirely different arenas were established for the exertion of force: the Gaza Strip and the West Bank. The role of the two types of violence—withheld and eruptive—differs in the two arenas, and the need to legitimize eruptive violence has likewise taken different forms. Under a regime that has no legitimacy—certainly the case in the Occupied Territories—no stable gap can be maintained between suspending and unleashing force, and the effectiveness of the ruling apparatus does not depend on regulated transition from one to the other.

When discussing the violence practiced in the Occupied Territories, one should be careful not to mistake withheld violence for a potential force actualized, and the eruption of that force should not be conceived of as suspended as long as certain legal and political conditions are not met. Instead, one should examine the actual forms of eruptive violence, on the one hand, and the deployment patterns of withheld violence, on the other, and account for the different ways they are practiced in the Gaza Strip and in the West Bank. Under Israeli occupation of the territories, these two forms of violence belong to two distinct spheres of action and may take place simultaneously without being related to each other. This happened for the first time in the Occupied Territories in an organized fashion toward the end of the First Intifada in the late 1980s, when the extrajudicial deployment of special undercover army units (the *mista'rvim*) to kill or injure resistance leaders and activists became routine. It happened again, much more extensively, with the outbreak of the Second [al-Aqsa] Intifada. Under the control apparatus maintained in the Occupied Territories, the entire space has become penetrable to both types of violence, and the relation between them is no longer one of potential and fulfillment. The apparatus of withheld violence is constantly active and does not remain a mere potential threat; eruptive violence is always in the offing. The force wielded by the control apparatus might materialize anywhere, and its emergence does not necessarily express the realization of potential force identified by conventional codes. Without ever materializing as eruptive, withheld, contained force inflicts continuous violence upon objects, bodies, and minds.

If the two forms of violence are taken to constitute a continuum, the threat of eruptive violence is all the more tangible the further away one moves from its suspended form. The threat it emanates increases, and the time needed to carry out that threat is reduced. This is, of course, an assumed continuum. In actual fact, observing Israeli violence in action in the Occupied Territories, it becomes evident that, on the one hand, the violent outburst, the *passage à l'acte*, does not always originate in the manifest presence of potential violence. On the other hand, countless foci of potential violence are visible throughout the dominated space, and the mere presence of potential violence suffices to prohibit, direct, and administer life, inflict bodily injury, and crush the life texture of an entire population. Our main distinction is, therefore, between withheld violence and eruptive violence.

There are indeed places in the Occupied Territories and situations in which continuity is evident between the two types of violence. But we argue that such continuity has now become the exception to the rule. For there to be such continuity between withheld violence and eruptive violence, conventions known to both the government and its subjects should be in effect. These include temporary or permanent zoning of land as private and public, as well as accessible and inaccessible areas, respectively penetrable and impenetrable to the infliction of sanctioned violence, and a space of action where both government's officials and the governed partake in restoring conventions when they are breached. Such conventions and demarcations, which have always been fragile in the Occupied Territories, have been systematically ignored since the outbreak of the Second Intifada and no such space of political action exists. The accepted rules can be set aside at any moment. The army can penetrate any demarcated site, such as the ministries of the Palestinian Authority and private homes and public places—mosques, schools, hospitals, and cemeteries—with a violence that leaves its victims helpless.

Withheld violence is suspended violence whose potential dimension—usually invisible—is made visible and displayed conspicuously. Violent force acts by flaunting its potential. Here it is not merely a declared or referred authority, the publishing of fiscal balances, or the parading of titles and uniforms. It is the *display* of the "thing in itself." It is not "the thing in itself," of course (the shot or blast), only its display, but the display is real (an actual weapon-carrying body, or at times, just the weapons). It is not a symbolic presentation—the force is present, not just represented. It acts through its actual presence. In a gang fight or a tribal feud, dispersing demonstrators or strikers, preparing for war, or even in war itself, the display of violence plays a central role. When the display of violence is regulated through cultural and legal codes that are considered legitimate, it might be a part of the strategy of struggle between the parties to the power relations, a strategy employed without actually having to exert violence. Such display might use decoys or simulation, of course. One can try to scare through exaggeration or belittling in order to mislead, but these possibilities stem from the role that is already assigned to the visibility of violent force. However, lacking cultural and legal codes agreed upon by the parties, the display of violence always constitutes the use of violence.

Suspended violence, either insinuated or withheld, is an active force because it is the unfulfilled possibility of eruptive violence that might manifest itself at any moment.[11] The expected outburst works because it deters, while the suspended outburst works because it enables a space of negotiation, retreat, escape, and counterthreats. Unrealized potential works, not only because it might be fulfilled, but also because it might not be. The presence of power in withheld violence should be conceived of here, not as a necessary phase on the way to actually erupting, as though that were an objective that would eventually be achieved, but as a presencing of the potential either to erupt or not to erupt, to be or not to be an eruption of violence.[12] The more intense such presencing of power is, and the more effectively it is deployed in space and time, the greater the power of potential to act *as* potential, that is, to administer, direct, block, expand, grab, diminish, redivide, abandon, establish borders and breach them, to injure, and even kill, precisely by not being exercised as brute force. One should add that as soon as withheld violence replaces the insinuated violence of the "proper" regime as a major tool of domination, insinuated violence, too, becomes afflicted, is less insinuated, and functions as display (or presencing) and not merely a representation of the potential.

Withheld violence tends to be contagious. During political crises, a state of emergency, war, or under occupation, when the law is suspended or imposed and subjects persist in their resistance, there are no permanent arrangements for the presence of withheld violence, and the rules for realizing its potential are drawn up ad hoc, changing according to the "situation on the ground." In such situations, when the suspending effect of withheld violence intensifies, there is an intrinsic tendency to blur differences between this kind of violence and eruptive violence, and the governed are trapped in a state of constant threat to their well-being, their lives, and their possessions.

RULING APPARATUSES

Violence, in both its forms, is the main ruling apparatus in the Occupied Territories. But in order to comprehend how violence functions, we must step back and place it in the context of other ruling apparatuses. One may distinguish three ruling apparatuses (in Althusser's sense of this term, i.e., practices that shape individuals as subjects of power and reproduce power relations)[13] involved on a daily basis in the rule of a modern state, each with its own ideological component: the judicial-sovereign apparatus that establishes general law, interprets it, and enforces it in particular cases; the disciplinary apparatus that forms individuals into subjects and citizens; and the governmental apparatus that focuses on administering territories and populations, assuring the well-being and security of society at large.

Retreat to violence may take place in all three apparatuses, in their more or less ideological components, but only the judicial-sovereign apparatus functions by regularly combining eruptive violence and the law, because some of its organs sanction the violence exercised by the others. Within this framework, violence usually appears in some relation to law, as a war that aims to destroy existing law and instate new law, or as policing to preserve the existing law. The law, in its turn, might legitimize war or preparations for it, and the various forms of police violence, as well as its own retreat from and abandonment of land and population in states of emergency.

The flagrant presence of withheld violence in the Occupied Territories since the late 1990s is explained by the fact that Israel is unable to make significant use of ideology, law, or disciplinary mechanisms, which, prior to the Oslo period, and despite the negative effect of the First Intifada on these mechanisms, still mediated and reduced its need for violence. After the Oslo Accords, and more intensely since the second Intifada, the meaning and function of the "civil" apparatuses, like law and discipline, which have never been dismantled, have been transformed. They are still at work wherever the security forces encounter Palestinians, at checkpoints, in the offices handling applications for permits, on patrols, and during arrests, but they act as mere simulations of similar apparatuses of regulated sovereign rule. Of the three apparatuses mentioned above, the only one functioning properly in the Occupied Territories is the governmental apparatus whose main role is demographic control and separation. But because of the transfer of responsibilities to the Palestinian Authority that followed the Oslo Accords, and because of the population's sweeping resistance, this apparatus has been completely reduced to its functions of counting and classification in the service of "security," entirely giving up its caring functions (e.g., the provision of health, education, infrastructure, and so on).

In every respect connected with the responsibility for administering the life of Palestinians, Israel acts as though the Palestinian Authority were a foreign sovereign government. But whenever Palestinian governance touches on anything Israel defines as its "national" or "security" interest, the control apparatus persists in acting as a sovereign. For its part, the Palestinian Authority has since the Oslo Accords established the three branches of government, and some of its institutions do take care of the Palestinian population. However, in countless matters of legislation and government, customs, imports and exports, infrastructure, construction, industrialization, and, of course, law enforcement, its hands are tied.[14] Besides endless futile "peace talks," most encounters between the ruling apparatus and the Palestinian Authority are devoted to "security issues," where "security" is the privilege of Jews only, and Israel repeatedly demands that the PA provide it. Whatever the governing role played by the Palestinian Authority, it is both allowed and constrained by the control apparatus's exercise of withheld violence. Whenever "diplomatic" pressure fails, the resistance of the governed is contained through the exercise of violence, which is more or less integrated into the governmental mechanisms used to classify the Palestinian population and monitor the movements and activities of its members.

The Judicial Apparatus

The ruling apparatus's actions are still overwhelmingly authorized by legislation and subject to judicial scrutiny. Military commanders and officials usually act according to authority vested in them by law. But legal authorization is more or less the only remaining vestige of law in the ruling apparatus of the Territories, and it, too, has been breached, because the army has repeatedly disobeyed explicit orders of the High Court of Justice in the (quite rare) cases where rulings have favored Palestinians.[15]

De facto rulings take place through an elaborate system of "ruling by decrees" that has characterized colonial regimes since the late nineteenth century.[16] The law in the Occupied Territories is not an effective device of control, not only because the Palestinians do not recognize its legitimacy, but because the Israeli regime incessantly changes it, suspending and annulling laws. The military command inundates the area under its control and its subjects with orders and regulations, which keep changing, and seldom follows its own regulations.[17]

The rule of law in the Occupied Territories (the West Bank since the Israeli "disengagement" from Gaza) has thus been suspended in three different respects: first, it is suspended due to the state of occupation and military rule declared there in June 1967; second, military rule itself is suspended by ad hoc state-of-emergency regulations, which are changed sporadically by announcements by military commanders on the ground;[18] and, finally, Israeli law itself has also been suspended, inasmuch as the army has been knowingly and intentionally acting contrary to court rulings. Nevertheless, edicts and regulations proliferate in the West Bank, some in response to criticism by the Supreme Court when it is called upon to judge the lawfulness, reasonableness, or "proportionality" of the ruling apparatus's actions, regulations, policies, and decisions. Appeals to the Supreme Court, which are always heard in retrospect, mainly serve to give the Occupation regime a semblance of lawfulness, enabling the continuum of eruptive and withheld violence. The court maintains this façade of legitimacy whether or not its rulings are enforced; the rare cases in which a ruling in favor of Palestinian petitioners is enforced are precisely those that uphold the semblance of lawfulness—in the eyes of the occupiers, of course.

The Occupied Territories were not a legal vacuum prior to Israel's "disengagement" from the Gaza Strip, and this is still true of the West Bank today. The abuse of life at the hands of the Occupation regime is not due to some withdrawal of the law, but occurs thanks to a savage proliferation of legalities and illegalities and the creation of an extensive judicial patchwork that keeps changing the law itself, the regime's authorities and immunity, and the subject's own status before the law.[19] Under such conditions, subjects cannot—and are not supposed to—internalize the law. The difference between law and decree, decree and order, and between order and the presence of the uniformed person who administers it greatly diminishes and at times disappears altogether. Even under less duress, ruling by decree is chronically and outstandingly unstable, and in the Occupied Territories, this instability has been on the increase since the First Intifada. Because the rules that the subjects are supposed to follow change rapidly, it is impossible to rely on the validity of anything that is not accompanied by withheld violence. No order is worth the paper it is written on without the actual presence of the force that can implement it. The regime needs the massive presence of withheld violence in order to announce the rules and direct and dictate the behavior of its subjects with them. But the subjects, too, need this presence in order to be informed of the rules and to know how to calculate their everyday moves. In order to know which route to take to work, one must know where the checkpoint is placed; in order to decide whether even to bother going to work, one must know whether or not a curfew has been imposed during the night—and thus on and on, with every activity in every aspect of life.

Disciplinary Sites and Practices

Ever since the Oslo Accords, the Israeli regime no longer maintains disciplinary sites in the Occupied Territories. Prisons and detention centers are meant mainly to distance the inmates, rather than to shape them into disciplined subjects.[20] In their capacity as disciplining sites, prisons have paradoxically served the Palestinian rebels no less than they have served the Israeli government. Incarcerated Palestinian prisoners have used these closed disciplining sites to shape the disciplined subject of the Palestinian uprising. The disciplinary apparatuses functioning within Palestinian society are not subject to Israeli rule. As in an inverted mirror image of the way in which such apparatuses in Israel train and recruit their "subjects" for the struggle against Palestinians, the Palestinian apparatuses recruit their own "subjects" into the struggle against Israel (and since the Hamas takeover in the Gaza Strip, against Fatah or Hamas, respectively). They seek to shape the Palestinian population in whose lives they are involved into subjects who see this struggle as inevitable, as an arena of excellence, and as a vital dimension of any public activity.

Disciplinary practices are still maintained in nearly any encounter between Palestinians and the forces that exert withheld violence, and especially at the institutionalized points of friction: the checkpoints, interrogation rooms, and whatever is left of the civil administration. But this disciplining—which takes place under absolutely illegitimate conditions set by the disciplining power— fulfills a local, ad hoc role. The Palestinians are taught how to behave when crossing a checkpoint, how to address an official in the district coordination office, how to gain benefits in detention cells. What the Palestinian learns in an encounter with the regime in one venue, however, does not teach the Palestinian subject what to expect in other encounters in other venues. Moreover, he or she ought to learn precisely this: that it is pointless to internalize rules of conduct, for these constantly change and must be deciphered anew in every encounter with the regime. Only two things will be repeated in nearly every encounter: the absolute submission of the Palestinian to the representative of Israel, and the need to relearn again and again what is expected in order either to please power or to avoid it. The sporadic disciplinary practices that do occur do not construct a reliable subject. Quite the contrary, perhaps. The almost unlimited authority that the security forces have to change the rules is a way of producing a subject who is inherently unreliable. Any unaccounted-for Palestinian is therefore suspect and must be supervised. The rules of discipline, like the law, need the immediate presence of withheld violence. Neither the judicial apparatus nor the disciplinary practices can produce the "remote-control" effect that typifies disciplinary apparatuses in a modern state. Paradoxically, therefore, instead of reducing violence (at least withheld violence) by means of nonviolent governing apparatuses, any appeal to the letter of the law and to disciplinary norms in the Occupied Territories requires the intensification of withheld violence, without which the law and disciplinary norms would be ineffective.

Under conditions of political stability, the main effects of disciplinary apparatuses and ideological representation are to shape every individual as a subject of the sovereign power, and to cause subjects to internalize these power relations and accept their position and status within them. Without the rule of law, when power does not maintain effective disciplining sites or ideological mechanisms, the Palestinians in the Occupied Territories cannot be made subjects of the Israeli regime—unlike Palestinian citizens of Israel. The Palestinian in the Territories is neither a citizen of the regime nor submitted to it as *subjectus*,[21] and his or her obedience to it is only out of compulsion and fear. It is impossible to internalize this relationship without the violent presence of the ruling apparatus, or to formulate it as an inner voice, even if one is willing to accept the absolute submission it involves, because it is impossible to formulate as a rule what appears ad hoc, sporadically, except the rule of hopeless arbitrariness itself, of violence that might emerge at any moment, anywhere. The noncitizens, subjects in spite of themselves, who are ruled by means of violent force that suspends the law and acts in unmediated ways, do not internalize a thing. As far as they are concerned, power must always be overt, be just what it is on the surface of the area in its grip, in the endless game between the intensifying presence of withheld violence and spectacular instances of eruptive violence.

The law is perceived by Palestinians as an arbitrary force that does not regulate violence, but rather sanctions it, and the ruling power enjoys no legitimacy. Unmediated by discipline or ideology, the ruling apparatus therefore has to resort to withheld violence and must accompany it occasionally by eruptive violence and shorten the time needed to exert it. Instead of disciplining its subjects or educating them, it harms them. Instead of punishing them in corrective frameworks when they resist (or are perceived by it as resisters, or as intending to resist), the ruling apparatus kills, bombs, and demolishes. The need for rapidity is expressed in a denser deployment of violence in the Occupied Territories and the absolute penetrability of the whole area to Israeli forces, regardless of the geographical or urban route of movement. This need has constantly led to the development of new techniques of warfare in built-up areas, including razing of buildings, uprooting of trees and bushes (*hisufim*), and "swarming," a tactic in which troops avoid existing, familiar routes (where Palestinians might ambush them) and move in as straight a line as possible, sometimes literally through house walls, equipped with gear and accompanied by professionals whose purpose it is to remove any obstacle in their way. Anyone they encounter on the way—standing in or crossing the straight line that connects them to their target—risks losing his or her life for having been in the wrong place at the wrong time.[22]

Israeli use of what Amira Hass calls "weapons of light construction" to raze buildings, dig trenches, lay obstacles, and seal wells in the Occupied Territories (Hass 2003), which has totally changed the Palestinian habitat, is mostly not an eruption of uncontrolled violence in response to resistance. Rather, it is a calculated use of technology to wreck buildings, smash objects, and degrade spaces without directly affecting humans. Harm to humans is a by-product, but usually not the direct purpose. The rationale behind such harm is demographic: separating, assembling, and compressing populations, which at times includes transferring individuals or relatively small groups, in what human rights groups have called "quiet transfer." Such acts are carried out by changing the law and using loopholes in it to make Palestinians lose their residency rights (Stein 1997), or through the widespread destruction accompanying warfare and the creation of "buffer zones" close to fences in the Gaza Strip, or through space-shaping "civilian" enterprises such as the construction of the separation wall and the paving of bypass roads in the West Bank.[23]

The Israeli regime acts in the Occupied Territories first and foremost as a *demographic* ruling apparatus through the systematic separation of Jewish citizens (colonists, soldiers, and visitors from Israel) from Palestinian subjects, through the territorial separation of Jews and Palestinians, and through the separation of the various habitats of the Palestinians, a separation that has been progressively increased since the 1990s. Until the outbreak of the First Intifada, this apparatus—first presided over by military governors and military administration and later by the "civil administration," subject to army commanders in the Territories—still attended in whatever limited way to the needs of the Palestinian population and bore minimal responsibility for administering a normal everyday life and addressing problems. However, since the First Intifada, this apparatus has been retracted and has gradually deteriorated. The Oslo Accords gave the Palestinian Authority responsibility for governing in Areas A and B, and the services provided by the Occupation regime to residents of Area C were further reduced. After the Second Intifada broke out, Israel all but ceased any governing that meant providing care for the subjugated Palestinian population. In 2002–4, in repressing the Second Intifada, it systematically destroyed Palestinian administrative apparatuses. But the Israeli demographic apparatus has not been removed. It has only changed its purpose. To achieve the fullest possible control and surveillance of movement by Palestinians in the Occupied Territories, it now works to hone and perfect the separation mechanisms and regime of movement implemented in the Occupied Territories, sporadically after the First Gulf War, at times following the suicide bombings of the 1990s, and systematically and continuously since the outbreak of the Second Intifada. Controlling movement requires classification, tracking, counting, and locating by "the demographic branch" of the ruling apparatus, which creates an incessant supply of more and more distinctions, some on the basis of geographical location, others based on demographic data (gender, age, state of health), employment, or "security"—a separate category that might, at any given moment, include any one of the other categories or all of them at once.

This highly sophisticated system incessantly produces and is nourished by detailed knowledge of populations, topography, and movements, as well as the capacity for classification, surveillance, investigation, reconnaissance, informing, incrimination, arrest, and detention. Withheld violence is essential, while eruptive violence tends to be used with caution and only in a limited way. When it erupts, violence disrupts movement arrangements, makes information gathering cumbersome, forces the separated to mix and breaks down the mingling of those who must be kept apart, hides what seeks visibility and exposes what seeks to remain hidden, making it necessary to count again, to locate, classify, and reclassify. People disappear or appear unexpectedly, and at times, the system even results in Jews mingling with Arabs. In short, eruptive violence tends to loss of control, making withheld violence all the more important. This measured, precise presence of the security forces promises maximal control and applies withheld violence at the lowest cost. This violence works along traffic routes, at checkpoints, in flash patrols, and at the entrances of homes in the planned and meticulous combination of armed soldiers and computers, of the magnetic pass card and the rifle, of passage permits and checkpoints that deny movement, of the sweeping blockage of movement throughout an entire region and the filtering of traffic by personal supervision of each and every individual passenger. But it is the lowest cost only because the goal is the separation of Jews and Palestinians, citizens and subjects, and nothing, of course, is self-evident about this.

It means the active rejection of two other possibilities that always loom on the horizon: withdrawal from the Territories, giving up control of their inhabitants, or annexing the Territories and naturalizing their residents.

VIOLENCE-PREVENTING VIOLENCE

The daily price that withheld violence demands of the Palestinians is exorbitant. As noncitizens, they lack the legal shield that enables citizens to negotiate the way they are ruled legally and politically. Their access to the Israeli legal system is curbed, and the help it can provide them is negligible. Nor does the Palestinian—as a nonsubject—see himself or herself as a part of some social whole that the government is supposed to represent. The Palestinian is a subject who may only submit or resist and force the ruling apparatus either to intensify withheld violence or respond directly in violent eruptions. The persistence of Palestinian resistance for over six years during the Second Intifada and the perseverance of the Gazans for over a decade of closures and partial siege show an unusual degree of resilience in the face of such violence, which forces the apparatus to deploy its withheld violence ever more broadly and to instigate more frequent eruptions of direct violence. The Palestinians in the West Bank—and until the disengagement, in the Gaza Strip as well—cannot publicly display their own withheld violence for fear of Israel destroying its machinery. The violence they direct at Israelis is nearly always eruptive, for withheld violence has an overt, ongoing presence that is markedly lacking in the violence of the terrorist or guerrilla. In circumstances of absolute inferiority, violent actions against soldiers and civilians alike reflect acknowledgment of weakness—an understanding that other channels of resistance (political, legal, or civil) cannot bring about any change in power relations. Under such circumstances, violent forms of resistance have provided the Israeli authorities with their principal excuse for intensifying their use of violence, both withheld and eruptive.

The truth, however, is that most of the time, the majority of Palestinians are afraid to resort to withheld violence of their own. Since they cannot totally give in to the dictates of the ruling apparatus either, they try to survive through improvisation and manipulation, looking for ways out, calculating the costs of daily activity, deciding every morning anew which path to take, how to dress for the inspection at the checkpoint, which permits to bring along, how to avoid encounters with the forces on the ground, and how to address the soldiers. They must not be perceived as threatening, yet they cannot afford to remain without resources for coping with the situation. But this is precisely what happens to them all the time. They are forever suspect, at least as long as they retain their ability to speak back to the ruling power in its own tongue—force—and at times only for taking the liberty of a level gaze. At any moment, they might be left resourceless, empty-handed. For the ruling apparatus, their resistance lies, not just in their actions, but in their mere presence, their insistence on staying.

According to the official Israeli doctrine, all Israeli mechanisms of violence active in the Occupied Territories fulfill "security needs," namely, preventing direct Palestinian violence against Israeli citizens. Observation of many of the situations in which withheld and eruptive violence are used by Israel shows that they were intended to prevent direct or indirect Palestinian violence against the ruling apparatus. Despite the fact that it is not a sovereign power, and that even in disciplinary sites it prefers violence to discipline, the ruling apparatus possesses mechanisms of self-preservation and seeks to inscribe its scheme of power relations in the minds of its Palestinian subjects. Official spokespersons tend to ignore the role which the continual, massive Israeli use of violence, both withheld and eruptive, plays in promoting violent and nonviolent resistance on the Arab side. In the same vein, they miss the role of Israeli violence in creating its own justification in the eyes of many Israeli Jews.

The majority of Palestinians do not resort to violence, but rather try to act in a civil mode. A few Palestinians still—or again—try to affect Israeli public discourse. Others pursue a legal struggle, organize civil disobedience, or take part in the efforts to mobilize international pressure on Israel. The most important recent development, however, is the spread of various forms of civil disobedience, mostly in the context of some villages' struggle against the separation wall, organized and coordinated with groups of Israelis from the "radical Left" and international supporters. The response of the ruling apparatus to this exemplary multinational nonviolent struggle has been to force it to become both national (i.e., Palestinian) and violent, either by simply defining it as such, and then raiding homes in the middle of the night in order to arrest Palestinian activists, or by reacting with force to the weekly demonstrations so as to provoke violent reactions. The army, so it seems, cannot afford to act otherwise. The violence associated with Palestinian resistance has a definite and crucial role in the overall economy of violence in the Occupied Territories, while civilized forms of disobedience and resistance pose obstacles that (at least until recently, when the army began to plan for the possibility of a unilateral Palestinian declaration of independence) threaten to undermine the smooth reproduction of power relations. This smooth reproduction needs sporadic armed resistance and terrorist attacks. With every such attack, official spokespersons hurry to announce that deterrence is never total, and that Israel has no choice but to persist in trying to prevent violent resistance. Journalists and politicians echo them repeatedly. Thus violence is presented as violence-preventing violence, as violence exercised so as to enable the apparatus to be the last to resort to violence. But the latest violent eruption is always the last of an infinite series—another, new "last one" will follow shortly.

The lull between one outburst and another has grown longer since 2005. After the suppression of the Second Intifada and the election of a Hamas government in Gaza, most Palestinian violence has been committed by Hamas and by the relatively small Islamic Jihad organization, focusing on Israeli towns and villages near the Gaza Strip, and even this resistance has been mostly subdued since Operation Cast Lead. But the dynamic has remained the same. Nearly every eruption of Palestinian violence provokes or retroactively justifies an outburst of Israeli violence. The latest outburst usually creates the conditions for the next eruption, and so on, seemingly ad infinitum. Victory will follow the latest blow, but the latest blow contains defeat (it, too, only temporary, of course), which will follow the next eruption of the other side. The real difference, at least as regards violence, is not between victory and defeat but rather between more and less lethal, destructive and spectacular violence. By this token, the Palestinians are losing, naturally: over 6,500 dead and 35,000 wounded since the beginning of the First Intifada and until August 2010, as opposed to 1,095 Israeli dead and about 6,500 wounded.[24]

In October 2000, after the collapse of the latest round of "peace talks" in Camp David, since they were unable to see any other way of getting rid of the occupier, the Palestinians also resorted to violence. In doing so, they refused to distinguish between the Israeli military and civil apparatuses.[25] Israeli soldiers and police generally use violence when ordered to do so by their commanders and those who authorize them (although this is not necessarily true of most colonists, whose use of violence is hardly ever authorized and follows no rules).[26] The instructions change constantly, however, leaving vast room for the personal judgment of officers and soldiers, who over time have become nearly immune to legal charges, even in cases of deviation from explicit instructions. Violence is always justified in the name of "security," which means security for Jews only, as it presupposes the very separation on which it relies. In the name of security most of the Israeli public and its political leadership are willing to accept the reduction of relations with Palestinians to various forms of violence and to live with the vast injuries inflicted, not only upon Palestinians, but also on Israeli citizens. They regard the need to risk the lives of Israeli soldiers as self-evident and prefer to ignore the mental and moral damage that follows military service in the Occupied Territories. Political considerations, on the rare occasions in which they are taken into account, might delay an eruption of violence or hurry it along, but in any case, they come only after the military need for action has been established. Legal considerations, if they enter into the picture at all, nearly always appear in retrospect only, when an action that has inflicted greater "collateral damage" than anticipated must be justified.

The two parties to this struggle are in each other's grip. They condition each other. The reacting force adopts the reasoning of the acting force, even as it attempts to free itself of the deadlock. But the relations between Israeli violence and Palestinian violence are not symmetrical, and not only because of the relations of submission and the obvious difference in armed might. In most cases, the Palestinians have neither the ability nor the means to respond violently to the violence used against them, and the violence that they do resort to erupts in places where they recognize openings in the web of withheld violence in which they are caught. This use of violence against Israelis does not reflect (let alone derive from) Palestinians' conception of the regime they wish to establish or the power by which they wish to be ruled. It is not meant to preserve an existing regime, but rather to free them from the grip of one. It does not necessarily express recognition of the authority of central Palestinian ruling institutions, or the authority of any regime whatsoever. On the other hand, when Israeli security forces use violence, withheld or eruptive, they act on behalf of the state and as a part of it, authorized by it in the name of the law and for the preservation of law and order. In their actions, they assert themselves as subjects of this regime and endow recognition and legitimacy both to the regime and to its ruling apparatus, to forms of exerting violence as well as to the models of justification that accompany them and the recruitment mechanisms that enable them.

Contrary to the popular opinion that "the merry-go-round of violence" is a direct result of terrorist attacks, Israelis do not resort to violence because they are subject to terrorism, but rather because using violence is a fundamental part of their ruling apparatus in the Occupied Territories, all the more so when they define the area as a war zone. Terrorist attacks and Qassam rockets change the intensity of reprisal, not its basic format: an endless game of withheld and eruptive, spectacular violence, which depend on each other and feed off each other, jointly compensating for the lack of other functioning ruling apparatuses. The division of labor between the two kinds of violence has no expression in the language of the regime. Israel's eruptive violence is always described by its spokespersons as an unavoidable response to Palestinian violence, threats, and disobedience, while its withheld violence is presented as an unavoidable substitute for "law and order" and as a preventive, defensive measure against Palestinian violence.

From the point of view of the governed, at least, eruptive violence tends to appear and disappear without any evident rationale. Withheld violence is present, changes its deployment, or becomes invisible according to an explicit rationale, which changes incessantly, but nonetheless permits informed guesses and reconstruction by the governed. Civil struggle against withheld violence cannot appeal against the illegality of the Occupation, and it clearly takes a toll. Still, because of the semblance of legality that is assumed in acts such as land dispossession or road blockage, it remains possible in principle to reduce withheld violence by judicial and political means. Eruptive violence, however, has no obvious link to withheld violence or to the rules it supposedly represents. If there are rules that guide it, they are clandestine, and eruptive violence is thus all the harder to rein in, control, or resist in legal ways.

For the Occupation authorities, every Palestinian is a potential source of unbridled eruptive violence—which is to say, "terrorism." If it does not erupt right now, it did yesterday or it will tomorrow; if not through this or that person, then through his or her neighbors or relatives. From the perspective of the Occupation regime, the Palestinian by his or her mere presence is both "an addressee" or "receiver" of violence and an accumulation of withheld violence that is just waiting for the right moment to erupt. This potential of eruption is not so much a function of the Palestinians' politics and mode of resistance, however, as of their position in the entire economy of violence. But unlike the flagrant withheld violence that the Israeli regime exercises from behind a façade of legality, withheld violence on the part of Palestinians is both forbidden and a challenge to such lawfulness. It is thus necessarily concealed, and exposing it requires an effort. One needs to threaten, constrict, restrict movement, and monitor it, penetrate in order to carry out surveillance, carry out surveillance in order to penetrate, make arrests in order to investigate and investigate in order to make arrests, ruin cultivated farmland (razing for the sake of exposing), impose closures and curfews. Violence-preventing violence produces violence just as much as it reduces violence. It constantly inflicts injuries on bodies, alive and inert, and destroys their common spaces. But it shapes new spaces and establishes new structures. It invents mechanisms and methods, sows anxieties and fears, beliefs and opinions, agents and dangers galore. This violence has a totalizing nature—without it, so we are told, everyone would be vulnerable. For its sake, everyone can be made vulnerable. It does not cease to act. It can hardly stop, or accept agreements that declare a ceasefire.

A pause in this cycle of violence always just means a longer stay at the pole of withheld violence—no attempt is made to stop the pendulum swinging between the two poles, hiding their simultaneous existence and thwarting every effort to construct alternative ruling apparatuses. In this economy of violence, the use of withheld violence does not mean its reduction or restraint, and its eruption does not bring any relief. The borders of this economy of violence are temporary and fluid. It is perpetually building walls and fences, but where necessary, it breaks them down.[27]

THE SUBSTITUTE

The distinction we have proposed here between eruptive and withheld violence echoes—but does not overlap with and cannot be reduced to—an important distinction formulated (and deconstructed) by Walter Benjamin when he differentiated between "lawmaking" violence (e.g., through a revolution or coup) and "law-preserving" violence (by police and military forces acting on behalf of the law).[28] Lawmaking violence is always joined by vast eruptions of force acting directly upon bodies, whereas in law-preserving violence, force is both suspended and present in the form of the policeman or soldier, the club or the rifle, and such suspended presence is a necessary condition for the enforcement of law and the maintenance of "the rule of law" in all senses of this phrase. This is all true, but not sufficient. At any moment, violence constructing law anew must *also* be preserved as *withheld* violence, lest it dissipate before establishing the new political order. Law-preserving violence, on the other hand, always contains traces of eruptive violence too, as Benjamin himself pointed out when discussing the police.[29] The police are supposed to act as an institution authorized to use violence in order to preserve a law that it has not established and to maintain a gap between lawmaking and law-preserving violence. But, in fact, through its violent performance, the police both reiterate and proliferate lawmaking violence at the very moment that law is preserved, and the opposition between the two types of violence is deconstructed through the performance that is supposed to reiterate it.

This deconstructed opposition is precisely what one cannot ascribe to with-held violence. Whereas the army or police violence to which Benjamin refers both constructs the law and preserves it, withheld violence, which we identify with the Occupation regime, neither constructs the law nor preserves it. It is not a tool of the law at all. Rather, the law is a tool in the hands of those exert-ing withheld violence. They use the law to give legal guise—either in advance or in retrospect—to orders and edicts that shelter and sanction withheld vio-lence, legitimizing it where its legality is questionable. The situations in which we observe withheld violence are those in which the law is recruited to sanction the orders and edicts of the military authorities substituting for it in an area not originally under its jurisdiction. Force is exerted under the authority vested in the military commander, and his actions are—in principle—subject to legal scrutiny, but that is precisely all that is left of legality. The authority vested in the government to damage, destroy, and kill is vast, and its victims have almost no way of knowing the rules of the activity that harms them or how to defend themselves against it. The law—as a differentiated sphere of texts and practices, the rules of which can be known a priori, and whose players all enjoy essentially equal access to its resources and negotiating positions within it—is no longer applicable. It is suspended without any proper warning (therefore, one can-not speak of the violence involved as law-preserving), and no other law is con-structed (therefore one cannot speak of it as law-constituting violence), except for the ad hoc orders that contain entire judicial and enforcement systems *in potentiam*, from the authority to arrest all the way up to the authority to execute.

The violent struggle under such conditions is not for instating alternative laws or preserving an existing legal system, but rather for *preserving the suspen-sion* of the realm of right as described here and the conditions under which such a suspension will persist within the law itself. The entire economy of violence functions as a means to preserve the occupied territory in a state of emergency, in which the exception has become the rule and rights—not only particular rights but the right to have rights—have been permanently or occasionally sus-pended. The violation of rights (just like eruptive violence), is kept exceptional, for suspended rights cannot be violated. Thus, the suspension of eruptive vio-lence (which withheld violence embodies) goes hand in hand with the suspen-sion of law (embodied in the endless series of edicts that suspend rights), until ultimately withheld violence takes the place of law as a state apparatus.

We distinguish here between deferment (*hash'haya* in Hebrew) and sus-pension (*hash'aaya*). Deferment indicates a temporary absence of what may or might appear, or be realized at any moment. In the meantime, its appearance or disappearance is deferred. Suspension indicates the declaration by a ruling or bureaucratic authority of the temporary revocation of a rule or law that are not altogether annulled themselves. Under "normal" conditions of rule by a lawful regime, when the need arises to exercise violence in order to preserve both the regime and the law, what is suspended, but not deferred, is "law itself" (or the constitution). Under normal conditions, every juridical clarification is based on the deferred display of "law itself," whose validity in some particular case has yet to be clarified. Any juridical ruling is a temporary apparition of the law, embodied in the case ruled on, but this embodiment is temporary until the next court ruling, until the next controversy, or the next case that will demand that the ruling be delayed and that the interpretation, which had previously appeared clear and final, be suspended. The deferred law and suspended interpretation are part and parcel of a properly functioning judicial system. They hover above bustling legal-interpretative activity like a seductive ghost, an unfixed signified over whose representation numerous signifiers are busy competing. Law-preserving violence—both withheld and eruptive—has to keep this signified hovering in order to maintain an open space for discussing the question "What does the law say?" But when civil law is suspended in favor of an elaborate system of decrees, procedures, and ad hoc orders, the deferment of eruptive violence is a substitute for the role played by deferring the presence of the law itself in a proper ruling and judicial system.

Israeli law has crept into the Occupied Palestinian Territories through several channels: enforcement of Israeli law in the areas annexed to Jerusalem, but in a way that left the Palestinian residents of Jerusalem with the fragile, hybrid status of "permanent residents" who might lose their right of residence should they leave the area for too long a time;[30] a gradual—by now almost full—application of the law to all Jewish colonies in the Territories;[31] the authorization of the military commander in the Territories (and some of his subordinates), by force of emergency regulations, to issue regulations and edicts that regulate the everyday lives of Palestinians there;[32] subjecting such authority to the juridical criticism of the High Court of Justice;[33] and finally, disarming such criticism by a long series of rulings in which the court avoids interfering in the state's considerations (such as on the issue of "targeted killings") or sanctions them retroactively (such as the ruling allowing construction of the separation wall beyond the Green Line).The Knesset itself applied the emergency regulations to the Territories and renews their application every year, and the military commander's decisions are subject to review by the High Court of Justice, placing the Occupied Territories (or the West Bank since 2005) and their inhabitants under the jurisdiction of Israeli law. But this legal inclusion is at the same time a means of exclusion, for the same emergency regulations allow Israel to repudiate its responsibilities as the actual sovereign power in the Occupied Territories and ignore the international law that supposedly protects the occupied Palestinians from the occupying power.

Both establishing rules and suspending them are validated by emergency regulations that were meant to regulate an exceptional situation, but have long since become a permanent tool of control in a permanent state of emergency. In fact there is no *permanent* distinction between the rule and the exception to the rule, for the rule that applies to Palestinians in a certain matter at a certain place is itself an exception to the rule that applies to Israeli citizens in the Occupied Territories, or to Palestinian residents in other matters in other places. Furthermore, the higher the level of violence—especially since the outbreak of the Second Intifada—the more decentralized the authority to establish rules and suspend them, to make exceptions to the rule, or to act regardless of any rules, under rapidly changing circumstances. The local military commander and his subordinates have the authority to use their own judgment and break established rules at any point—not just at any checkpoint and other designated sites, but wherever encounters between the security forces and Palestinians is expected.

When civil law is suspended and subjects are defined as noncitizens, the escalation of withheld violence does not preserve the law, but rather replaces it, without ever ceasing to be legitimated. Withheld violence replaces the suspended judicial system with a system of rules and regulations, exceptions, and ad hoc rulings, while deriving a semblance of legality from the very judicial system that has been suspended. The differences between a regulation and an ad hoc order, and between the latter and an order on the ground, have been almost completely erased. Eventually, the presence of withheld violence—the soldier at the checkpoint, the policeman at the inspection post, the troops operating the bulldozer—sets the rule: where traffic stops, who is permitted to proceed, what is to be demolished.

Essentially, withheld violence can turn into an eruption of violence at any moment, but must not be considered in terms of unfulfilled potential. The potential of withheld violence is fulfilled in its noneruption at least as much as in its eruption, and in fact, the institutionalization of such violence marks a systematic separation of suspension and eruption. Usually, the people whose presence embodies withheld violence are not particularly adept at using the weapons they wield, and they only rarely make use of them. One must not confuse the mentality and practices of the checkpoint with those of killing. If something goes wrong, they will summon others more skilled than themselves. Naturally, there are exceptions, but, however frequent,[34] such exceptions are usually the result of overexertion in a lawless zone and of regarding lives as already forsaken. They have no systemic rationale and are sometimes simply perceived as a sign of a failure of the control system, indication that the apparatus is overburdened. In this context, one must understand the great investment made by the Israeli government, as part of the attempt to suppress the Second Intifada, to improve the service at the checkpoints and even to construct some of them as relatively modern installations that appear or are intended to appear—at least by the government—to be border crossings.

Essentially, withheld violence can be rationalized to a certain extent and might become the object of civil negotiation over "humanitarianizing" the regime of movement by placing officers in charge of humanitarian matters and introducing humanitarian training for checkpoint operators.[35] One might always try to teach the armed forces to speak politely, respect others, take the trouble not to violate rights unnecessarily, avoid superfluous humiliation, and follow instructions as long as they are in force. The Occupation authorities even expect the subjects to appreciate the protection they receive from these armed troops. Everyone knows that, whether their conduct is more or less rational, more or less polite, they are a buffer between the bare bodies of the subjects and the thing itself.

PERMANENT SOLUTIONS

What is "the thing itself," whose appearance in the Occupied Territories withheld violence works to defer and suspend? It is neither Israeli law nor simply Palestinian political independence, but rather the emergence of a radically different order. This other thing could take the form either of total lawlessness, threatening to destroy everything, or of the abolition of the Occupation and the reinstitution of a law as a branch of civil government. We would like to call this radically different order "the permanent solution."

A permanent solution is what continues to hover, ghostlike, over the entire economy of violence in the Territories, just as law itself hovers over withheld violence in a normal civil regime. What is suspended is either the declaration of total war or the total abolition of the Occupation. Every local act of withheld violence, every act of control by means of suspension, draws its power from the ongoing suspension of the permanent solution. The suspension of the permanent solution is a "singular point,"[36] which might develop in two opposing directions, and thus contains as virtual two opposing situations: annexation of the Territories, naturalization of their Palestinian residents, and full implementation of the rule of law, on the one hand, or total war, on the other. These two potential "final" outcomes of the events the ruling apparatus seeks to control construct ruling relations and interfere with them by an intricate set of suspensions and deferments.

The Occupation, essentially a provisional state, has evolved into a permanent ruling structure, which seeks to remain just what it is: an Israeli occupation regime. Its "temporariness" lends this structure its legitimacy, at least in the eyes of most Israelis, as well as of most Americans, because it is utterly impossible to reach agreement on either of the two opposed states that might replace it. The Occupation "protects" both the Israelis and the Palestinians from one of two worst-case scenarios (worst, in Israeli eyes, of course): either a war that would include Nakba-like ethnic cleansing and elimination of the Palestinian national movement, or Israel's annexation of the Territories, making their Palestinian residents equal Israeli citizens.

Withheld violence does have a restraining effect, but this restraint must be understood here in two opposing senses: as the restraining, not just of Palestinian violence, but also of the Israeli power of destruction, not just as replacing the law, but also as preserving a semblance of a "lawful" situation. The massive presence of withheld violence everywhere allows the suspension of an outburst of much more widespread military violence and even the suspension of declared, total war. It enables the ruling apparatus to function lawlessly, without any judicial form, with no education or disciplining, but also *without war*. Such a war, were it to break out under the present circumstances, with the Palestinians lacking military force, would mean either their expulsion or their annihilation. It would lead to one or another form of "permanent solution" of the conflict, for the Territories are already occupied, and there is no enemy to be defeated. But the Palestinians are not being annihilated, just as they are not being assimilated. They are neither being eradicated nor made citizens. The deferment of full-fledged annexation is the flip side of suspension. Annexation would add three and a half million non-Jewish subjects to those officially governed by the Israeli state, which could then no longer be called Jewish. It would become a binational democracy if those new subjects were granted citizenship. For the state to continue to deny them rights of citizenship would be for it formally to admit to being an apartheid regime.

Postponing the War

The Occupation was the result of a brief war between states, but the term has applied only to the Palestinian territories in the West Bank and the Gaza Strip. The Golan Heights were annexed and "cleansed" of their Syrian residents, and Israel withdrew from the Sinai Peninsula after less than fifteen years, following the peace agreement with Egypt. The all-out struggle against the Palestinian residents of the Occupied Territories was consolidated into a total military campaign only after the Camp David peace talks of the summer of 2000 failed and the Second Intifada broke out. Even then, it was not war. Until the 1982 war in Lebanon, Israel managed to neutralize any political organizing and uprising in the Occupied Territories, as well as the influence of Palestinian national organizing outside the Territories upon life within them. In 1982, however, Israel fought a total war against the Palestinian national movement on Lebanese soil, explicitly intending to annihilate it.[37] This war included a massive ground invasion, bombing heavily populated areas with aircraft and artillery, and a lengthy siege of Beirut, the capital of a sovereign state. Thousands of Palestinians and Lebanese citizens were killed, the civil and economic fabric of life in southern Lebanon was seriously damaged, and leaders of the Palestinian national movement and its official bodies were forced to leave Lebanon and settle for exile in Tunisia. James Ron (2003) identifies the Lebanese arena as Israel's frontier since the 1980s and distinguishes between administering a population of noncitizens in a "ghetto" and reckless war against a frontier population. We may add that the professed intention—and certainly the effect—of the first Lebanon War was to enable Israel to continue administering a Palestinian ghetto in the Occupied Territories. The Lebanon war was thus another means (precisely like withheld violence) for postponing or replacing war in the Territories, enabling further control of the Palestinians there without their naturalization, expulsion, or annihilation.

In the Occupied Territories, warfare has remained tentative. For many years now, the Israeli struggle against Palestinians living there has been an all-out struggle—not just the takeover of a regime or land, annexation, or dispossession, but a total change in the overall fabric of Palestinian life. This struggle has transformed Palestinian space, landscape, and urban environments, drastically

constricting Palestinians' freedom of movement, blocking economic development, dismantling some social institutions and eroding the authority of others.
But notwithstanding the widespread use of armed force, brutal "operations,"
and occasional massive mobilization of troops, this struggle has never been
conducted as a real war. At least not in the Occupied Territories.

Such an all-out struggle against a large indigenous population has been a
familiar characteristic of colonization processes in different parts of the world,
no less than the pendulum of relations between withheld and eruptive violence
in which this struggle takes place. Under typical colonial European modes of
control from the sixteenth until the late nineteenth centuries, all-out struggle did occasionally turn into total war: across North America and Australia,
in South Africa, and throughout the Russian (and later Soviet) Empire, entire regions were cleansed of their indigenous populations. "Natives" were
crowded into reservations, their social frameworks shattered, their social strata
collapsed, their family dynasties terminated, their cultures turned into labo-
ratories for anthropologists and a collection of folklore objects for curio deal-
ers and tourists. The geopolitical conditions under which Israeli rule has been
maintained in the Occupied Palestinian Territories since the late twentieth century, as well as the nature of Jewish Israeli society's recruitment into its colonization project (a recruitment often tormented, self-righteous, and full of
contradictions), place enormous obstacles in the way of any attempt to conduct the all-out struggle against the Palestinians in the Territories as a total war.
In 1982, the first war in Lebanon could—just barely—be presented as a survival
struggle, but in a way that never really gained widespread public legitimacy, because the PLO was presented as a hostile army posing a threat to the actual existence of the State of Israel, and a distinction was made (verbally, not necessarily
on the battlefield) between it and the Palestinian population. In the Occupied
Territories, such a distinction has been impossible at least since the First Intifada. The struggle therefore has to be an all-out one, but cannot—for the time
being—be conducted as a war.

Yet total war has hovered—and still does—as a real option over any local
confrontation and has turned into a routine issue in the discourse over necessary responses to Palestinian aggression in the Gaza Strip. Since preparations began for the "disengagement," Israel's spokespeople have never ceased
their threats of total war if the Qassam rocket launchings resume or intensify.[38]
These indeed have resumed and intensified, and have been followed by Israeli
operations to eliminate Palestinian resistance. The threat of total war hovers

anew over every such operation (e.g., "reoccupation" of the Gaza Strip in order to "drain the swamp" or "purge the area of terrorist nests"). There are plenty of examples. The military operations are often perceived and presented as preparatory to far more sweeping campaigns, still held back as contingency plans. An operation that was supposed to last a few hours might eventually go on for weeks or months. At any moment, the number of detainees, the expelled, or the dead might double or triple. Instead of demolishing a row of houses in the heart of a city, the whole city might be devastated. Instead of hundreds of dunam of farm land, thousands could be razed. But in the meantime, there are always political, moral, and even military reasons for the decision not to extend the operation, in spite of the temptation to do so, reasons to postpone its second or third phase for the time being, to withdraw before the announced date and still assure "us" that "all our objectives were achieved." This was true even of 2009's Operation Cast Lead. Total war and the utter disaster it would wreak have always been reserved as a distant threat, but the line between the reckless phantasm of violence and the restrained violence actually exerted is drawn more flexibly than ever. The threshold of violence that the Israeli public conceives of as unbearable and unjustifiable is modified again and again according to operational circumstances, which include but can never be reduced to Palestinian resistance. As a result, more people are willing to comply and live with deeds that were previously regarded as "inconceivable."

Postponing Annexation and Catastrophe

Since annexation of the Occupied Territories and the naturalization of their Palestinian inhabitants is ruled out of the question, Israel's responsibility for the life and well-being of three and a half million noncitizens who have no political rights has become a matter of international humanitarian law. This was especially clear during and following the Second Intifada, when the Israeli reaction was the exacerbation of a process that had already begun during the period of the Oslo Accords: turning the state of emergency into a permanent condition, reducing the number of ruling apparatuses in charge of the lives of its subjects, and (as a matter of security) diminishing their existence to the mere potential for violent attacks that they embody, on the one hand, and to their mere survival (a matter of humanitarian concern), on the other.

Until the outbreak of the Second Intifada, the Palestinians' political existence, as perceived by the Israeli authorities, was reduced to their status as subjects in the literal meaning of the term: those subjected, or who should be subjected, to the ruling power. This reduction process, which has been ongoing and has intensified since the beginning of the Second Intifada, peaked during the Israeli "disengagement" from the Gaza Strip. The Palestinians ceased to be defined simply as those subjected to power. Their existence was reduced to that of moving bodies that interest the ruling apparatus in two ways only. First, as recipients of humanitarian aid, which the government allows out of anxiety over the possible consequences in Israel and abroad of their dying en masse if a "humanitarian crisis" were to develop; this obliges the government to let nongovernmental and international organizations provide the minimum conditions needed to keep the Palestinians alive. Second, as suspects, a nuisance, a disturbance, or threat, and hence the targets of either withheld or eruptive violence. In any other sense, the Palestinians' life-world is no-man's-land in the eyes of the ruling apparatus. They are not subjects, but an abandoned population. This abandonment and shirking of responsibility do not stem from neglect, negligence, or failure on the part of the regime. They are inherent and systematic.

The abandoning of Palestinians takes place between two death threats: the individual death of the agent of violence ("the suicide bomber") and mass death resulting from a humanitarian disaster. The former is a pretext for containing the abandoned Palestinians within a system of surveillance more rigorous than ever before, while the latter is an excuse for making the area in which the abandoned Palestinians are enclosed accessible to welfare organizations the world over for active participation in the globalization of the conflict in general and for administering Palestinian life in particular. Although the Oslo Accords assigned part of the responsibility for the administering of Palestinian life over to the Palestinian Authority, the Israeli reaction to the Second Intifada shattered the PA's ability to function, and the main responsibility for running Palestinian life was assumed by welfare bodies, nongovernmental organizations, UN agencies, and local charities, both secular and religious.[39] The ruling apparatus takes the liberty to deter and even sabotage the activity of these groups whenever it spots a threat to security, familiarly a sweeping consideration, while explicitly encouraging their activity whenever it fears an approaching humanitarian crisis.

The catastrophe is deferred for the same reasons that war is deferred, perhaps, but why are the Palestinians allowed to remain on the threshold of catastrophe? Surely not for the same reasons that they are made to remain noncitizens. Denial of citizenship does not necessitate abandonment to disaster conditions, and, as we have seen, the Occupation regime long treated Palestinians as subjects whose existence had to be facilitated no less than their lives had to be administered. The First Intifada marked the emergence of a political space whose existence Israel had not previously allowed. In the Oslo Accords, Israel recognized this space and enabled its institutionalization. Thus it sought to destroy, though not officially, the option that had been left open in the first twenty years of the Occupation: naturalizing the Palestinians and assimilating them into Israel's political sphere. Abandoning the Palestinians to disaster conditions—especially in the Gaza Strip, where economic conditions had always been worse than in the West Bank and further deteriorated following the disengagement—is a result of the decision to control and dominate them without actually ruling them, and certainly without governing them. More accurately, abandoning the Gaza Strip and pushing its population to the brink of humanitarian catastrophe has become a mode of governance specifically designated for this region.

5 ABANDONING GAZA

UNRULY AND UNWANTED

The creation of the Gaza Strip as a separate territorial unit was a product of the conquest of large parts of Palestine by Jewish forces in 1948 and the declaration of the State of Israel in a territory that included lands allocated to the Palestinian state according to the UN Partition Plan. Since then, the Strip has had a special status in Israeli political and military discourse. Even before its occupation in 1967, it had been seen as a "wasps' nest"—an exceptional appendage that was both a threat and a burden. In 1948, Israel conquered neighboring areas in the Negev Desert and temporarily in the northern Sinai Peninsula, along with other territories that were meant to be part of the Palestinian state, but it did not attack the Gaza Strip. The Rhodes Armistice agreements, signed in March 1949 between the State of Israel and Egypt, approved Egyptian rule in the Strip. Gaza became a haven for Palestinians who had been expelled from the territories conquered by Jewish forces and were settled in hastily constructed refugee camps.

Egypt controlled the Strip without annexing it. Reluctant to assume full governing responsibilities, it ruled Gaza as a closed, separate colony and did little to alleviate the harsh economic conditions resulting from the Strip being excised from the rest of Palestine in 1948. At the same time, until the Sinai War in 1956, Egypt supported the Palestinian armed struggle against Israel, which was launched from the Strip. This made the area subject to repeated Israeli of-

An earlier version of this chapter appeared as Ariela Azoulay and Adi Ophir, "Abandoning Gaza," in *Agamben and Colonialism*, ed. Marcelo Svirsky and Simone Bignall (Edinburgh: Edinburgh University Press, 2012).

fensives—described as "retaliations"—and helped Israel justify its conquest of the Sinai Peninsula in November 1956. This conquest took place—after some hesitation—only at the last stage of the Sinai War, after the main Egyptian force in the Sinai had been destroyed. Soon thereafter, when it was forced by the United States and the USSR to withdraw from the Sinai, Israel tried to hold on to the Strip in order to prevent the return of the Egyptian army to Gaza. Hoping to persuade the superpowers to agree to its rule in Gaza, it stated that it was ready to consider sharing power with the United Nations and would naturalize some of the Strip's inhabitants, also offering to resettle an unspecified number of refugees inside Israel.[1] Israel was forced to withdraw from Gaza, but a special concern for Gaza's refugees, both as a "security threat" and as a "humanitarian problem," has persisted ever since, making the Gaza Strip exceptional in more than one way.

When the war broke out in June 1967, Moshe Dayan, Israel's minister of defense, had reservations about occupying the Strip, with its overpopulated and quite militant refugee camps. Ground forces entered the Strip only on the second day of the fighting and apparently against his judgment. Some 60 percent of the Strip's inhabitants were refugees from territories conquered by Israel in 1948 and their descendants.[2] Most of them lived in the refugee camps, and they had not relinquished their demand to return to their villages of origin. An Israeli newspaper caricature that portrayed the refugees as trapped inside a football, with Egyptian, Syrian, and Jordanian feet kicking it to and fro, aptly expressed Israel's denial of its responsibility for the creation of this massive population of refugees and the attribution of that responsibility to the Arab states hosting the refugees.

The Occupation in 1967 did not change Israel's refusal to bear any special responsibility for the Palestinian refugees it had created in 1948. But soon after the war ended, and throughout the first two decades of the Occupation, Israel acted—both in the West Bank and in Gaza—as a colonial power that assumed governmental responsibilities for the population under its control. Even then, the overpopulated Gaza Strip was perceived as a special problem, and calls to get rid of this piece of territory somehow (rather than strengthening Israel's grip on it) were frequently heard across the political spectrum.[3] When the Labor party came to power following the 1992 elections, Israel's desire to be rid of responsibility for Gaza achieved a respectable political guise under the plan named "Gaza first," which the minister of foreign affairs at the time, Shimon Peres, was eager to promote. Peres proposed using the partial transfer of governing authority to the Palestinians in Gaza "to run their own show" as a means to change direction in the Israeli-Palestinian conflict, setting a new horizon for the political process.

Israel's shirking of responsibility for administering the life of Palestinians was significantly facilitated by the Oslo Accords (1993). The withdrawal of the Israeli army from most of the populated areas of the Gaza Strip and the transfer of certain governmental responsibilities to the quasi-autonomous Palestinian Authority were seen by many as a great advantage for Israel. Indeed, when Yasser Arafat entered it with his armed militias in July 1994, the Israeli interest in the Strip and its inhabitants was quick to evaporate: "After the 1994 retreat, Gaza was considered dead news," the correspondent Shlomi Eldar recalled. "We sang 'Goodbye, Gaza' and built a tight separation fence around it. It no longer interested us. Let them all perish in there."[4]

This change in the Israeli attitude to Gaza was made concrete mere days after the signing of the Oslo Accord, even before the "peace celebrations" had died down. The ruling apparatus imposed long-term closure on the Gaza Strip, turning it into a separate, sealed enclave, disconnecting thousands of workers from their sources of livelihood in Israel proper, while shirking all responsibility for finding them alternative employment. Furthermore, the movement of goods and raw materials was hindered by border crossings, deterring potential investors and foreign investors who sought cheap labor in the Gaza Strip, but cleared out as soon as they realized the costs and conditions of passage.[5] As Sara Roy details, the Gaza Strip was made subject to a process of economic "de-development."[6] Within a few years, the Strip—an impoverished, overpopulated territory that had managed to sustain itself in spite of the process of economic degradation imposed upon it by the Occupation regime—became a humanitarian basket case.

Most of the contact Israelis had with Palestinians inside the Strip was at this time restricted to the realm of security, including the safe movement of Israelis to and from Jewish settlements, whose expansion had never ceased. All other contact took place at crossings, control of which was now tighter and tighter. Plans to build a port in Gaza rapidly evaporated; the Dahaniya airport promised in the Oslo Accord was made functional only briefly; "safe passage" between the Gaza Strip and the West Bank began to operate in October 1999, but it ceased after a mere nine months.[7] All the while, the Israeli military presence on the ground persisted along the Strip's main roads and outer borders, dissecting it into four regions—respective of the Israeli colonies and their connecting bypass roads—that could easily be separated from one another. However, Israel's military hold on the Strip was already partly managed from the sea and in the air.

During the Oslo period there were, of course, other aspects to the new form of control in Gaza. The Strip had previously been a nearly continuous region, exclusively populated by Palestinians and controlled by the Palestinian Authority within the constraints set by the Accords. The PA was authorized to administer most facets of everyday life and a considerable part of the Strip's economic activity, as well as economic, legal, and administrative planning within the enclave. Various economic initiatives emerged under the auspices of different international organizations, and with the mediation of Israeli officials and entrepreneurs; new housing projects, hotels, and public institutions were built, and new sources of employment were created inside the Strip, courtesy of the disproportionate expansion of the PA's civil and military government apparatuses.

However, the Israeli decision to go on controlling Gaza as a prison, separating and abandoning it at the same time, sabotaged investment in its economic development and steadily worsened its economic situation.[8] When Israel's civil and military colonial presence in the Gaza Strip ended, its division into four separate area cells ended as well. Instead, new dividing lines appeared, at first within close range of the fence surrounding Gaza, and later deep in the heart of the Strip. When firing was renewed after the disengagement, the army declared areas near the fence out of bounds to Palestinians, no-man's-land into which artillery shells were fired in order to hinder Qassam rocket launchers from moving freely. Sporadic combat activity was also resumed in those areas, where violence often erupts, depending on available intelligence and the visible presence of "armed insurgents."

The withdrawal of the controlling apparatus from the Gaza Strip and the dismantling of the Jewish colonies there created a new situation, unprecedented since the outset of the Occupation: one side of the border between the Gaza Strip and Israel was inhabited by Israeli citizens; the other, by Palestinian noncitizens. The exclusion of the latter from the Israeli political system has been presented ever since as if it had always already been a fact of political life in the region. The Sharon government declared that with the dismantling of the Israeli settlements and the withdrawal of army forces from the Gaza Strip, the Occupation there had come to an end, and Israel no longer bore any responsibility for this territory and its inhabitants. This has been reaffirmed by several rulings of the Israeli High Court of Justice, rejecting petitions from NGOs and Gaza Strip inhabitants demanding that the state provide the means for Palestinians to receive "welfare controlled by Israel"— for example, by opening Gaza's border crossings for import and export, and by granting Gazans permission to visit relatives or study in the West Bank, or to enter Israel for medical treatment unavailable in the Gaza Strip. Relying on (and interpreting) both Israeli and international law, the court ruled that the State of Israel owes Gazans nothing but minimal humanitarian aid, which in actual fact means nothing more than allowing international organizations to send necessary supplies. Both the government and the High Court ignore the obvious fact that "ending the Occupation has not ended Israel's effective control of the Gaza Strip and its surroundings."[9] Disregarding the claim by the Israeli Center for the Legal Protection of Freedom of Movement (Gisha) that Israel effectively controls the Strip and is answerable for it under the Hague Convention of 1907 and the Fourth Geneva Convention, the High Court of Justice ruled in two separate cases that the disengagement and the Israeli government's promise to do "everything in its power to prevent a humanitarian crisis in the Gaza Strip" has rendered the issue "theoretical, without any practical outcome."[10]

The court thereby accepted the Israeli government's position and ruled that its responsibility for Gaza can be reduced to its duty to prevent humanitarian disaster. In doing so, the court ignored the fact that the condition of Palestinians in the Gaza Strip is a direct consequence of their imprisonment within the giant holding pen that Israel has erected for them (with Egypt's tacit cooperation). In fact, the court effectively excluded the Palestinians from its field of vision. For the Supreme Court of Justice, the inhabitants of the Gaza Strip are no longer subjects of Israel. The court has failed to recognize that, precisely for this reason, the Gazans are still nonsubjects *of* the Israeli state, that is, they are still ruled by Israel as its nonsubjects. Their semi-autonomous elected government is incapable either of forming a state or of running it, but this statelessness is precisely the form and effect of their relation to a certain state—Israel—that has deprived them of their own statehood and does everything it can to keep them abandoned, forsaken between a suspended war and a suspended catastrophe. The conditions under which Palestinians live and die, love and work, raise children and pray to God, are determined—to an extent unprecedented in the contemporary world—by a series of quite simple acts of state. The "disengagement" constituted the Gaza Strip as a no-man's-land, whose entire population has become a client of humanitarian agencies. The Strip is excepted from Israeli law and out of range of Israeli sovereign responsibility, but completely within its rule and control, effectively preventing the emergence of any other power that could assume the responsibility of a sovereign government. The Palestinians in Gaza are the abandoned people of the Israeli regime.

In fact, abandonment has been an official Israeli policy in Gaza since the beginning of the Second Intifada. No longer perceived as a subject with an identity who must be subjugated but also cared for, the Palestinian was tagged as a client of humanitarian aid, a hunted person, a name on an elimination list, a dot on the electronic display in an operations room or a military pilot's cockpit. Despite having shirked its duties toward some of its subjects, the Israeli regime has not relinquished the sovereign's ultimate authority: the right to take life. Even before the disengagement, the Gaza Strip contained 1.5 million exceptions to the rule, people living on the threshold of the law, as well as on the brink of catastrophe. In response to Palestinian armed resistance during the Second Intifada, Israel adopted the policy of targeted killings—assassinations by decree that take place when persons presumably identified as suspected of "terrorist activity" are targeted from helicopters and unmanned aerial vehicles (UAV), often also killing many others who happen to be near the target. Most of them have been carried out in the Gaza Strip, where the density of the population makes everyone vulnerable. Combined with the siege, the rationing of basic supplies, and liberalization of the rules of engagement, the new policy has turned each and every inhabitant of the Strip into *homo sacer*, in the sense that the Italian philosopher Giorgio Agamben gives this term, which is to say, a person included in the juridical order solely in the form of its exclusion, that is, he is not protected by the law and his killing is unpunishable. At the same time, his killing cannot be considered as a sacrifice that makes sense in a religious or divine economy, hence he is included in the religious sphere in the form of his exclusion from that economy.[11] Although it assumes the authority to kill them, the sovereign power is no longer obliged to protect the Palestinians in the Strip. They have become fair game: killing or hurting them is permissible and goes unpunished; those involved in injuring them enjoy immunity; finally, their self-sacrifice is not recognized as such (at least by Israel), and their deaths can assume no transcendent value.[12]

However apt the metaphor of *homo sacer*, one should not be misled into thinking of abandoned Palestinians as passive victims. As a policy, abandonment is a response to active, persistent, and often painful Palestinian resistance, not a reflection of their passivity. Nowhere is this clearer than in the context of the way Palestinians handle the deaths of their people who have been lost in the struggle against Israel. The Israeli sovereign state has never succeeded in controlling Palestinian representation of death and sacrifice. By withdrawing from the densely populated areas in the Gaza Strip, Israel suffered a certain weakening of its grip on the way Palestinians take leave of their dead. For as long as the ruling apparatus administered the Palestinians' lives, it was able to intervene violently and extensively in the management of their regard for their dead, and it did this from the very beginning of the Occupation by setting the dates of funerals, violently dispersing funeral and memorial processions, and displaying withheld violence in the very space where funerals took place.[13] This insistence on administrating Palestinian deaths decreased and nearly ceased when Israel relinquished control of Palestinian daily life after the Oslo Accords.

The Palestinians, for their part, turned self-sacrifice into a lethal mode of operation and treated their dead as martyrs. Everyone who died in the struggle against the Occupation was declared a *shaheed* (witness), who had not only sacrificed his own life for a noble cause but bore witness to the conditions of his abandonment. Clearly, "abandonment" means different things to the two sides, resulting in different kinds of strategies. For the Israeli ruling power, the Palestinians are indeed abandoned and rendered entirely vulnerable, *homines sacri*; for the Palestinians, the abandoned who have died become *shaheed*s and through their deaths actively sanctify their common struggle. The Palestinian mass funerals, mourning tents, and memorial ceremonies have always been sites of resistance; but when Israel withdrew its full control following the Oslo Accords, the Palestinians were able to manage their own representations of death and their leave-taking from the dead, and through a celebration of death, turn abandoned life into sanctified life.

The withdrawal of Israeli military forces from the Gaza Strip, together with the administrative apparatus dealing with civilian population (slight or malfunctioning though it was), has turned the Strip into a zone of exception where biopolitical control of life has been delegated by the state to humanitarian organizations, while the state itself exercises violence that has little or no relation to the law. In the Gaza Strip, it is certainly true that, as Agamben puts it, "humanitarian organizations . . . can only grasp human life in the figure of bare and sacred life, and therefore, despite themselves, maintain a secret solidarity with the very power they ought to fight."[14] However, in this case, the solidarity is not secret, as we shall show below, but a professed rule of the game both for state authorities and humanitarian activists.

This is not due so much to the naïveté and limited power of the humanitarian organizations, however, as to the "humanitarianization" of the ruling apparatus, that is, the systematic integration of humanitarian agencies of various kinds into the government of the Gaza Strip. The withdrawal of Israeli law and other state formations from the Strip at the time of the "disengagement" was combined with the closure of the area, which often turned into a full-scale siege. This combination made humanitarian intervention both possible and necessary. Israel announced that its rule in the Gaza Strip was terminated, and so from the point of view of the Israeli legal system (represented by the government and accepted by the court), Israeli law is no longer applicable in the Strip; it has not been suspended but rather abolished there altogether. The area has been declared ex-territorial. Only the occasional suspension of humanitarian assistance—on which the Palestinians rely for their very subsistence—brings Gaza back into the realm of Israeli rule and restores the fundamental relationship of inclusive exclusion between the sovereign and the exception. This suspension, and the resumption of full-scale siege, remains potentially at Israel's disposal, even since the opening of the Rafah crossing by Egyptian authorities in June 2011.

Gaza is a demarcated area, entirely within the scope of Israeli power, in which the production of scarcity is the rule and famine is the exception, whose use as a means of governance is never ruled out. Perpetuating an ongoing "low-profile" disaster and postponing a large-scale regime-made one is Israel's way of containing the Gaza Strip within its sphere of rule. As we shall see below, this includes a rule of law, at least as far as the operations of the Israeli army and security apparatus are concerned.

ON THE BRINK OF CATASTROPHE

Under the Oslo Accords, the Gaza Strip was fenced in with barbed wire, and when the Second Intifada broke out in October 2000, this closure gradually became a full-fledged siege. Economic de-development rapidly deteriorated into a humanitarian crisis, which continually threatens to become a humanitarian catastrophe. After Israel's disengagement in August 2005, ground control inside the Strip was replaced by full peripheral Israeli ground control, plus control of the air and the sea,[15] as well as occasional ground incursions and airborne attacks. Gaza was enclosed, like a holding pen, with entry and exit permitted only rarely, and only to a few individuals, and altogether prohibited over long stretches of time, because the crossings are often closed. Passage to Egypt, too, while not under official Israeli control, is indirectly subject to full Israeli monitoring.[16] Gaza's territorial waters are fully controlled by the Israeli air force. Remote-controlled surveillance enables comprehensive local monitoring of every individual moving within the area.

This monitoring is based on census data that Israel has been withholding in spite of its commitment under the Oslo Accords in 1995 to transfer this information to the Palestinians. Israel did not register hundreds of Gazans who had relocated to the West Bank and were then forced to move back to the Strip.[17] The fence continues to contain the Strip within the Israeli "customs shell," so that all goods imported to it through Israeli-controlled terminals can be taxed. This fence has not eliminated the connection of the Strip to the Israeli power grid and telecommunications networks based inside Israel. Gaza cannot sustain itself without the ongoing supply of electrical power, fuel, food, and raw materials that reaches it through Israel. Before the disengagement, the severe shortage of various medical services sent hundreds of Gazans into Israel for medical treatment,[18] and this issue remains unresolved to this day. Containers with goods that are not qualified as urgent humanitarian aid according to the Israeli authorities pile up on the Israeli side. Farm produce imported by the Gaza Strip decomposes at the crossings because of long delays, while Gazan produce rots on the other side of the fence, inflicting heavy financial losses on merchants. The Strip has remained under full siege. Allegedly, the siege was a response to the abduction of the Israeli corporal Gilad Shalit by Palestinian combatants in 2006, but it was not lifted after his release in October 2011. From time to time, the Strip is bombarded from the sea and from the air and raided by special forces, whether in response to scattered rockets fired on neighboring Israeli villages and towns or, allegedly, to preempt such attacks. Every once in a while, too, individuals presumed to be "terrorists" are targeted and killed from the air.

Under these circumstances, the threat of catastrophe is neither the result of the military activity or economic policy of a "strong state" nor a consequence of the fiascoes of a "weak state" surrendering to the violence of paramilitary groups; it is rather the result of the *withdrawal of a part* of the ruling apparatus of a strong state—Israel—from a defined territory kept under strict closure. The administration of justice, law enforcement, and welfare has been withdrawn. The closure of the Strip and—until the disengagement—its spatial fragmentation have prevented Palestinian governing bodies from effectively replacing the withdrawn governing apparatuses by looking after the population abandoned by Israel. Hence the need to *prevent* catastrophe (without removing its causes) has become an essential component in the structure of Israel's control of the Strip.

In 2003, following more than two years of Palestinian uprising and Israeli oppression, Jean Ziegler, the special envoy of the UN secretary-general, stated plainly that the Occupied Palestinian Territories were "on the verge of humanitarian catastrophe." The Israeli authorities "acknowledged that there is a humanitarian crisis in the Territories," he added. "They did not contest the statistics indicating a rise in the extent of malnutrition and poverty among Palestinians."[19] Similar figures and formulations documenting the humanitarian disaster in the Gaza Strip have appeared in numerous reports of various international organizations, as well as on behalf of foreign governments and parliaments. The multiplicity of such reports is noteworthy; the Occupied Palestinian Territories are certainly one of the most thoroughly documented disaster areas in the world.[20]

Although Israel has continually obstructed the work of organizations who provide aid to the Territories, such as the UN Relief and Works Agency for Palestine Refugees (UNRWA), Oxfam, USAID, and the International Red Cross, it has remained officially and practically committed to preventing the Territories from crossing this dangerous threshold. "There will be no hunger in Palestine," members of the control apparatus have repeatedly insisted,[21] and they have made sure that cases of local want do not turn into outright starvation. UNRWA supplemented the flour it provided with iron, for example, thus preventing the Palestinians from crossing the threshold of malnourishment, but without moving them further away from it.[22]

The ruling apparatus quickly adopted the humanitarian discourse and institutionalized its ties with the humanitarian organizations. "In the order of operation, among the targets cited for operational attack and the men wanted for elimination or capture, the following article [i.e., order] relates to the humanitarian realm," in the words of Lieutenant Colonel Orli Malka, chief of foreign relations and international organizations at COGAT (Coordinator of Government Activities in the Territories).[23] The Israeli government is aware of the catastrophic implications of the regimentation of movement and acknowledges that its military actions perhaps create the humanitarian crisis. It is prepared to monitor the changing threshold of the crisis that requires intervention, employing the means of surveillance, point of view, and language of the humanitarian organizations: "Israel will prepare itself to provide [for] humanitarian needs. . . . No, there will be no hunger. But this policy is extremely clear. There will be no hunger in the Territories, no way," Malka stated.[24]

In June 2007, the hostility between the Hamas government in Gaza, elected in January of that year, and the PLO, which lost the election, deteriorated into violent clashes between the two parties. The PLO tightened its control in the West Bank, and the Hamas government in the Strip disconnected itself from the Palestinian Authority in the West Bank and dismantled the Fatah apparatus in Gaza. Israel's response, backed by its main allies, the United States and many European countries, was to boycott the Hamas government and impose a siege on the Strip. Ever since, Israel has invested much effort in counteracting the Hamas government's operations, reducing its capacity to a minimum. Any service provision beyond the most basic humanitarian aid has been consistently sabotaged. In September 2007, the Israeli government asked its defense forces, Ministry of Foreign Affairs, and juridical bodies to prepare a plan "that would address all military and civilian aspects of impacting the services provided by Israel to the Gaza Strip."[25] As part of this economic rationalization, the Israeli army was asked to propose a "price tag" for the launching of Qassam rockets and mortar shells by Palestinians in Gaza. In October, the cabinet decided to disconnect areas around the fence from the power grid during the evening hours. A few days later, the Israeli prime minister asserted that cutting off power would not lead to a humanitarian crisis.[26]

At the end of October 2007, the government's legal adviser intervened and forbade the army to cut off power or the fuel supply to the Gaza Strip.[27] However, he did not rule out rationing them. The judicial arm and the military disputed the rationing of vital services, not Israel's actual right to turn the supply of these services into a means of control, monitoring, and collective punishment. Two weeks later, an arrangement was reached, and the legal adviser agreed in principle to a new plan by the defense apparatus, aimed at restricting the power supply to the Strip. "According to the plan, the principle of 'blackout Gaza' is changed." Instead of blacking out neighborhoods or parts of the Strip for foreseeable periods of time, the entire power supply would be reduced and limited through "current pacers" installed on all power lines in the region. These power limiters would enable Israel to provide the Strip with less electricity per day, but the responsibility for "distributing the reduced amount of power will lie with the consumers, namely, the Gaza authorities. . . . Increased consumption of electricity would bring about power cuts and short-circuits—and Gazans will have to make do with less. . . . This will ensure the continued power supply for humanitarian needs and the Hamas government will no longer be able to blame Israel for power cuts at a hospital, for example."[28]

The initial brutality of the policy decision proposed by the Ministry of Defense was restrained by the Ministry of Justice, the result being a more finely honed tool for creating humanitarian disaster in Gaza and monitoring its limits. Like the delivery of food to the West Bank through "back-to-back" transfers from one truck to another, a method introduced at the beginning of the Second Intifada,[29] current pacers are a tool that generates disaster, while at the same time limiting it, meting it out to the "proper degree." The legal instruction given to the Ministry of Defense clearly had a dual purpose. On the one hand, the instruction turned the disaster threshold into a means of governance. One could, then, always claim that the threshold had not been crossed, that the minimum conditions for Palestinian existence have not been impacted, and so forth. On the other hand, the decision pushed the responsibility for "impacting life" itself onto the Palestinians, making them full partners in the creation of want and the onset of disaster conditions.

Gradually, since the disengagement from Gaza, a sophisticated mechanism for the creation of controlled scarcity in the Strip has emerged. Documents relating to the Gaza closure policy released by the Israeli Defense Ministry reveal a series of rules (whose existence had long been suspected)[30] controlling and blocking the transfer of goods into the Strip, with formulas for calculating the amounts of commodities allowed into the Strip. These rules and formulas guided the ruling apparatus from the disengagement (August 2005) until the end of May 2010, when Israel succumbed to international pressure. This pressure has mounted in response to the deadly attack by the Israeli navy on a Turkish flotilla that tried to break the siege on Gaza. The documents reveal a policy geared at monitoring basic products entering the Gaza Strip, including basic food products and fuel, controlling the amount of those products, and keeping the decision-makers current.[31] According to the documents, the state approved "a policy of deliberate reduction" for basic goods in the Gaza Strip. The state set a "lower warning line" to give advance warning of expected shortages of a particular item, but at the same time approved ignoring that warning if the good in question was subject to a policy of "deliberate reduction." Moreover, the state set an "upper red line," above which even basic humanitarian items could be blocked.[32]

The creation of scarcity has little to do with "security reasons," of course. The decision whether to permit or prohibit an item is largely based on "the public perception of the product" and "whether it is viewed as a luxury." In other words, goods characterized as "luxury" items—such as chocolate and paper—are banned. The procedures determine that the list of permitted goods "will not be released to those not specified," meaning that merchants in Gaza cannot know what they are permitted to purchase. But the most important aspect of the policy in the context of our argument is that the Israeli Defense Ministry created a series of formulas to compute product inventory. The calculations are presumed to allow COGAT to measure what is called the "breathing span." By dividing the inventory in the Strip by the predefined daily consumption needs of residents, the formula calculates the number of days it takes for residents of Gaza to exhaust their "breathing span" and run out of basic products.

Prior to the Second Intifada, 1,700 trucks a day crossed the Karni terminal. At the later stages of that Intifada, about 350 trucks a day got through: "This lifeline supplies only a quantity that could keep Gaza alive. No more, no less."[33] After the "disengagement," the crossing was closed nearly half the time, and even on days when it was opened, no more than 150–200 trucks a day got through, although 400 trucks were actually set as the minimum required for Gaza not to starve.[34] Israeli control of Gaza's gates and the near-total isolation of the Strip from the rest of the world has enabled the Israeli ruling apparatus to establish the unemployment rate and the level of malnutrition in the Strip, as well as to set income levels, production potential, and the modes and rate of distributing food and medication by international organizations.[35] In the present era of economic globalization, the actual isolation of a very densely populated area from its entire surroundings over an extended period of time amounts to creating disaster conditions inside the isolated area and obstructing efforts to cope with disaster as it happens. By monitoring the entry and exit gates, Israel is capable of setting the patterns for the disaster's expansion and intensity. This kind of governance through "catastrophization" is a new component in a new economy of violence.[36] Closure of the Strip, economic strangulation, and the destruction of civil infrastructures greatly exacerbate the impact of every single person wounded or killed, every demolished home, every damaged public building, in turn escalating economic deterioration and the ability to maintain normal life activity of any kind.

Excluded, surrounded, and isolated, the existence of the Strip's inhabitants has been reduced in the eyes of the Israeli government to the mere presence of mouths to be fed with the barest minimum.[37] Everyone is aware of the fact that opening the gates to human movement and goods is a humanitarian issue. It is brought up as a humanitarian problem in every round of meetings and following every violent attack. Even when the gates are closed, on days when violence rises and tensions mount, closure is perceived as temporary, and after a few days, or weeks at the most, the transfer of humanitarian aid is renewed, and exit permits are sometimes even granted to the ailing and the wounded who need medical treatment outside the Strip. Punitive actions such as severance from the electrical power grid or fuel supply are taken in a measured, calculated manner, in an effort to impact for the sake of exerting pressure but also to halt a dramatic deterioration of the humanitarian situation just in time. By closing the gates of the Strip and disconnecting its electricity supply, Israel could, if it wanted, create famine within a matter of days or weeks. But so far it has been made clear that such severe measures are not on the table. Israel is ready to approach the threshold of catastrophe in a controlled manner, but not to cross it.

Clearly, the threshold of catastrophe has never been a fixed line. Since the 1970s, the humanitarian conditions considered unbearable and the interventions considered permissible have undergone significant erosion. During the First Intifada, every local curfew that lasted over a week threatened to cross the line, but this hardly ever resulted in exceptional humanitarian intervention. In 2007, after long weeks of closure and fragmentation into separate "area cells," impacting the fabric of life of hundreds of thousands, this situation became the rule, and extensive humanitarian activity of numerous local and international organizations has created a new life routine. Prior to the Oslo process, hardly any nongovernmental organizations shared the burden of responsibility with the Israeli government for the population in the Territories, except for UNRWA, which provided mainly for the inhabitants of the refugee camps. Only 10 percent of UNRWA's budget was allotted to supplying food directly to the needy. In 2007, about ten organizations were providing food in the Occupied Territories, with UNRWA handling over half of the population in the Strip, where thousands of families live outside the refugee camps; 54 percent of its budget was then dedicated to direct aid for the needy (UNRWA 2007). Catastrophe—actual and extensive disaster—is in the air, more concrete than ever, and the Israeli control apparatus, UN agencies, and NGOs collaborate in acting on their commitment not to allow this threat to materialize, thus keeping the humanitarian indicators below the threshold.

The occasional "humanitarian gestures" that the Israeli government is willing to make within the ritual of negotiating the terms of negotiation, or in response to the Palestinian internal struggle, remain essentially symbolic. When concrete, they are a part of the measures that would be taken in any case to avoid crossing the threshold of catastrophe. When violence intensifies, the Israeli administration takes special care to prevent disaster as soon as the threshold appears to have been crossed. This occurred, for example, during the short civil war in which Hamas took over the Gaza Strip and distanced forces loyal to Fatah in June 2007. When the crisis broke out, most of the humanitarian organizations active in the Strip published emergency reports that predicted full closure of the Strip and calculated how long the available basic food supplies, fuel, and medicine would last.[38] However, a few days after violence broke out, Israel allowed supply trucks to enter the Strip, carrying provisions from UNRWA, the UN World Food Program, and the International Red Cross, and vaccines supplied by UNICEF. These were successfully delivered in spite of the fact that these organizations had to coordinate delivery with the boycotted Hamas government. Starvation was prevented, but the Strip remained under siege, and goods not included in the humanitarian basket remained stuck in Israel. Additional damage was done to the sinking Palestinian economy, which became all the more dependent upon international aid, as well as on the willingness of the Israeli government to open a "humanitarian safety valve" in the wall surrounding the Strip.

The Israeli disengagement has changed the status and significance of Palestinian civilians in the Strip. They are now not only objects of attack, manipulation, and domination; their suffering has become an asset at stake for the rival parties. The ability to calculate, demonstrate, and predict this suffering has acquired strategic significance. Through the combined and orchestrated use of siege, violent attacks, and humanitarian practices, catastrophization has become a major means of ruling the Gazans. Once the threshold of catastrophe has been more or less established, the scope for abandoning the population in a designated area is identified and can be used perspicaciously as a means of control. One can estimate in advance for how long the terminals can remain closed and the supply of food, water, fuel, electricity, and medications cut.

A space has thus been designated in which the suffering of the population becomes a legitimate instrument. Calculating the number of calories and hospital beds and the amounts of clean water and fuel required become crucial in the instrumentalization of human suffering and its integration into the Israeli war machine. Humanitarianism has become a branch of the military, and humanitarian knowledge, expertise, and practices have been directly and indirectly incorporated into the military apparatus.

This new constellation became plainly evident during Operation Cast Lead, the massive Israeli assault on the Strip that started in the last days of December 2008, following weeks of rocket attacks. The assault lasted three weeks; about 1,400 people were killed and more than 11,000 housing units and 1,500 shops, factories, and public administration buildings were destroyed or damaged.[39]

Given the population density in the Strip, the ratio between lives lost and houses destroyed—1,400 lives to 1,000 housing units, or roughly eight houses for every person killed—is telling. It is explained by the care Israeli soldiers took to reduce civilian casualties and the surgical precision with which houses were bombed, blown up, or bulldozed. This does not mean that more care could not have been exercised, even by military standards and accepting the military point of view. Reports abound on brutality, negligence, and indifference to Palestinian life, especially among the rank and file.[40] However, considering the planning, the tactics, the kinds of weapon used, and the role of the "embedded lawyers" in approving and restraining operations, it becomes clear that the army's policy was to spread destruction while keeping the number of "noncombatants" killed as low as possible, in conformity with international humanitarian law—as interpreted by the Israeli state's legal experts (see Weizman 2009). "We did not wish to kill Palestinians, we wanted to hit them in their pockets," a military strategist said in a closed meeting convened at Tel Aviv University to discuss Judge Richard Goldstone's *Report of the United Nations Fact Finding Mission on the Gaza Conflict*.[41]

These words do not exhaust the motives behind the ferocity of the Israeli show of force at the time, but they certainly represent the rationale of the ruling apparatus. Hitting Palestinians in their pockets means impoverishing them further, adding to scarcity in an already defunct economy. In most cases, the aim of the extensive use of violence was not death but destruction. Food shortages and sanitary conditions had been bad for a long time before the attack, and new traumatized public spaces have been created as a result of the destruction of thousands of overcrowded houses and their replacement with temporary tents. Violence has become an instrument for producing and managing catastrophe subject to legal restraints. Warning the inhabitants—usually by cell-phone announcement minutes before striking at a house—has, for example, become a common practice. Catastrophe management has achieved two things at once: immense destruction of the Palestinian urban environment—which does not, however, create an immediate, dramatic change in the variables that determine the threshold of humanitarian emergency—and respect for what the Israeli experts conceive of as the legal use of force by the military. Humanitarian aid has long since replaced labor and commerce in Gaza. The destruction inflicted on the Strip in January 2009 was precise action of the kind that keeps life on the brink of catastrophe, without crossing the red lines of the humanitarian charts and giving rise to new emergency claims.

Since the official declaration that Israel had terminated its rule there, the administration of catastrophe in the Gaza Strip has taken the form of including the excluded and abandoning the governed. Invoking Agamben's conception of the state of exception, in which application of the law is suspended but remains in force, and life is put under a ban, we would like here to stress a clear difference between such a state and the state of emergency in the Gaza Strip: the exceptional status imposed on Gaza by Israel is the suspension, not of the law, but of humanitarian provisions, threatening to bring about "a real humanitarian emergency" but indefinitely suspending it. Referring to an apparent lacuna in the state of exception, Agamben writes:

> The lacuna is not within the law [*la legge*], but concerns its relation to reality, the very possibility of its application. It is as if the juridical order [*il diritto*] contained an essential fracture between the position of the law and its application, which in extreme situations, can be filled only by means of the state of exception, that is, by creating a zone in which application is suspended, but that the law [*la legge*], as such, remains in force.[42]

Clearly, in the case of the Gaza Strip, this structure has been inverted. What remains in force is not the law but the authorization to use force beyond the realm where the law applies, and to use it in order to create a fracture in the biopolitical (humanitarian) order (from which the law has been excepted), and not the juridical one. The aim is to suspend the provision of essential means of subsistence, so that the threat of catastrophe, though suspended, remains in force. If there is a law whose suspension is relevant in this situation, it is not the law of the Israeli sovereign but the sovereign-less law of nations, international humanitarian law and its major conventions, which are constantly invoked here by all protagonists, Israeli judges and lawyers included.

THE ISRAELI REGIME

Part 3

6 THE CONCEPTUAL SCHEME

The ruling apparatus in the Occupied Territories is an integral part of the political regime of the State of Israel, not the temporary and external appendage that it is often imagined to be in Israeli legal and political discourse. Once this is taken seriously into consideration, Israel's regime appears as "a regime that is not one" but rather a combination of two distinct regimes that, albeit dual, exists in its unity and is headed by one government.

After almost half a century of occupation, it is hard to deny that as a system of government, the Israeli regime is grounded in and articulated through two distinct ruling apparatuses, one that operates mostly in "the Territories" and the other mostly in "Israel proper." The distinctions and imbrication between these two governmental subsystems are blurred, subject to much debate, and continuously reinscribed. The links and differences between the two ruling apparatuses are essential to each and create a unique combination, which we attempt to decipher here. Our discussion of the Israeli regime is limited to the questions arising from this linkage of the two separate systems existing within it. We wish to conceptualize this regime in the context of the control that it has exercised for some forty-five years over the Occupied Territories, its expanding colonizing project, and its military rule of three and a half million Palestinian noncitizens stripped of civil rights.

Being aware of the traps of dominant ideology, we would like to start this conceptual work by clarifying our conceptual toolbox by way of a short lexicon in which some of the concepts crucial for our analysis are set out at some length. This should help us avoid certain confusions prevalent, not only in

Israeli political discourse, but in much of the research about Israel, where so often the state is confused with its regime or with the nation to which it supposedly belongs, and structural elements of the regime are presented as contingent state projects.

RULING POWER

Ruling power is power that rules or that rule endows with power, authority, the means to enforce its rule. The Hebrew term, whose distinct, hard-to-translate meaning we have been presupposing throughout this work, is *shilton*. Were "power" not so heavily laden with connotations, and "rule" so ambiguous and confusing when used in certain contexts, we could have avoided the cumbersome term "ruling power." The King James Bible translates the two occurrences of *shilton* in the Hebrew Bible as "power," and this choice has been retained in some modern translations as well: "Where the word of a king *is*, there is power [*shilton*]" (Eccles. 8:4; KJV). The author of Ecclesiastes is very clear: *shilton* is de facto, enforceable authority; no man, not even a king, therefore has "power in the day of death" (ibid., 8:8). *Shilton* is hegemony and supremacy that lies in what Agamben calls "a threshold" or "zone" of "indistinction" between fact and right (Agamben 1998, 18, and passim). It is neither an authorized power that cannot be enforced nor an exercise of force that claims no authority (a claim that may be refused by its addressees, but must be recognized as such—a claim to have authority to use force).

This means that a street gang can have *shilton* in a neighborhood without forming an official or even unofficial government, and that a weak government of a weak state has no *shilton* in many areas where its authority cannot be enforced. This also means that "government," even in the wide sense of this term (as used, for example, by Locke in his *Two Treatises of Government*, and in the entire tradition derived from it) cannot be equated with *shilton*. *Shilton* cannot be reduced to government, while the latter may include various functions that expand the relation between ruling power and its subject beyond what is necessary for ruling itself (which is precisely Foucault's point in articulating and reconstructing a genealogy of a whole realm of "governmentality" (Foucault 2007, esp. chaps. 4 and 9). Phrased differently, in modern states, ruling powers exercise their rule through the governments they have; if governments are entrusted with ruling power, it is only because they embody this power, which none of its branches, not even the ensemble of these branches can exhaust.

Regime, state, ruling apparatus, and government should be understood as specific, historically determined and evolving formations of ruling power and its complex relations with those whom it rules or claims to rule. Most of this section is devoted to explicating the first three of these terms as we are using them in this work, and articulating the distinction among them. The fourth term, government, is less frequently used in this work. We think of government as that element of a ruling power whose de jure authority has been generally established (regardless of how much it can be contested) and whose function in the modern state has expanded in the modern state much beyond ruling. The power at work in the Occupied Territories has hardly ever enjoyed de jure authority in the eyes of those it rules. It has often exceeded its de jure authorization even in terms of the Israeli judicial system, and many of its agents are not employed or authorized by the government. We have therefore usually opted to use "ruling apparatus" when referring to concrete actions, operations, and the use of withheld and erupting violence, and "ruling power" when referring to the supreme authority itself.

Ruling power is the regular existence of asymmetrical power relations between the powers that be—that is, those authorized to command—and those required to obey. These power relations revolve around a real or imagined center and require a hierarchy of authority and subordination. In the modern state, political rule is the regulation and institutionalization of asymmetrical power relations within a more or less defined territory, over a more or less defined governed population. The relationship of ruling power and the governed people is never symmetrical. A sovereign power is authorized to set territorial boundaries as well as to control the composition of its governed population, at least as far as incoming members are concerned, in time of peace, and more generally in times of war and emergency. Only some of the governed are entitled to partake in governing, rise to power, and change the regime. Their identity and the rules for their participation are constitutive elements of any regime, and they vary in different regimes. Apparently, the limits of such participation and its rules precede the operation of the concrete government and are supposed to curb it; in actual fact, however, the powers that be set these limits, and their enforcement is one of their main tasks. The governed always already find themselves bound by a governing power that enforces association and partnership within borders not of their own choosing; a struggle by the governed to change the form or extent of their participation in the government embodies the demand to redefine the regime that sets borders for the government.

Political rule in the modern state has developed on two separate but linked planes of differentiation. First, an increasingly intricate system of control and governance was made distinctly separate from the ruler himself—prince, king, emperor—on the one hand, and from the governed public—people, nation, community—on the other. Ruling power in the modern state might draw its authority from the governed public, but it is never identical with it; it might be vested in one individual, but never, even in the most autocratic of regimes, can the exercise of government be reduced to the ruler's will or personality.[2] On the second plane, a clear distinction has been established between political rule and other social spheres, first and foremost, civil society and its market, and the religious sphere. Mechanisms that protected the relative autonomy of those spheres but also protected power from being usurped or monopolized by certain religious or economic forces have gradually evolved and become part of the structure of the modern state. The government's legal authority to use violence is a de jure (if not de facto) monopoly, distinct from the economic power of nonruling bodies, and from religious or any other spiritual authority.[3]

In the eighteenth century, new *governing* bodies began to evolve, administering the lives and bodies of individuals and multitudes. While this biopolitical apparatus has been colonizing more and more domains of the life-world, it has never been fully subordinated to the government. Unlike organs of law enforcement and the exercise of violence by the government, many biopolitical bodies of governance are more often decentralized, based on the "unbiased," "apolitical" knowledge of experts, and are easily privatized. Although these governing biopolitical mechanisms are relatively decentralized and autonomous, their authority to intervene and its extent are either granted by the government or can, at any given moment, become subject to its regulations and intervention.

The government in a modern state is authorized to regulate power relations of all kinds and in all walks of life. Through new legislation or emergency regulations it may always reverse its withdrawal and withhold intervention in certain areas or in situations it defines as extreme or exceptional. Such withdrawal may be a matter of liberation or abandonment, and its areas and direction are important features of any regime. Striving to extricate power relations from their arbitrariness and randomness, the government regulates them, relates them to a source of authority, and legitimizes them. Regulating power relations, however, might entail the use of force. Political rule is the authority to exercise force in order to dictate and administer power relations of all kinds through the enforcement or suspension of the law.

Political rule is *the imagined dimension* of the act of rule that the governed tend to ascribe to concrete figures of power authorized to exert various kinds of force. The soldier, the tax collector, the municipal veterinarian, or the school principal are usually seen as extensions of a power older and larger than the authority they exercise. This extension is imagined but not imaginary; it links the proliferation of figures and positions of authority to one source, integrating a concrete holder of authority within a *comprehensive general, unified hierarchical structure* of authorization.[4] The imaginative faculty is required because neither the linkage nor the structure and its hierarchy are perceived directly in the mere presence or action of the one who claims authority. But this is by no means some wild imagination, because failure to obey the rules often invokes more agents who claim authority and exercise force in the name of the same government.

An imagined, more or less unified figure of rule (or ruling power) under which the multiple branches of government are assembled is a condition for participating in the political game. Without this imagined dimension of power, any encounter with power's representative would turn into a forceful taking of control, while in practice such encounters usually reiterate existing hierarchies and familiar relations of subordination between a ruling authority and those it governs. When the unified figure of rule is imagined and its agents recognized, the need to retake control and dominate government anew is reduced, for even if the legitimacy of the governing power is contested, its representatives are recognized and their authority to use violence and other sanctions is acknowledged—at least as authority from *their* point of view.

The ruling power in the modern state is imagined as singular, embodied in one government, but always acts in the plural, and not only through the government's official arms. Its imagined unity can never appear as such but is manifested, rather, in a partial and fragmented way, through some of its aspects. The hierarchy among the various authorities of which this power consists is not always clear and stable. Still, usually even at a time when authorities clash, the parties do need and presuppose a unified image of the ruling power. As long as it does not completely dissipate into two separate entities neither of which accepts the authority of the other (usually meaning partition of the state itself), the contested matter does not call into question the unity of the ruling power but rather the authority to represent it and make decisions on its behalf. On principle, the division of authority among various branches of government takes place as a differentiation within a whole that is supposed to ensure that whole's endurance and stability. This unified figure of power is often no less crucial for the governed who oppose the governing power or wish to be liberated from it than for citizens who consciously support it or thoughtlessly partake in it.

The daily business of ruling helps that power to veil both the event of seizing power and the violence exercised to preserve and activate it with a thick texture of relations between focal points of authorization and authority. Various kinds of such relations exist, in accordance with various differentiations within the governed population. Some of the governed are invited to take part in ruling and governance, or recruited to join one of the power's arms, partake in shaping it, and above all else identify with it and with its aims. Others are ordered or forced to do so. The government may interfere, care for, provide, harass, neglect, or be utterly indifferent, and these attitudes are often the medium through which it accomplishes and sustains the differentiation of the governed population into various groups.

Whether caring or oppressing, the ruling power might be perceived as a normal everyday part of one's life-world, the home environment to which people wish to belong, or as a sort of resource to be acquired, possessed, and used. It might, however, also appear alien, separate, inaccessible, aloof, and overbearing. All these possibilities contain an imagined component that endows the ruling power with force, unity, rationale, and will, concealing the primary aim of any powers that be—to continue ruling, to perpetuate themselves—and enabling them to recruit the governed for their various projects, or at least to preserve their subordination.

State projects undertaken by the government cannot be reduced to the plans and policies through which they are realized. Such projects become consolidated and take place over long periods of time as initiatives, plans, policies, resources, technologies, and means are jointly orchestrated toward a common end. Such a project is a long-term strategy that has no one source or a single subject as its author; it does, however, have a clear goal, a logic that harnesses means to ends, mobilizing people and resources, and a capacity for self-preservation.[5] Openly or tacitly, willingly or not, projects may work to reproduce the regime or to transform it. Large construction projects, wars, efforts to civilize, convert, or secularize, the methodical expropriation or destruction of entire habitats, transfer of populations or their annihilation—all of these projects bear the imprint of a certain regime, while reproducing or transforming it.

But even the most centralist projects—the Great Wall of China, the Napoleonic Wars, Kemal Atatürk's secularization of Turkish society, to name a few—were always particularized into a myriad acts and events carried out by numerous emissaries of the governing power and their various appendices.

THE RULING APPARATUS

A ruling apparatus is the concrete interface by which the ruling power administers the lives of the governed. By putting various institutions at its service and orchestrating their actions, the ruling apparatus ensures the provision of various public services, exerts and regulates violence, protects some of the governed while attacking or abandoning others, monitors the distribution of resources and bestows titles and authority, records a joint past, and plans a joint future. The relations, tensions, and conflicts among various ruling apparatuses and the way these reflect and affect the unified, imagined figure of the ruling power are an important feature of the regime. Conceived and imagined through this unitary figure, the ruling apparatus becomes the unfolding of power's multiple faces. But when the ruling power is not recognized as such or is entirely alienated from the governed, in cases of revolt or secession, for example, the ruling apparatus is unveiled as the apparatus of *control and domination*, which needs to take control again and again with every single act of governance. When this is not the case, however, the ruling apparatus, being a collection of concrete mechanisms in which relations are established between rulers and ruled and by which the ruling power operates, serves as the "space of appearance" of the regime itself. This is the plane in which one must locate, diagnose, and define not only the ruling power but the regime, which is the structure that gives power its form, both concrete and imagined. When a regime is an object of study, the ruling apparatus is the field to be observed.

THE STATE

The modern state is a distinct form of organizing political power and creating the actual ensemble and imagined totality that binds governing power and the governed. It is the organization and totalization of the powers that be, their institutions, within a delineated territory. Equally modern states are governed by different regimes, although they may be similar in the general form of organizing political power and its representation as a totality that binds governing power and the governed and is defined in relation to a specific demarcated territory.

The state is also a super-institution particularized into a multiplicity of apparatuses that rule and manage life. When the totality that binds governing power and the governed in a given territory is represented as a legal and historical entity, a persona that receives international recognition, it bestows upon its ruling apparatuses the status, validity, and purpose of their actions. The most common modern form of constructing this totality is the nation-state. The nation is often perceived as the subject of the state, and the state as the means of fulfilling that nation's self-determination and sovereignty.

Two principal conceptions of nationhood must be distinguished here: nation as a distinct ethnic group with its shared history, habitat, and culture (Hebrew: *leom*); and nation as a group of citizens subject to the rule of the state (Hebrew: *umma*). In the first case, the state is a means to achieve the nation's vocation and historical destiny, to protect its alleged historical rights, security, and well-being; in the second, the nation is the effect of the constitution of the state as a totalizing mechanism of governance and rule. Following Azmi Bishara, we shall call the former "the ethnic nation" and the latter "the civic nation" (or the citizenry).[1] In many nation-states, the nation is conceived along ethnic lines, but a clear congruence of the nation and the state's citizenry is very rare.

Either way, through its various mechanisms of control and governance, the state is instrumental in nation-building, creating or shaping the nation as a group to which individuals can feel they belong and with which they can identify. A group that defines itself as a nation but lacks a state of its own strives to fill this function, however partially, through more or less autonomous national institutions and various cultural elites. Such was the role of the Jewish "Yishuv Institutions" and the "Arab Action Committee" in Palestine before the founding of the State of Israel; for Palestinians, after the founding of the state, it was, and largely still is, the role of the PLO. National (ethnic) movements tend to nationalize and monopolize state apparatuses, and represent them as serving the interests, aspirations, and goals of the nation, which is constructed in turn as a subject with a past, a future, and a destiny. The nation thus becomes the sole owner of the state and its territory, regardless of the actual governed population, alienating those who do not recognize themselves in the image of the national subject propagated by the state.

The construction of civic nationhood in the nation-state usually detaches the privileged citizenry as a group from the governed population as a whole, and the construction of ethnic nationhood enhances this separation. In an ethnic nation-state, such gaps create at least three distinct governed groups: citizens who are members of the nation that "monopolizes" the state; other citizens of the state, conceived of as "minorities"; noncitizens who are governed but hardly counted. In some ethnic nation-states—for example, the Balkan states after the disintegration of Yugoslavia, the Czech Republic after World War II, and Israel since its foundation—there is a fourth group, usually an indigenous population expelled through ethnic cleansing, which is associated with the state by being entirely excluded from it, and therefore may be considered the un-ruled. The four groups usually differ in their access to power and to public discourse and the rights that protect them from power's excesses. The differences between the groups and the mobility from one group to another are among a state's most important characteristics.

REGIME

By regime we do not mean a particular ruling group, certainly not an authoritarian one, but a system of rule or, more precisely, an abstract form with a relatively stable outline, an idea of sorts of the relations between a government and the governed, and of various groups of governed among themselves. The recurrence of this form is accomplished and made recognizable in and through reiteration of relations among the various elements: branches of government, groups of governed, spheres of action, and so on. Regime structures webs of relations, lines of separation and association, modes of authorization, events and processes of intervention and management, and the struggle to transform all of the above, which, in their turn, shape the regime and reproduce it—or transform it.

Regime is a structure of differences separating the main groups in the governed population. One can usually discern a single decisive difference that governs, limits, and is articulated through all other differences. The decisive difference is the one establishing the basic grid of differentiations among the population groups regarding their protection from and by the ruling power, their access to that power, their rights, duties, and opportunities. Beyond the principles of separation and difference, regime is a more or less closed set of features and rules essential to a specific form of rule and governance, not all of them explicit, that regulate relations among the various branches of the government and between them and social spheres of action that have been separated from the governing power and enjoy relative autonomy: civil society in its economic and political aspects, religion, science, or art, and so forth. This set of rules is manifested in the different mechanisms of the ruling apparatus and in the structural link between them.

192 THE ISRAELI REGIME

In order to endure, this structure needs real existence and its reproduction is ensured by the mechanisms of the ruling apparatus. The mechanisms themselves might act similarly under different governments and different regimes and still remain intact even when power changes hands and the regime is altered. The French sociologist Pierre Bourdieu (1980) used the Latin term *habitus* to describe the array of skills, tendencies of action, and coordinated expectations needed by the individual in order to know how to participate in the various cultural, social, and political games he/she is faced with in different realms of social action, how to move within these fields and find one's way among them. The knowledge, techniques, and practices unique to every mechanism of rule, and the special habitus unique to the people who operate it, are supposed to depend upon the nature of this realm more than upon the maxims and rules of the regime, and to be subject to experts in their field more than to the players in the political domain. But these mechanisms do not operate in a vacuum, and their systemic ties are essential for the regime's structure and existence. Outright regime change might alter the apparatuses, just as gradual, implicit changes in this system itself might reshape the regime. Regimes are distinct, discrete forms and thus, for a regime to change, a threshold needs to be crossed. This threshold, however, is no less imagined than the regime itself. Its crossing necessitates the reconceptualization of the gap between the regime's concrete formation and its idea. Such reconceptualization is a part of the attempt to change a regime or expose changes that have already taken place in it.

This could also be presented as follows: regime is a way of regulating, more or less permanently, the division of authorities and resources among the various governed groups, as well as of the formation of relations among the various elements that have been separated in the modern state. Similar patterns of regulation recur in the government's actions and are embodied by its institutions. The various bodies and technologies of governing are supposed to ensure not only the existence of a certain ruling power and its government but the form of regime whereby changes of power are regulated. They bear the *imprint of the regime*, embodying its unique structure, and inscribe it in all realms of their intervention. Relations between the ruling power and the governed are manifested and embodied in power's modes of intervention in different spheres of action, in the limitations that these can impose upon the governing power, bestowing or denying legitimacy, intervening in changes of government, and participating in governance itself, but also in the ways in which the government may and can achieve obedience, recruit the governed to its various projects, enhance or modify difference among groups of governed and use such differences to reproduce the regime or transform it. Change of government and regime transformation are distinct processes that may or may not entail each other (a new government may initiate a regime change, and a new regime may be established without overthrowing the old government). Regime change may or may not involve an informed decision of the main officeholders in the government, of the multitude of the governed or political agents, or of any institutions that function in between. Regime change may happen abruptly, through a series of dramatic decisions or events that no one fails to notice, or gradually, through a planned transition of power in which many are called upon to participate. Some regime changes, however, take place quietly, without coups or revolutions, through change in the inner grammar of separations that structure the regime and the patterns of relations among its various elements. We assume, then, that regime change is not merely a matter of definition and does not necessarily occur when it is declared. Since regime is a form, its change means crossing a certain threshold, after which a new form emerges. Recognition of the emerging form may be quite late to arrive and its declaration too early. The question of the threshold or "the real change" is itself contested and is part of what is at stake in various struggles. Our attempt to describe the emergence of a new regime in Israel-Palestine is no exception.

However, our intervention differs from many others in one respect: we do not conceive of regime as an ideal type and do not measure historical events and social structures in light of such a type. We avoid the often discussed question (in Israeli theoretical and political discourse, at least) of whether or not Israel meets the minimum conditions to be considered as this or that type of regime: democracy, apartheid, and so on. We try rather to extract the form from the historical reality we have interpreted.

The regime's ideal type often serves as a kind of political compass and a basis for the critique of institutions, which assumes that the gap between the ideal and its materialization can and should be narrowed. This normative critique all too often fails to come to terms with the complex reality it purports to judge. By going in the opposite direction, from the phenomenology of the ruling apparatus and the totality of relations between governing power and the governed to the regime formation, we allow the emergence in discourse—in thought and articulation—of a new form, for which we may yet lack a name. It may not fit any ideal type from the rather limited repertoire of regimes recognized by political philosophers or political scientists—but without its analysis, no critique is possible.

The regime is never given as a fait accompli. The reiteration of its form through webs of power relations and of its basic grammar embedded in the ruling apparatus is achieved or fails to be achieved through the exercise of power of all kinds. The question of regime, the attempts to use ideal types to represent or criticize the powers that be, and a theoretical intervention like ours all belong to the same field where this exercise of power takes place, the regime takes shape, and its form emerges. Therefore, rather than asking whether the regime in Israel suits the ideal type termed "democracy" (according to whichever conception), we shall question the role of discursive efforts (political and legal, by the governing power as well as by the citizenry) to define the regime as democratic and measure its deviations from an ideal model.

PROJECTS AND REGIME

The differential matrix of separations and oppression (hence ever more zones of friction) is the blueprint of the Israeli regime. One should keep in mind that this blueprint differentially serves—in quite distinct ways—diverse state projects, which, in their turn, reproduce but also transform the matrix as a whole. The matrix lends support and justification to various projects that mobilize and enact various state apparatuses. These projects, in their turn, articulate the matrix of separation and oppression in space and time and reproduce it as the regime's blueprint. In order to clarify and elaborate this point, we should dwell on the relations between regime and state projects.

Regime is the highest, most abstract level of organization of reproducible political forms. A tool—something like a gun, a roadblock, street lights, a bulldozer, an ID card—is an instance of the lowest level of organization. In between regimes and instruments, one finds state projects and policies, modes of operation, technologies of governing and domination, techniques of control and intervention, collection of data and production of symbols. A tool can also be a mode of operation or a technology of government; its role depends upon the way, the frequency, and intensity of its use and integration with other elements. A roadblock, for example, is a tool that may be integrated into a technique, a mode of operation, or a technology of governing. Roadblocks along with a few guns and documents that grant their holders the right of passage make up a checkpoint. Some checkpoints consist of more tools than others, and their operation requires more sophisticated skills (hence a technique). More important, they usually do not function alone; they constitute a whole network, integrated into the road system, and together they form a mechanism for movement control—hence a mode of operation. Clusters of techniques and modes of operation controlled by state authorities form a state apparatus.

The use of tools and techniques often betrays the intention of their inventor and users, undermining planned policies and professed objectives. A mode of operation can be used for very different purposes, regardless of the state apparatus that resorts to it. Thus a checkpoint may be used to collect taxes or separate people, to ease the flow of certain kinds of people and slow down others, and so on. Hence a different level of organization is that of policy. A policy is a planned effort to coordinate a variety of modes of operation, using different techniques and tools to achieve a more or less coherent purpose.

A project exists at a level of organization higher than that of instruments, techniques, and modes of operation: it is a set of policies coordinated to achieve what may be described as an end that justifies its means; only rarely does it need further justification. State projects mobilize a vast number of tools, techniques, and modes of operation and cover a vast area of activity. The actions taken to achieve the goals of these projects tend to have long-lasting effects—both intended and unintended—on the living conditions of the entire governed population, citizens and noncitizens alike, or a significant part of it. The end in view may justify the effects retroactively, but in order to explain them, one should take into account the dynamics created by the modes of operation animating a project and the constraints imposed by the regime to frame and contain it.

Thus an electronic fence, for example, may become part of a state's mode of operation in the realm of movement control; a specific system of movement may serve a policy that seeks to keep the number of illegal workers below a certain threshold; immigration policy and the control of workers' movement may serve a neoliberal project; they may also be part of a different nationalist project. These projects might conflict locally but still feed each other in a way that preserves and reproduces the template of the regime. Governments may exercise policies that do or do not follow a certain set of state projects; many nongovernmental actors may contest or support policies because they see them as linked to state, national, or class projects that they wish to promote or undermine. Policies, like modes of operation, may reproduce or undermine the regimes within which they are carried out, but their effects are often contradictory, ruling each other out, or accumulate slowly and dissipate quickly. Projects often involve numerous state apparatuses, national movements, or large corporations, but at the same time they may amplify the reproductive or transformative force of local agents and modes of operation.

A regime is an ideal structure that should be imagined on the basis of the regularity of the rules and practices it guides, and by which it is reproduced. Projects are more or less concerted sets of actions motivated and directed toward a goal, for which they mobilize state apparatuses and resources. Usually this goal is unachievable as such; there is always more to be done, conquered, or reformed, and the movement becomes perpetual. A state project, too, has a form, of course, but this form is not determined by the motivation and intentions of the people involved; it is, rather, shaped by certain dialectics between the regime that constrain and enable the project and the particular modes of operation seeking to implement it. Regimes are truly distinct when they mobilize and constrain projects, policies, and modes of operations in a distinct way.

A regime is a constellation of elements made up of various state projects, multiple policies, and numerous modes of operation. At least one of these projects should take care of the regime's reproduction, the endurance of the form of relations among its various, multiple elements. But a regime is associated with multiple projects and these are not easily reconcilable. Regime is a form that keeps changing even in the absence of straightforward resistance, because its reproduction depends on modes of operation, policies, and projects pregnant with unintended consequences. Regimes frame, call for, make possible, and constrain projects; projects reproduce, but also reform, transform, and, more rarely, undermine regimes.

SOVEREIGNTY

Sovereignty is a way of describing the top of the ruling hierarchy and the structure of authorization resulting therefrom. It presupposes the hierarchical organization of the ruling power and its claim to monopoly over the legitimate use of violence in a given territory. Distinction should be made here between state sovereignty and the sovereignty of a ruling power in the state. The former is an aspect of an international order of things whereby the state is the highest recognized form of authorized governance within a given territory. By this order, essentially, there is no longer any place on the globe that is not a territorial part of a state (or, in some rare cases, the control over which is arranged by agreement among states). Likewise, there are no people who are not defined as bound to some sovereign power or other: as its citizens or as its noncitizens (whether because they have been denied or not yet granted citizenship). A ruling power is considered sovereign when the sovereign ruling powers of other states recognize it as a supreme power authorized to regulate all forms of power relations within the territory over which it rules.

A sovereign power within a state assumes or claims the sovereignty of the state. The sovereignty of this power consists in the authority to impose closure on any matter in dispute, in any political, legal, financial, or administrative discussion, to bring such a discussion, dispute, or violent conflict to an end, and to declare the continuation of the dispute or conflict, or of some of its forms, to be unlawful. Often, the sovereign is ascribed with power and authority that are singular, indivisible, unified, and relatively stable. Damage to the unity and stability of sovereignty as an institution has usually been considered weakness of the government itself.

Following and revising Carl Schmitt's notion of sovereignty, we give up this image of unity and emphasize *the moment of decision* that aims to produce *an effect of absolute closure upon* the matter at stake, on the one hand, and to the ruling authority that takes the decision, on the other. The sovereign decision pretends to put an end to the clash between the governing power and the governed, of the branches of government among themselves, or of the governed among themselves. Sovereign closures may be brutally imposed or readily accepted. They may be exercised through killing or granting amnesty, suspension of the law or legislation, issuing a decree or annulling one—as long as further possibility of legitimate contestation of struggle is no longer legitimate, and all who persist in their struggle are outlawed, marginalized, oppressed, excluded, or eliminated by means considered legitimate even when they are illegal.

The authorized pretension "to put an end to it" might be ascribed to and manifested by all echelons of the ruling apparatus, from the lowest official of the internal revenue service, the traffic policeman, or city parking inspector up to the highest ranks of government. The authority to put an end might shift among leaders of the army, government, or the juridical system. It might reside in parliament or on the battlefield, in the gray corridors of bureaucracy or the hallowed halls of justice. When the military commander orders the erection of a fence, ignoring the protests of those who own or use the partitioned land, he appears sovereign. Once a judicial authority agrees to continue—and then put an end to—the legal dispute regarding that land, the presiding judge appears to be the sovereign. And when the lower-ranking military commander at the site orders suspension of the dismantling of the fence, thus overlooking the court's ruling, then he—the junior commander—has actually made the latest

198 THE ISRAELI REGIME

sovereign decision. Sovereignty is always provisional, partial, split among various ruling positions, and negotiable among holders of power and authority, between governing power and the governed, unlike its inherent pretension to be final and decisive and issued by the highest and clearly recognizable authority.

In a modern state, the government draws its legitimacy from its pretense to define and act on behalf of the common interest shared by the ruling power and its governed subjects. This shared interest might take the form of an interest in the future, security, well-being, development, growth or expansion of a state, a nation, or a people. The supreme justification for the government's acts is formulated as the interest that the ruling power claims to share with its subjects. Less frequently, it is presented as stemming from the duty to protect the regime or refrain from altering it. But the question of what the good of the state or the people is, and to what the regime's precepts are committed, is an open one, which many aspire to answer. So, too, is the question of what the supreme principle or source of justification of the ruling power is: the state, the nation, the people, the regime, or that power itself. The sovereign power stands out among all rival authorities in this dispute by claiming to be the final authority to determine the interests at stake and what principle of justification should be preferred. The decision to place the good of the state or of the nation above the law has a familiar paradigmatic form: declaring an exception because of which some laws may be suspended, or declaring a state of emergency and suspension of the constitution as a whole.

The authority to decide on the exception, which defines sovereignty according to Schmitt,[6] is actually only *one* of sovereignty's several typical features, and only in certain constellations of the legal system within the ruling apparatus does it become the supreme factor. Even then, the sovereign power does not act in a void, and any of its most final decisions may be thrown back into the legal, political, or military field from which they are supposed to be extracted.

Various thinkers from Jean Bodin and Thomas Hobbes to contemporary theorists of liberal democracy have believed that the stability and functioning of the state depend on the existence of a single, unified, clear, and distinct sovereign authority. Such an authority is never the case in actual states, but a certain continuum may be discerned in terms of divisions and instability within the government and the ability of any authority to reclaim "the closure authority," namely, the authority to put an end to any dispute, procedure, or project. In a representative democracy where the rule of law is respected, the demos—that is, the citizenry—is considered sovereign, because every once in a while, citizens eligible to vote can disestablish the existing government and replace many of its authorized officeholders. But this limited moment of sovereign authority granted to the citizens should be juxtaposed with a myriad of other moments of sovereign decisions spread across the entire sphere of governance.

This distribution of moments of sovereign decision, the possible negotiation that precedes and follows such decisions, and the level of centralization in each of them is another feature that characterizes and differentiates regimes. A recognizable, relatively stable pattern of distribution characterizes any rule of law. In a liberal democracy, the principles of distributing sovereign decisions among the three branches of government are part of the constitution but are also negotiable among the various authorities within the government, and between the latter and the governed. In an absolute monarchy or under tyranny, it is of the utmost importance to represent the distribution of sovereign decisions as emanating from the sovereign power itself, grounded in its supreme authority, no matter how dispersed and distant from the highest seat of power they actually are. In a democracy, it is of the utmost importance to represent this distribution as emanating from the "people." In a militarized colonial regime that characteristically rules by decrees (as opposed to the rule of law), sovereign moments are dispersed and distributed in an unstable manner among the state security forces and settler militias, and this unstable distribution is of the essence.[7]

POLITICAL SPACE

This is a space of relations, actions, and communication that occur wherever people live, assemble, come into contact and speak with one another, negotiate, or influence one another's actions. The existence of such a space is its own end, and it precedes the supposedly collective interests of the group(s) that share(s) it, because it is through this space that a group comes into being.[8]

Regimes differ in the way ruling power sets limits and establishes boundaries for political space. Usually, the government cannot take over political space in its entirety, leaving no residue of exchange free of its dictates, and subjugating the people who inhabit this space to its rules and orders. As Hannah Arendt showed, the effort to completely and systematically eliminate political space is a hallmark of totalitarian regimes. On the other hand, the principle of open access to that space is a precondition for a modern liberal democracy, and its realization is an ongoing task and challenge for government and governed alike. From the government's point of view, political space is a source of legitimacy, but also of excess that must be contained and of instability to be stabilized. From the point of view of the governed, political space is a crucial resource in their attempts to benefit from power and be protected from its harm.

The fact that in democracies many citizens might become a part of the government, and that many agents of this power will eventually become simple citizens again, softens the decisive difference between the governmental point of view and the civil one but cannot entirely erase it. Whoever has been elected or appointed to rule takes a position that he or she wishes to preserve or reinforce, and expand the authority that is ascribed to it. The inherent interests embodied in such a position—the authority, responsibility, access to information, and subjection to other ruling figures or dependence on them—determine the point of view, which is structurally and principally different from those of the governed, who do not bear governing responsibility, do not enjoy such authority, and do not compete for power. This difference is irreducible (even though its scope and costs for the governed vary), and its removal, as it were, does not express liberation but rather the disavowal of the way one is governed. This difference is grounded in the actual ruling relation itself, which in various given situations splits the planes of action, the field of vision and discourse, along the essential divide between those authorized to command and those bound to obey.

The difference between the ruling power and the governed is played out and articulated in two related but distinct planes: the plane of being governed; the plane of sharing government and partaking in governance. The political space is where this (often ignored) distinction comes into the open and is partly bridged at the same time. Limitations and possibilities of action on one plane do not necessarily reflect those existing on the other. Thus, subjects of an enlightened monarch may be protected from the caprices of a power that they can never share, while citizens in a democracy might be governed poorly, being directly exposed to the whims and delusions of a ruling power in which they can fully share.

Wherever power is problematized, the political space is open. The government might try to impose rigid rules of entry into that space and harsh restrictions over negotiable issues, but it could never entirely destroy the potential of resistance and preempt the attempts of the governed to violate the rules limiting their access to the political space or to create it where it is least expected. Once in the political space, the governed may strive to change the conditions under which they are governed or the form and extent to which they may share in government (or both). These are two different—and not always compatible—directions of action, and different groups in the governed population have different stakes in them. Some groups are better protected than others, some groups have a larger share in power than others, and the former cannot simply be identified with or mistaken for the latter. This difference between the two planes is an important characteristic of any regime and crucial for understanding the Israeli regime.

.   .   .

Our main claim in what follows is that the Israeli Occupation should not be perceived as a distinct project but rather as a regime, not as a task of the governing power but rather as a separate, uniquely characterized form of political rule. Perceiving the Occupation as a task and the difficulty of seeing it as a regime may help us explain the special temporality of the Occupation and its disrupted spatial borders, the willingness to accept colonization, and even join it, but also the transition, with hardly a jolt, from colonization to separation. Finally, the invisibility of occupation as a regime and the naturalness with which it is accepted as a project amalgamate the two parts of the Israeli regime and recruit most Israelis subjected to a civil-democratic regime to cooperate with the maintenance of the tyrannical regime in the Occupied Territories, while still regarding themselves as citizens of a democracy.

7 STRUCTURAL DIVISIONS AND STATE PROJECTS

TWO PLANES OF POWER

We broach the question of the Israeli regime with two assumptions. First, the occupation of the Palestinian Territories in 1967 and the subjection of three and a half million Palestinians to Israeli rule have lasted long enough—over four decades—to be counted as a constitutive element of the Israeli regime. Second, the various ways in which the Occupied Territories and their Palestinian populations are separated and excluded from the main body politic, geography, law code, and bureaucracy of the Jewish state are precisely the ways in which they are governed, and any attempt to characterize the Israeli regime must take this mechanism of separation into account.

The (theoretical) situation would be simple if we could now claim one of two things: that only Jews can be citizens of the Jewish state, or that the main dividing line is not between Jews and non-Jews, but rather between Israeli citizens and noncitizens, and that this division overrules national, ethnic, and geographical ones. The first claim is obviously false, for almost 20 percent of the Israeli citizenry is non-Jewish. The second claim overlooks differences in the accessibility of civic status: the distribution of rights between the two national groups and their ability to use them. Jewish immigrants are guaranteed civil status by the Law of Return (and they need not even be naturalized before taking advantage of the biased distribution of rights and resources), while non-Jews can hardly be naturalized at all; prevention by law of the return of Palestinian refugees to their land; legal and administrative discrimination of non-Jews seeking naturalization in order to be reunited with their spouses, children, or parents who are citizens; differences in rights to buy and access land, unequal distribution of government spending, investments in infrastructure, education, and so on.[1] In other words, the (theoretical) situation is not simple, because neither of the two principles of division—civil and national—can be reduced to or subsumed under the other.

The two divisions are neither mutually exclusive nor necessarily consequential. They coexist and converge under one governing power, not subjugated to each other but rather intersecting, with no stable hierarchy between them, and they are articulated differently in the two planes of governance: sharing power and being governed. The national or ethnic difference is decisive as to participation in governing power. The civil difference, on the other hand, is decisive as regards the state of being governed. We must, then, go back and examine the two differences, the civil and the national, in regard to the two planes of political existence.

The Plane of Being Governed

The three and a half million noncitizens in the Occupied Territories are governed quite differently from Israel's seven and a half million citizens. The two groups are entitled to different protection under the law, and they are exposed to the violence of the governing power to a different extent and in different ways. The vulnerability of Palestinian noncitizens in the Territories, their exposure to state and settler violence, and to the effects of the ruling apparatus's harsh measures, cannot be compared to that of Palestinian Israeli citizens, however severely deficient their civil status is.

The Plane of Sharing Power

This is the decisive plane for articulating the national difference. Palestinian noncitizens have no legal access to the Israeli political sphere. They are overlooked, not represented, and their voice can be heard almost solely through demonstrations, acts of violence, appeals to the High Court of Justice, or within the narrow frameworks of diplomatic negotiations. Until the outset of the Oslo process they played a marginal part in the lowest echelons of the ruling apparatus in the Occupied Territories, as officeholders at the municipal level, clerks, teachers, or collaborators. Since the establishment of the Palestinian Authority, they have had limited freedom to share its governing powers. But they have never been allowed to take part in shaping the government that constrains the Palestinian Authority and continues to rule them over and above it. Palestinian citizens of Israel, on the other hand, take part in the democratic game: they vote in elections and are represented in the Knesset (parliament), serve in local government in various capacities, are appointed as judges, and fill some lower positions in public administration and the diplomatic service. If they are Bedouin, they may—and if they are Druze, they must—serve in the army as well.

Such participation is not negligible but very limited. The representation of Arab citizens in the judicial system and diplomatic service is minimal, far from reflecting their numbers in the population of the state. They are consistently distanced from senior positions, both appointed and elected, they are not members of the government cabinet or coalition,[2] and in the Knesset, they are underrepresented in major committees and excluded from briefings in "security-sensitive" committees for obvious lack of "security clearance."

The influence Palestinians have on the ruling power in Israel is far more limited than that of organized Jewish groups outside Israel. No Arab party has ever been part of a coalition that formed a government, and the need for a "Jewish majority"[3] for deciding on any issue of political importance is expressed openly and accepted by the majority of Jewish members of the house. The ongoing political harassment and legal persecution of Knesset members such as Azmi Bishara, Jamal Zahalka, Hanin Zu'abi, and Sheikh Ra'ed Salah is the most ostensible example of nonrecognition of the Arabs' right to take part in the government, and it is merely the tip of the iceberg in the current frenzy of suspicion and incitement against Arab members of the Knesset. Relative representation of Arabs in the Knesset (10 percent at most) has never corresponded to their percentage in Israel's citizenry (nearly double that). In the media, their representation is an even smaller percentage. This exclusion is not explicit by law, does not formally stem from the definition of Israel as a Jewish state, and is not necessarily dictated by the principle of national self-determination.[4] But it is a systematic and structural exclusion nevertheless, and it actually plays an important part in shaping Israel as a uniquely Jewish state: a state that only Jews control, with hardly any non-Jewish participation in its administration.

The dual division (citizens vs. noncitizens and Jews vs. non-Jews) is manifested differently on the planes of relations between the government and the governed. If only citizens are considered, excluding Palestinian citizens from participation in the government can be understood as a more or less "natural" expression of "ethnic democracy,"[5] or as a repairable defect of liberal democracy. However, the distinction between the two planes of power relations reflects the national difference, is shaped by it, and serves it as well. This national difference is at one and the same time a product of a stable distinction between the two planes and the source of its legitimacy. Within the democratic institutions of "Israel proper," the distinction between the two planes allows for the persistence of inequality between the national groups on the one plane and relative equality on the other; at the same time, the national difference enables the separation between the two planes, reducing access to governing power without impacting democratic equality.

In a liberal democracy, where citizens are more or less equally endowed with and share rights protecting them from the excesses of the government, it is difficult to stabilize the distinction between the two planes of relation to the ruling power. All citizens can in principle become members of the government, and in that capacity they are always also governed, just like everyone else. In Israel proper, this distinction is relatively stable, because it is based on national differences and reproduces them—the essential structure of the existing regime is flexible enough to tolerate the formal equality of rights for non-Jewish citizens as long as their status as governed is concerned, but it cannot tolerate an equal sharing of power. In the Occupied Territories, the difference between the two planes is even more radical, because it coincides with the ethno-national difference that intersects the two planes of power relations in the same way, and does not affect the difference between them. Jews share in power and benefit from its protection because they are Jews; Palestinians have no political status; they can serve the governing power without partaking in it and are expected to accept its rule without being given any kind of protection on its behalf. On both planes, national identity is the sole determining factor. In Israel proper, however, Palestinian citizens are entitled to a citizen's rights, even if less so than Jewish citizens. Druze citizens must, and Bedouin citizens may volunteer to serve in the army but they can rarely occupy high-ranking positions in any ruling apparatus.

Ethnicity and geography determine status in entirely different ways for citizens and for noncitizens, adding further differentiation to the governed population. Ethnic distinctions have important consequences for Jewish and non-Jewish citizens alike. For *noncitizens*, however, the consequences of ethnicity are slight; the decisive difference, dwarfing all others, is geographical: whether one lives in the Gaza Strip, the northern West Bank, the southern West Bank, or the Jerusalem district. One's official address, which is often different from one's place of residence, determines the extent and kind of governmental care to which one is entitled and the violent intervention to which one is exposed. Palestinian citizens may be harassed and persecuted, neglected and discriminated against because they are non-Jews, but they are not legally be forsaken by the state or eliminated. Palestinian noncitizens, however, can lawfully be abducted, expelled, eliminated, or completely abandoned. These are essential differences that intersect all dimensions of the regime and its ruling apparatus, and penetrate all realms of life of its governed subjects.

Thus Palestinians in the Occupied Territories can be abandoned by the ruling power and exposed to its violence precisely because they are noncitizens. The Palestinian citizens of Israel can be disposed of, discriminated against, and continuously disempowered precisely because they are non-Jews. The complete exclusion of the former, and the partial exclusion of the latter (by denying their access to the echelons of power) significantly reduces the number of Palestinians eligible to vote and organize politically, and significantly constrains the power of those eligible to take part in the political process. The Jewish state can thus adopt certain principles of democratic rule in Israel proper because these do not seem to endanger the principle of a Jewish majority and the image of the state as Jewish.

The democratic institutions that function in Israel proper enable—or are at least supposed to enable—political organization and even a certain measure of social mobility for members of the national minority. Social mobility and its political manifestation might jeopardize the monopoly held by the dominant national group over state institutions and hence the permanent quest for ways to limit them without giving up the rules of the democratic game. The "solutions" lie in different legal administrative measures, in discriminatory bureaucratic practices based on geo-ethnic demarcations and spatial segregation,[6] and in an ethnic-civic habitus shared by most Jewish citizens, who pride themselves in their democracy, while naturalizing the tacit exclusion of Arabs from governing positions and structural discrimination against them in the housing and labor markets.[7]

This difference—between two principles of dividing a governed population and two planes in which they are inscribed—is so decisive that, in fact, two different regimes really exist alongside each other: an occupation regime in the Occupied Palestinian Territories, and an ethnic democracy within Israel proper. In both quasi-separate regimes, the determining principle is the national one, but it has a different meaning in each, because one is basically meant for citizens only and the other for noncitizens, and the national partition differentiates between two kinds of citizens in the first and between citizens and noncitizens in the second. The civil partition intersects the regime structure in all its dimensions, differentially shaping the relations within the state, distinguishing two separate colonial projects, reaching every branch of the intricate ruling apparatus, and touching upon every aspect of life of the governed.

This double exclusion of Palestinians, as non-Jews and as noncitizens, is not only one of the structural features of the two regimes but also an endless, ongoing project. The dual structure of the regime can be maintained only as long as the double exclusion is not compromised, and it can be achieved through democratic means (i.e., the election of the government in Israel proper and the checks and balances to which it is subject) only as long as the two systems of exclusion are kept apart. Both of these missions face resistance by Palestinian citizens and noncitizens and hence require continual investment of power and resources, and yield new technologies of control, dispossession, and (mis)representation. The split between the two regimes is the condition for the democratic element of the Israeli regime; the link between the two places this democracy in the service of colonial oppression and military dictatorship.

At this point it may be tempting to see domination of the Territories as a *project* consisting of a series of political rulings, colonial practices, legislation, and procedures especially designed to achieve the goal of the Zionist project since its inception—the Judaization of the Land of Israel as a whole by colonization of its frontier. However, what originally began as a project, or actually as a series of projects, escalated and solidified into a unique, rigid, sustainable system of government, a regime that reproduces itself and imposes constraints on all governmental actions, plans, and initiatives in its realm, as well as upon all those taking place within Israel proper. Instead of looking at the Occupation as a project, we propose to read it as one system of government in a dual regime that structures a series of projects, which together work to reproduce the regime, transforming it while preserving its basic grammar. To demonstrate this, a more diachronic perspective is necessary.

1948

The Israeli regime came into being in May 1948 , when the British Mandate over Palestine ended and the State of Israel was established. The main blueprint of this regime, consolidated in the late 1950s, changed gradually. However, with the occupation of the Territories in 1967, a decisive change took place. In order to explain this properly, one must first briefly describe what Meron Benvenisti calls the "first Israeli republic," which lasted up to 1967.[8] At the basis of the regime formation that commenced in 1948 lies a violent transformation of the body politic and a differential control of two separated national groups, only one of which—the Jews—can have a real share in political power. Three major state projects that had preceded the establishment of the state had been woven together to form the Israeli regime, and enabled its reproduction over time:

1. A majoritarian project aiming to achieve a Jewish majority within the State of Israel through Jewish immigration and Arab emigration (forced and voluntary), and the exclusion of non-Jews from most governing institutions.

2. A colonial project meant to take over vast areas, to found new, exclusively Jewish towns and villages, and to reduce the Arab presence throughout these areas.

3. A destruction project meant to demolish large parts of the Palestinian habitat, annihilate traces of civil Jewish-Arab relations, reduce the physical and symbolic presence of the Palestinians, build over the ruins of their homes, and change the country's landscape and infrastructure.

The two first projects consolidated within what was called "the Zionist project" and combined ideologies, action formations, local initiatives, and various technologies of governance that had developed ever since the onset of Zionist settlement in Palestine. The destruction project budded as a series of sporadic, local initiatives on the morrow of the Partition Plan in late 1947 and expanded when the British Mandate came to an end, combining military and colonial practices.[9] Immediately following the Partition Plan, all three became state projects based on British governing mechanisms, on the one hand, and on the organizations and the governing rationale developed by the Zionist movement since the 1920s, on the other. The new state was founded with boundaries far vaster than those allotted the Jews under the Partition Plan, and it expelled most of the Arabs living within them. It was both directly and indirectly responsible for the displacement of the Palestinian majority that had lived in the area declared as Israel, and for the transformation of the landscape, where the Palestinian presence was gradually eliminated.

Less than a year after the end of the British Mandate, Jewish forces had taken over 78 percent of Palestine west of the Jordan River. These months of fighting were the phase of constituent violence, the violence that instituted the Israeli regime. Arab opposition to the Partition Plan was—and has been—presented ever since as the reason and justification for expulsion and expropriation, but these policies were not accidental, inevitable results of a war fought for other causes. As has often been acknowledged, they were the aim of the colonial and majoritarian Zionist projects that preceded the Israeli regime and of the violence that constituted it.[10] This violence was instrumental for the new regime and helped the new state represent itself as a decolonized nation-state and rapidly repress its own colonial dimension. The use of violence was also necessary for continuing the first two Zionist projects and adding the new project of destruction, for each of these projects harmed the Palestinians and generated resistance that was often violent. Even when the Palestinians became a minority in Israel, it was necessary to ensure that they would not place obstacles on the path of the Zionist projects.

The phase of constituent violence that terminated with armistice agreements in March 1949 came to be known as Israel's "War of Independence" and is depicted as a war of survival or a war of national liberation. This, however, was not simply a "war of survival," if only because Jewish insistence on establishing a regime in which the Arabs residents of the country would not be able to share power contributed directly to creating the existential threat. Nor was it a "war of liberation," because the colonial power—the British Mandate—had left of its own accord. The Palestinians were not oppressors from whom Jews had to be liberated. They were not even party to the armistice talks conducted with the Arab states, where agreements were signed that framed them and sealed their fate as stateless. These agreements led to international recognition of Israel as the state of the Jews, accepting the armistice lines as the de facto borders that defined its territory. Because military forces from Jordan, Egypt, and Syria intervened on behalf of the Palestinians, and that intervention ended in armistice agreements, the usurpation of power by one ethnic group in Palestine and the suppression of the other could be narrated as a war between two equal political entities, a conflict between states.

Against the background of the demise of European Jewry and the presence of Jewish refugees throughout the European continent, the regime gained immediate legitimacy in and support from some countries, most importantly from the USSR, and partial, hesitant, and gradual legitimacy in most Western countries. However, the actual existence of the Jewish state and its right to exist as a *Jewish* state have not been seriously contested in the West ever since. The destruction inflicted upon the Palestinians has become a lingering "refugee problem," whose resolution—it is generally believed—must be achieved without undermining the Jewish supremacy in the new state.

The effort to legitimize the new regime had to ignore more than a hundred civil contracts between Jews and Arabs, achieved locally throughout the country in order to prevent violence and hostilities, and to dismiss their potential to serve a different form of coexistence (Azoulay 2012). The new regime met with opposition from three groups: the Palestinians who had been expelled from their land for the sake of creating a Jewish majority, and whose right of return the regime consistently denied; the Palestinians remaining in Palestine; and groups of Jews who did not favor the partition of Palestine, opposed the expulsion of Arabs, and objected to the massive exertion of violence. Little is known about the number of these Jews; their opposition was silenced and denied access to public space, and no data was gathered about it. The opposition included anti-Zionist ultra-orthodox Jews, communists, veterans of the Jewish Peace Alliances, Brit Shalom and Kedma Mizracha, and Jews who traded with Arabs and others who had Arab neighbors and friends. It is likely that among the many who refused to enlist in the Israeli army or shirked the first draft in August 1948,[11] quite a few did not agree with the goals of enlistment.

Jewish opposition rapidly dissolved, but Arab resistance remained intact. This resistance, within and without, along with the government's reluctance to complete the expulsion and proceed too fast and openly with the destruction project (which only few perceived as such) meant that none of the two other projects that had shaped the new regime and now became state projects could be completed. Nor were any of the goals that the regime had already achieved ensured. For the sake of stability and continuity, it had to persist in executing the state projects, which required the recruitment of a large number of citizens. Pre-state Zionist ideological narratives depicting the majoritarian and colonial projects as natural and inevitable were reiterated without accounting for the major change in power relations that had taken place in the meantime, while the destruction project was never acknowledged as such. Acts of expulsion, demolition, confiscation, and expropriation were denied or consciousness of them was repressed. If need arose, they were presented as a part of a necessary policy and a just war. Under such circumstances, a new project grew and established itself: the project of regime preservation.

Each of the three Israeli state projects contributed in some measure to filling the gap between the way in which the government treated the three groups it ruled and separated: Jewish citizens, Arab citizens subject to military rule, and the expelled Palestinians who became refugees. Being denied the right of return and unwilling or unable to integrate into their host countries they became a designated group whom the Jewish state refused to rule. However, this did not suffice. In order to preserve the regime, those Palestinians remaining in Israel had to be isolated from their brothers in the West Bank, Gaza Strip, and refugee camps, and excluded from sharing power in the ruling apparatus of the new state. The weak Jewish opposition that opposed the *étatisation* of the Jewish nation and the ethnic nationalization of the state apparatus—had to be further marginalized. While the 150,000 Palestinians who remained in Israel were placed under military government, many of the democratic practices and institutions of the Zionist movement were adopted by the state. However, this institutional shift had to be supplemented with ideological work to maintain its democratic nature. One had to forget the recent colonial past of the Zionist movement and stress the fate of the Jews during and after World War II as a nation of victims, refugees, and persecuted people, dismiss as irrelevant or illegitimate the Palestinian majority who opposed the creation of this regime, and establish the expulsion of Palestinians as an irreversible act.

The Jewish citizenry was quickly socialized into the logic and justifying narrative of the new regime by various means, ideological and coercive, aiming to turn them into willing partners and recruit them for various projects. The creation and establishment of a new political habitus that enabled the Jewish governed not to recognize the disaster that they as citizens—or their fellow Jewish citizens—had wrought upon non-Jews governed alongside them, past or present, was central. The violence inflicted on the Palestinian governed was presented as self-inflicted and their deportation as voluntary; Palestinian opposition to the Partition Plan was presented as a ground and reason, excuse, and justification for anything that had happened to Palestinians ever since November 1947—as though agreement to the Partition Plan had been the only logical political and moral option. The outcome of the disaster was alternately denied and justified, and the Jews' role in its creation was repressed. The devastation of European Jewry and the fact that Jewish survivors found refuge in the State of Israel served to justify not only the creation of a Jewish state but also the Palestinian disaster that went along with it, as though the new reality were an act of historical rectification, exonerating Israeli Jews from any responsibility for or link to the disaster they had caused.

The Palestinians' opposition to the new regime facilitated the presentation of them as an "exterior," an enemy threatening the integrity of the regime and the existence of the state (which were equated). The annihilation of Europe's Jews, the Arab forces from neighboring states joining the Palestinian side during the violent struggle that took place immediately after the founding of the state, and the threats made by Arab regimes against the "Zionist entity" all contributed to the construction of reality in terms of a war of survival imposed upon the Jews, a "no choice" war with no end in sight, in which every Jew was obliged to take part. Against this historical background, we must now look briefly at the three major Israeli state projects.

COLONIZATION AND MAJORITARIANISM

Formally, and from the state's point of view, Israel was established as a democracy and its citizens were granted equal rights. Ethnic cleansing in 1947–49 and Jewish immigration in the years that followed reduced the Palestinian population to less than 10 percent of the citizenry and made the contradiction between pronounced democratic principles and the Zionist claim of a Jewish nation-state somewhat less visible and more tolerable—for Israeli Jews, at least. Most of them considered Israel a democracy even as it prevented the Palestinians refugees from repatriating after the war, took over most of their land and property, and imposed severe restrictions on the movement and activities of the remaining Palestinian population during eighteen years of military government. The subjection of the Palestinian minority to martial law and the dispossession of those who became refugees were conceived of in terms of the inevitability of emergency law and justified as an exception to the legal system, which pretended not to undermine its democratic principles. Martial law also provided a pretext for the other state project at work throughout the country: a project of destruction that reshaped the landscape, erased such traces of Palestinian presence as still existed, separated Palestinians from Jews in the remaining mixed towns, and minimized opportunities for civil coexistence.

But in the early 1960s, new trends appeared in Israeli politics. Groups seeking liberalization of the economy and democratization of the regime were growing stronger. These aspired to a less centralist regime that would improve the standard of living, especially for the middle class, expand individual freedoms, and change the relation between the state projects for which the public was expected to exert itself. At the same time, more voices were heard struggling to end the military government of Palestinian citizens of Israel. National liberals, Zionist leftists, and Arab leaders joined in the struggle against the military government, which was in fact a separation regime imposing an inferior status upon Arab citizens and constituting a convenient platform for their ongoing dispossession. Martial law was repealed in December 1966. If the tendencies expressed by this change of policy had been carried on uninterruptedly and the territory and population under Israeli domination had not expanded after the war of June 1967, a steady process of democratization of the Israeli regime might conceivably have occurred. But the abolition of the military separation regime at the end of 1966 turned out to be a mere passing episode. The war in 1967 was the harbinger of a new separation regime—stable, stronger, and much less democratic.

The regime constituted in 1948 and the one that began consolidating after the occupation of the Territories in 1967 form a continuum, and they exhibit quite a few similarities. The main one is national separation and the identification of the political demos with the Jewish nation, while discriminating against and oppressing the Palestinians. But these similarities cannot blur the crucial structural differences between the two regimes, especially with regard to the containment and separation of the governed Palestinians and their exclusion from sharing power.

The regime of the "first Israeli republic" (1948–67) was shaped by the exclusion of Arabs from the land, from the public sphere, and from governing bodies, and by the expansion of Jews throughout the territory defined as Israeli. Reduced Palestinian presence was obtained by expelling and displacing hundreds of thousands of Palestinians, sealing the borders to prevent their return. At the same time, the rapid absorption and settlement of Jewish immigrants from the refugee camps in Europe and from all Arab countries helped to establish a clear Jewish majority. Under such conditions, the colonial project and the majoritarian project were congruent and mutually empowering. Most state apparatuses worked to promote these two projects, in which enormous resources were invested, and they were joined by numerous local initiatives.

The situation in June 1967 was radically different. The two projects—colonial and majoritarian—quickly adjusted themselves to the addition of vast territories and a large Palestinian population to Israel's domain of control, defined new arenas for action, and developed tools accordingly. In the first decade, the colonial project that turned to the new territories was reluctant, hesitant, and subject to dispute and contestation within Jewish political society. At the same time, a new, hardly disputed colonial initiative took place in the Galilee, whereby small Jewish localities were built adjacent to and topographically above Palestinian villages and towns. The settlement of the Galilee had an explicit majoritarian aim—it was officially defined as the "Judaization of the Galilee." Majority-minority relations in this part of the country were perceived as a national problem that required state intervention, and colonization provided a means to solve it.

The settlement project in the Occupied Territories, on the other hand, was torn between two approaches at the time. The first, shared by "left-wing" or "dovish" parties and exemplified in the "Alon Plan" to partition the West Bank between Israel and Jordan wished to promote the colonial project within the strictures of the majoritarian one and limit Jewish expansion to areas relatively free of Palestinian localities. The second, advocated by the so-called hawkish or right-wing parties and led by Gush Emunim, ignored or postponed the question of a Jewish majority and sought to obtain, not a Jewish majority, but rather a Jewish presence throughout the Occupied Territories.

The interplay between the two projects was framed and limited by the negation of three known modes of action. On the one hand, as Israeli society grew more liberal and the international community became less tolerant of mass expulsion of Palestinians from the Occupied Territories, this no longer seemed possible or desirable. On the other hand, the need to preserve a Jewish majority among the state's citizens had become an axiom accepted by most Israeli Jews, hence the option of naturalizing Palestinians as Israeli citizens was also ruled out. And in between these two negations, there was a third one that created the temporal framework both projects needed: withdrawal from the Territories was either precluded (by the Right) or postponed indefinitely (by the Left).

The direct result of this triple negation was that the Palestinians in the Occupied Territories had to be ruled as noncitizens. An essential structural tension and friction were thus interposed between the two projects, resulting in discrepancies that were usually blurred and made to be forgotten. The majoritarian project worked to keep Palestinians out and preserve the separation between interior and exterior (first in physical space, and then gradually and mainly in economic and juridical space); the colonial project expanded into what had been defined as exterior, risking the Jewish majority in some areas, while trying to interiorize others so as not to jeopardize the Jewish majority.[12] As the latter approach gained ground, and in view of the new demographic reality and the frequent interaction of Jews and Palestinians in various spheres, above all in the economy, maintaining a Jewish majority became no longer merely a quantitative matter but a qualitative one as well. In various situations, whether in employment or trade, real estate or services, the Palestinians—devoid of rights—were not permitted to organize, could not demand their rights, and were kept subaltern in order to preserve Jewish supremacy in every field of interaction.

Aliya, that is, fostering and absorbing Jewish immigration to Palestine/Israel has always been conceived of as the major, most decisive instrument of the majoritarian project. But before the disintegration of the Soviet Bloc, only a few visionaries believed that this project could cope with the significant de-mographic shift created by the war of 1967. The Zionist Left has always seen this shift as a strong argument against annexation of the Territories, and against Jewish expansion into densely populated Palestinian areas in general. In the early 1990s, the demographic balance shifted once again because of Russian im-migration. But in the late 1990s, and especially after the collapse of the negotia-tions under the Oslo Accords, something else changed: the nonpartner dogma gained ground, mainstream Israelis realized that "the conflict" was not going anywhere and that Israeli rule in the Territories was not going to end in the foreseeable future. Forceful naturalization of Palestinian noncitizens seemed out of the question, and a clear Jewish majority *not only in Israel proper but rather in the Territories* seemed crucial for maintaining the image of Israel as both Jewish and democratic.

This is the context for understanding the "disengagement" plan: about a dozen settlements and fifteen thousand settlers in the Gaza Strip were sacri-ficed in order to erase one and a half million Palestinians from the census, thus gaining a clearer Jewish majority in the rest of the land (along with some other political benefits in the international arena). As a mode of operation, disen-gagement has been very different from absorbing Jewish immigration, but the two are part and parcel of the same majoritarian project. The "disengagement" was an ingenious plan, because it allowed Israel to maintain its grip on Gaza and, at the same time, stage a separation between the population and the terri-tory that rids Israel of its responsibilities to the Palestinian population. It could be achieved, however, only at the expense of the colonial project.

As we have seen, the majoritarian project has often required that certain re-strictions be imposed upon the expansionist drive of the colonizing forces. The colonial project seeks to establish a Jewish presence in every bit of the land. The majoritarian project concerns population growth and decline and it takes geography into account when whole regions are about to lose their clearly Jew-ish majority (as happened in the Galilee, in the Jerusalem region, and in some other mixed cities inside the 1949 borders). The majoritarian project is also compatible with respect for individual human rights, but opposes the rights of Palestinians as a national group. For the Jewish colonial project, on the other hand, respect for human rights that restricts dispossession and forbids trans-fer of non-Jews is simply an obstacle, to be removed whenever possible. At the same time, the colonial project may be compatible with national rights—as long as these are respected within areas designated strictly for Palestinians.

After 1967, the creation of two systems of government generated a certain division of labor between an unruly colonial project, which only external pressure could restrain, and a more civilized colonization that takes place as part of the routine work of state apparatuses dealing with planning, housing, and population growth. The colonial project in the Territories was imposed by the military, to which it has never ceased assigning new tasks, heeding the colonists' new whims of adventure. This mode of expansion has inscribed the national separation in space. However, at the same time, it has never stopped creating more and more zones of Palestinian resistance and friction between Jews and Palestinians, thus requiring ever-new means of separation to avoid the harmful effects of such friction.

The majoritarian and colonial projects each have their own ways of articulating the split of the Israeli regime into two distinct systems of government: civil and military. They use, reaffirm, and reproduce the matrix of separation differently, respecting or ignoring the three types of separation in distinct ways, which may be used to characterize their basic modes of operation. Where separation and friction unfold differently within the different state projects is also where they most visibly clash or collaborate.

DESTRUCTION

Part of the violence exercised in the late 1940s took shape as a project of destruction and gained momentum with the advance of Jewish forces. Tens of thousands of Palestinian houses were destroyed in five hundred towns and villages during and right after the ethnic cleansing of 1948–49, and numerous others were destroyed in later land confiscation in the years prior to June 1967.[13] The destruction that usually took place after the displacement of the Palestinian inhabitants was meant mainly to create a new geopolitical landscape from which all traces of Arab presence had been erased. The new landscape was also supposed to support the Jewish claim to the land, while making the Palestinians aliens to it, whether without or within.

From 1967 on, the destruction project was no longer directed at "empty" villages and "abandoned" houses but rather at inhabited ones. Instead of being meant only to resettle Jews or change the landscape, destruction became a means of clearing thoroughfares in the refugee camps, punishing suspects of resistance, and undoing "illegal construction." Unlike the efforts seen within Israel proper to erase traces of the destruction and restore the scarred landscape, in nearly every episode of destruction in the Occupied Territories, restoration has been prevented and the rubble remains for a long period of time, bearing witness to the relations of control. Destruction has turned into a device for subduing resistance and controlling the Palestinian population, justified ad hoc, respective of local circumstances. These entail similar techniques and tools (bulldozers, explosives, bombs) but reflect different policies and are integrated into separate modes of operation. Understanding the destruction according to the way it is framed, represented, and justified by the ruling apparatus, however, misses the cumulative effect of repeated acts of destruction—keeping the Palestinians temporary residents in their own land, residents who have no private space to shelter in, and whose public space is spotted with ruins that proclaim and document the temporariness of their lives. This effect becomes clear when one realizes that house destruction has been an ongoing project since 1967: 24,813 Palestinian homes had been demolished up to July 2010.[14]

Destruction has continued within the Green Line as well, usually under the pretext of undoing "illegal construction." As a *policy*, it has been used differently when targeting Palestinian citizens and noncitizens in Gaza, the West Bank, East Jerusalem, and the Negev. A clear correlation can be seen here between the civil status of the victims, or lack of it, exposure to the threat of destruction, and the number of houses actually destroyed. As a *mode of operation*, it is not the last resort, not even within Israel proper, but it is a relatively available one, incorporating humanitarian concerns for those affected by the destruction's collateral damage, while ignoring the basic human rights of the direct victims. As a *means* it is used irrationally: manpower and tools invested in destruction are not related to any profitable production, while property and landscape are destroyed and treated as purely dispensable and superfluous; the very decision to destroy turns them into waste. The real effect of destruction is hardly ever accounted for: the ongoing destruction has enabled the change of landscape and the production of a physical reality that has suited the hegemonic historical narrative and sowed blindness to the Palestinian presence in the country. This is an embedded blindness in Jewish citizens, passed on from generation to generation. It does not enable one to see Palestinians as victims of a regime-made disaster; it makes the Palestinian demand to return groundless and proof of their intention "to destroy Israel." Ongoing destruction helps present the Palestinians as foreigners on their land, a minority in the Jewish homeland, temporary stateless refugees.

THE LIBERAL PROJECT

The colonial project did not go uncontested. As early as the late 1950s, Jews and Palestinians called for political liberalization in order to grant full political rights to the minority of Palestinians who had not been expelled. When the military government was abolished in 1966, there was a degree of political and economic liberalization and democratization, which continued at least till the Second Intifada in October 2000.

The liberal project has two separate but intertwined channels: economic and judicial-political. The liberal economic project began with opening the labor market to unorganized, rightless Palestinian labor. The capital market gradually fell in with the labor market and liberal tendencies have turned neoliberal. The outset of the liberal political project could already be detected in the late 1950s, in the struggle to abolish the military government; it peaked in the basic laws passed in the early 1990s, as interpreted by the Supreme Court, under the leadership of its president, Aharon Barak. This "judicial revolution" served as the basis for "lawfare" by various civil organizations on behalf of Palestinians in Israel and in the Occupied Territories. In spite of a few triumphs, however, it had no effect on the principles of separation of Jews and Arabs, and of citizens and noncitizens.

The two liberal projects, then, had a clear limit: they never doubted the Jewish monopoly on the state apparatus and the inclusive exclusion of Palestinians in the Occupied Territories. Thus, for example, the incorporation of Palestinian labor into the Israeli economy would not have been possible had it implied recognition of Palestinian workers' rights, including the right to unionize. Conflicts that broke out, especially between judicial liberalization and the majoritarian and colonial projects, were always managed within this framework. The liberal trends could disrupt or delay these projects, but they could not change their course. Various interventions by the Supreme Court might be mentioned here, mostly grounded in the new basic laws: a ruling concerning the acceptance of Palestinian citizens as residents in Jewish communities, a ruling about the status of Arabic as an official language, the intervention of the court to abolish discrimination in education of the Arab sector, and interventions of the Supreme Court in matters of violated human rights in the Occupied Territories. In many of the cases, the government managed to circumvent the rulings of the Supreme Court, delay their implementation, or sabotage them. Such failures and partial, mostly ephemeral, successes have been common in the liberal political project, whether before reaching the court, during the hearing, or following court rulings.

The politics of the Israeli economy became explicitly neoliberal at the time of the Oslo Accords, and neoliberal market forces played a full part in the redeployment of the ruling apparatus in the Territories and the privatization of some of its branches.[15] Most of the economic elite supported the Rabin government and were directly and indirectly involved in the peace talks and the implementation of the agreements. However, officials in the military and security apparatuses took senior positions in big corporations soon after their retirement. The prospect of new spaces in the region soon to be opened to Israeli corporations was part and parcel of the peace rhetoric at the time. Within this framework, industrial zones were created at the border crossings from Israel into the territory of the Palestinian Authority. These enabled Israeli capitalists to employ cheap Palestinian labor without letting Palestinians back into Israel proper. Israelis also played mediating roles in raising foreign money for the Palestinian Authority and the mushrooming NGOs working in the Territories. With the collapse of the Oslo Accords and the consolidation of the separation policy in the Occupied Territories, the same economic forces enabled the removal of Palestinians from the labor market and flooded it with foreign workers. Israel's integration into the globalized neoliberal economy also contributed to the flourishing of security and hi-tech industries that used (and are still using) the Occupied Territories as a laboratory for developing new tools of monitoring, surveillance, and interception, making Israeli companies a strong player in a growing international market of security devices.[16]

Hence, while Jewish colonization squarely contradicts judicial-political liberalism, it has both been quite nicely served by economic liberalization and neoliberalism and served them well. The liberal political project has become the business of a shrinking minority of politicians, lawyers, and human rights activists, and its main stronghold in the state apparatus has been the Supreme Court. This has been a very weak stronghold, because the court has fully accepted the separation between citizens and noncitizens, ignored some of the basic rules of the Geneva Convention regarding the protection of populations in occupied territories, and too easily accepted claims made by the security forces. The court has hardly ever contested the rule of the military government and the wisdom of its security experts, and has never confronted the basic question of the legality of the Jewish settlements in the Territories.

Within Israel proper, the liberal project supports those aspects of the regime limiting and constraining the majoritarian project, but without contesting the Jewish monopoly on governance and usually without proposing a clear response to the demonizing rhetoric of the "demographic threat." The collapse of the Oslo process in summer 2000, the Second Intifada, and the overall transformation of the international arena following 9/11 further weakened the forces engaged in the promotion of judicial liberalism and made them politically superfluous. After a brief opening, the government has been closed to Palestinian participation again, and the very demand to share this power has been interpreted as an existential threat.

However, the novelty of recent years does not lie in this exclusion but in the outspoken acceptance of the discriminatory dimension inherent in the Zionist project as a whole. More and more Jews are now ready to adopt racist discourse, demand constitutional institutionalization of discrimination against non-Jews, struggle to reestablish separation lines in places where they have been blurred, and try to shackle the Supreme Court in its discussion of the status of Palestinian citizens. At the same time, fewer Jews are ready to stand by their fellow Palestinians, and the space open for their political action constantly diminishes.

However, weakened though they are, the liberal forces are still active, liberal and democratic elements are still inscribed in Israeli law and Israel's political system, and the Israeli regime's need to brand itself as a democratic state has not vanished altogether. Most important, the regime in Israel proper is still distinctly different from that in the Occupied Territories. This difference exists in spite of the ethnocratic and racist processes taking place in Israel itself, and the strengthening majoritarian project west of the Green Line has not erased it.

PERPETUAL SEPARATIONS

All state projects are shaped by the major lines of separation that constitute the Israeli regime, while transforming and reproducing them in their own way. From the outset, the Occupation was a regime of separation in which the excluded part is contained and included as excluded. Everything separated remains inside; nothing is totally removed, distanced, or annihilated. Separation is dynamic, ongoing, and continuous, and its lines constantly change with respect to their geographic route, to their place in a three-dimensional social space, to their object (what is separated from what, who from whom, who from what), and to their relative weight. Since the 1990s, general closure and later the erection of the separation wall came to be presented as a part of the government's attempt to establish separation *in* the territories without really separating *from* the territories. However, separation as a framework of justification is but one element in separation as major mode of operation of the ruling apparatus. The symbolic proof of the fact that separation as such has never been the goal of the Occupation regime is the wall itself, separation's most visible icon, a gigantic instrument that has never been completed. Since contact is necessary for subjection, and the excluded Palestinians are also included in the regime that rules them as noncitizens, separation has become a perpetual movement that can never achieve its end and come to a full stop without causing the whole regime to collapse. The separation movement, which has never ceased to create friction and subjection, reproduces a regime that needs the perpetual regeneration of the work of separation.

Most Israelis (Jews and Palestinian alike) do not at all recognize the Occupation as a separate regime, and do not know "the other side of the moon," inasmuch as they certainly do not see themselves as subjected to this regime. Still, at least four groups of Israelis are subjugated at one and the same time to the two different regimes, move freely between them, and take part in both: settlers, employees of private companies providing services to the Occupation regime, administration officials, and soldiers who serve in the Occupied Territories, along with their families. The citizenship of these in Israel proper constitutes an extension of the military regime at the heart of the civilian regime that presents itself as a democracy. There is also an extension running in the opposite direction, of the civilian regime into the heart of the military regime: most of the actions taken by the ruling apparatus are legally authorized according to the rules of a democratically elected government, they are all subject to judicial scrutiny, and they are considered legitimate by a large majority of the citizenry.

We may now discern the invisible glue that enables the two parts of the doubled regime to be connected and prevents the duality from becoming a total split: this glue is the democratic image of the civilian regime in Israel proper. Everyone understands that Israel can be a democracy only if the Occupation is indeed temporary and external, but in fact, the inverse is no less true: most Israeli Jews still assume or wish to believe that Israel is a democracy and hence accept the Occupation as a form of rule that is declared to be both temporary and external. Those less concerned with the democratic image or real features of their regime—whose numbers have been rapidly growing of late—are more willing to give up both the externality and the temporality of the Occupation and accept their regime for what it is, a regime of separation. They would not admit that separation means apartheid, of course—they simply understand it as a necessary condition for having "a Jewish state." On this both "democrats" and those indifferent to democracy agree: the state is and must remain a Jewish one, and it matters little what the state does to render invisible the large non-Jewish population subjected to its rule. This is the state they are willing to serve and die for.

8 CIVIL RECRUITMENT

To summarize, we have argued that the ruling apparatus in the Occupied Territories is a separate military regime that coexists alongside the civil regime in Israel proper. The two regimes are nonetheless actually part of the same political system. They are not only linked but extend into each other. How does this connection that duplicates the Israeli regime work, then, splitting it into two halves, preventing their detachment from each other in spite of their separation, while at the same time blocking a full breach of the borders between them, even though each regime has emissaries present and active within the other? How is it possible to maintain an oppressive military regime whose ruling apparatus denies millions of people their freedom and rights, while free citizens, anxious for their rights, democratically elect the ruling power responsible for this occupation and enlist to defend it?

There is a ready answer to this question: the citizens of the civil regime participate in the Occupation because it is perceived as a national mission destined first and foremost to protect them. They believe the Occupation persists because of what they call terrorism and the obstinacy of the Palestinian leadership in rejecting Israel's generous peace offers. Israelis have no choice but to continue ruling the Territories by force so that armed Palestinian resistance will not shift from the Occupied Territories into Israel proper and make it a living hell. Reacting to this ready regurgitated answer, critics ask whether terrorism indeed perpetuates Occupation, or whether it is not rather the institutionalization of the Occupation that has intensified Palestinian resistance and generated terrorism, which one must fight regardless of one's view of the Occupation. Critics also point to the role of colonization in the continuation of the Occupation and the grooming of Palestinian terrorism and refuse to accept the absence of political agreement as a ground for both expanding the colonies and shirking responsibility for the well-being of Palestinians.

But such discussion misses the question we pose. The question is not about the linkage of motives and ideology to action (from quiet support to active participation in the ruling apparatus), but rather about the conditions that enable the existence of this hybrid—their coexistence—under a single governing power: two such vastly different forms of governance whose principles are mutually contradictory, and in the past each of which was often born of the ruins of the other. This chapter explores several ideological and political mechanisms responsible for the hybrid structure of the Israeli regime.

THE INVISIBLE REGIME

Occupation of the Palestinian territories in June 1967 was experienced by most Israelis as a whirlwind drama, and by many as a religious epiphany, even the harbinger of redemption, but the emergence of the new Israeli regime was slow and hardly noticeable. In the late 1960s, the *state* of occupation became a state *project*. In the 1970s, its scope grew considerably. Sometime in the early 1980s, the project was consolidated into a new *regime*, distinct but not entirely separate from the ethno-democratic regime that had persisted until June 1967.

When this distinct-but-not-separate regime appeared, the Israeli regime was doubled, its two faces attached to each other, Janus-like. Palestinian noncitizenship was *attached* to Israeli citizenship, and the Occupied Territories—their legal status left undetermined—were attached to sovereign Israeli space, which had already received international recognition (except for the status of Jerusalem). The spatial and civil separation of governing and governed discussed above help *separate the government in Israel from the ruling apparatus in the Occupied Territories*, isolate the former and emphasize its democratic features, while blurring and justifying the tyrannical features of the latter. By the same measure, the Palestinian governed are also separated from *the governing power that rules them*, while their participation in it—marginal and restricted as it may be—is denied. Together, these divisions and separations retain the image of the governing power as Jewish and the image of the Israeli regime as democratic. Each of these separations limits the integrity of the other and charges a high price to maintain it. No separation is fully realized, and the gap thus created produces chronic instability and a task that can never be fully accomplished.

These divisions are now integrated as components in a form of domination that has become its own end, the perpetuation of ruling by *inclusive separation*. However, each division is usually represented and conceived of without accounting for its systemic role, and is discussed and justified with respect to specific strategic objectives that it allegedly serves, such as preserving security, assuring the continuity of Jewish settlement, securing Israel's water reserves, and so on. These aims are presented as if they were consensual (among Jews, of course), and the use of separations as means for their implementation is almost indisputably accepted as within the authority of the government or the army. Indeed, in Israeli public discourse there is hardly any dispute with respect to these separations.

As strategic objectives, the principles of separation are explicitly formulated and discussed. But the form of control in which they play a systemic role goes unnoticed; its perpetuation is no one's goal, and no political party has turned it into a cause for struggle. Ruling Palestinians as noncitizens, imposing spatial divisions so as to block and monitor their movement or to create and protect "clean" Jewish areas are presented as things one prefers not to do, but must do nevertheless, as if by some force majeure. The principles of separation are accepted in public discourse in Israel as a kind of law of nature, a decree of fate, or at best, a kind of compromise imposed on the State of Israel by the actual presence of Palestinians who insist on staying and dare resist Israeli rule. But the Palestinians do stay and have turned this steadfastness into an ethos (*sumud*); geopolitical conditions make their expulsion an unrealistic mission, and the national (or ethnocratic) definition of the regime rules out their naturalization. Still, the principles of civil and spatial separation are not presented as a solution of the "Palestinian problem" or a way to end the Occupation, but rather as an efficient way to "manage the conflict." However, accepting the fact that this management—essentially temporary—will last into the foreseeable future also means accepting (without admitting it, of course) the fact that the means have become structural conditions.

The two principles of separation are seen as legitimate, not because they are conceived of as a solution, but precisely because no foreseeable solution appears, and they are presented as a substitute for a solution—a means to manage the conflict and ensure strategic objectives. Recognizing the temporality of the form of control in the Territories and refraining from a decision about their final status directly contribute to the misrecognition and legitimacy of Israel's dual regime. In other words, in order to gain legitimacy, the form of control must be presented as a strategy of the governing power, and its temporariness must be manifest and grounded in the various governing arrangements. This manifest temporariness, expressed in endless diplomatic talks as much as in numerous changes in the Occupation regime's regulations, is one of the dimensions of the regime. This presumed temporariness plays a significant role in the political sphere of the civil regime. Since the policies at work for securing the perpetuation of the dual structure of the Israeli regime are presented as strategies for conflict management during an interim period, their unilateral dimension is hardly ever contested.

This, then, is how the Occupation regime is introduced and discussed in Israeli public discourse: as a temporary, misrecognized form of control whose unilateral imposition on its Palestinian subjects is legitimate almost a priori. In this context, the Occupation regime is a project that can be broken down into a series of strategic decisions. Ruling the Territories by force is a necessary aspect of this project, a mission that citizens serving in the army are called upon to carry out from time to time, in collaboration with a small group of government functionaries and devoted settlers by the tens of thousands. Those who, more or less willingly, take part in this mission see themselves as working for Israel's security, not for the perpetuation of its regime. As a form of control and a sui generis system of government, the Occupation remains almost invisible.

ISRAELI JEWISH CIVIL HABITUS

Most Israeli Jews continue to regard their country as a democratic one, in which almost every resident is a citizen and all citizens enjoy equal civil status. They do not think of Israel's regime in terms of almost half a century of ruling the Occupied Territories. The policies that maintain and reproduce this regime are considered as legitimate and authorized democratically. This blind understanding is the only dimension of the civil separation that is almost impeccably concurrent with the spatial division, regardless of where it is delineated. Israelis, both "here" and "there," grasp the governing power exercised in their own habitat as "their own" and as separate from the means of control applied in the Occupied Territories. In their habitat, they expect to be ruled by law, as citizens for whom the transition from withheld to eruptive violence is authorized and regulated by the law and executed by a ruling apparatus accountable to and checked by the legislature and judiciary. Many of these citizens take their citizenship seriously, even employing highly developed civil tools and skills, and they protest in various ways when they detect a change or violation of the rule of law, or of the principles of separating the different au-thorities. However, they take for granted the absolute lack of such conditions under the Occupation regime.

Under the Occupation regime, violence erupts in an irregular manner and inflicts harm and humiliation when withheld. The ruling apparatus is not ac-countable to the legislature and is hardly ever checked by the judiciary; as re-gards Palestinian subjects, for all practical purposes, this apparatus at one and the same time legislates, executes, and judicially supervises its own actions. The regime thus maintained is not operated by aliens (although the government has tended to outsource some of its functions of late), but by citizens of the State of Israel.[1] When they cross the separation line between "their" regime and the other, they see no wrong in this mode of operation. The only place, then, where full and stable concurrence is found in the civil and spatial divisions is in the consciousness of Israeli citizens. The citizens of democratic Israel's political habitus, in Bourdieu's sense of the term,[2] are therefore an arm of the Occupa-tion and a key factor in understanding the Israeli regime.

Political habitus is the cluster of skills, tendencies, and expectations that makes possible the transformation of citizenship from a legal category with po-litical significance into a code of relations with the various branches of govern-ment, as well as with other citizens and noncitizens—a code for living together with others who are subject to the same government. When political habitus is (ethnically) nationalized and the nation is perceived in ethnic and partisan terms, the code of civil relations is dictated by the basic division into "our" na-tionals and other nationals, and basic civil—and universal—companionship is incurably impaired.

Civil habitus in Israel has been thoroughly nationalized. One's political habitus is largely acquired through socialization into military service, which is almost exclusively Jewish, and through the presence of military life and prepa-ration for it within the family, peer group, and school.[3] Despite the liberaliza-tion of civil society since the 1980s, Israeli Jewish and Israeli Palestinian civil society are profoundly separate. The few binational civil frameworks that do exist deal mainly with structural discrimination against Palestinian citizens. When citizens concern themselves with improving education in the school system, urban bicycle tracks, and green spaces, they usually do so in their own national grouping, replicating the separation of Jewish and non-Jewish citi-zens. Thus the basic solidarity of all those governed as citizens is gravely im-paired and almost any opposition to the government is usually carried as if it concerns only one national group, no matter how universal the matter at stake may be.

To the above should be added explicit ideological mechanisms. The Israeli educational system denies young citizens elementary historical and geopolitical knowledge, nurtures forgetting and ignorance, and disseminates falsehoods. Whole chapters in the history and culture of the Jews that do not coincide with the Zionist meta-narrative are excluded from school curricula. The narrative of the founding of the State of Israel does not, for example, include the Nakba—the expulsion of the Palestinians, making them refugees. To the extent that it is known at all, the fact that refugee status is a central characteristic of the national existence of the Palestinians—including the internally displaced in Israel proper—is seen as a natural aspect of Palestinians' being in the world. Israel's contributions to the failure of various peace initiatives from the 1950s down to the present are not mentioned. The Green Line has been erased from maps and from Israelis' consciousness, and the scope of the jurisdiction in which Israeli law applies is unknown to the public. The state, its regime, and often its government too, are treated as one and the same and are presented simply as concurrent with "the people [*am*] of Israel," a term that could have been used ambiguously, as referring to the entire Israeli demos but almost always refers to the Jewish nation alone. Civil disobedience is presented as treason, and refusal to do one's military duty in the Occupation forces is regarded as a direct threat to Israeli democracy.

The common denominator of all these forms of denying knowledge and nurturing ignorance is the effort to separate the citizenry (the civil nation) from the ethnic nation, drawing the image of the nation along the precepts of the Zionist narrative and blurring the difference between recruiting citizens for the government, the state, and the nation. The state apparatuses in Israel proper nationalize citizenship and systematically impair the development of civil habitus. They disrupt the citizens' orientation in their own life-world, limit their ability to perceive and conceptualize the political and social problems they share as citizens, their ability to weigh various modes of action and select them in an informed manner. Geography, history, architecture, archaeology, urban planning, culture, and literature are permanently recruited to help Jewish Israeli citizens forget or disregard what Jewish citizens *do to others* in the name of the State of Israel. Various practices that enhance ignorance such as restricting access to information, closing certain archives and limiting access to selected documents in others, erasing traces of localities and buildings—are all permanent fixtures in civil everyday life.[4] And they are not necessarily dictated or orchestrated by any authority. The clerk at the mapping center knows that he must cut away the Green Line from the old maps in his storeroom before handing them to a citizen; the tour guide knows how to tell the story of the ruin in front of which he stands, attributing it to Jewish history without mentioning the Arab village that existed at this very spot until merely a few decades ago; the selector at the airport knows whom he must question and further delay, regardless of the formal protocol; the official at the Ministry of the Interior knows he may harass the Palestinian facing him, asking for documents not required of Jews. Wherever one encounters the shadow of a Palestinian presence, in person, documents, or ruins, one might encounter similar practices of denial, repression, and discrimination.

Especially important are the denial of the Nakba (as if Palestinians are simply born refugees) and the erasure of the Green Line (making "the Territories" abstract and geographically flexible). Citizens are thus prevented from understanding the fact and significance of their own participation in a regime of inclusive and oppressive separation, and their perception of this participation as a "contribution to society" is made all the more comfortable. When civil habitus is thus recruited for the sake of the ethnic nation, *part of the governed represent the nation and the governing power instead of the governing power representing all of the governed*. Those Israeli citizens, a tiny minority, who are committed to the nation of citizens and see the state as accountable for the welfare of all are regarded as radical and often portrayed as "Israel haters."

(NON)ALIEN GOVERNMENT

The conception of the nation-state commonplace in Israeli public discourse assumes the existence of an ethnic nation as a defined political entity that has a right to self-determination. From the ethnic-national perspective, the state and its government are the nation's means to fulfill its self-determination. The state is the fullest expression of the nation's self-determination, and each of its apparatuses is supposed to serve the interests of the nation, its aspirations and vocation.[5] The nation is constructed as preceding the state, logically as well as spatially and temporally. The state is perceived as a stage in the nation's history. The state's territory is a contingent effect of the state's weakness or strength. It is the nation that should dictate its "natural" or "historical" borders, desirable demography, and the rules for joining the body politic to its state. The nation, not the state, is the whole that binds together the government and the governed subjected to it, contains their contradictions, and reconciles social divisions of all kinds. The nation's narratives and political imagination, replete as they are with blood and destiny, religious motifs and rhetoric, are interwoven into family life, private and collective memories, and the upbringing of individuals. The nation calls upon each and every one of its members to rise above utilitarian considerations—to the extent, even, of sacrificing his or her own life; it has immense power to mobilize individuals and recruit them for the national cause.

However, some important facts are missing from this nationalist conception of the nation, for which the state becomes a tool of self-realization. Missing is the state's immense contribution to constructing the nation as an ethnic group, as what frames the state's historical narrative, and determines the boundaries of its body politic. Missing also is the recognition of the role of various ruling apparatuses in teaching nationalism in the home and at school, at the workplace and in the army. For the state constructs nationhood in various ways, which are not merely "ideological," through legislation, censuses, naturalization laws, and exclusions.

The relation between nationhood and state, like the relation between sex and gender, is a result of historical construction whereby the "natural" component, too, as it were, owes its separate existence to apparatuses of cultural construction. Thus constructed, nationhood is a recruiting mechanism operated by state ruling apparatuses to ensure the obedience, partnership, and loyalty of members of the nation to the state's government. Since this nationhood is ethnic and many of the state's citizens and governed subjects do not belong to it, national mobilization means recruiting members of one governed group to support the government and regime that separate them from other groups, establishing and justifying the hierarchy that ranks them. When ethnic nationhood becomes state religion, the real competition is not between the nation and the state but rather between the nation and the citizenry. This is a competition between two separate discourses of citizenship and, more than that, between two types of political habitus. The first of these is *civil*, whereby the state and its government draw their legitimacy from the entire governed demos, the association of citizens; the primary civil commitment is to this civil association, and commitment to the state and its government is derived from that civil commitment. The second habitus is ethnic-*national*, whereby the state draws its legitimacy from expressing the self-determination of an ethnic nation, and the primary commitment is to that nation.

One decisive difference between a civil and an ethnic-national political habitus is the extent of the ruling power's alienation. No matter how republican a state becomes, civil habitus leaves a certain distance and alienation between the ruling power and the citizens. The government is supposed to present its justifications to the citizenry, receive its authority from it, and renew its authority by force of the agreement vested in it by the citizens. And vice versa: where distance remains, governing power appears alien, intrusive, and interfering. While there is still enough space for political action, civil solidarity flourishes, and citizens mobilize to curb the government and limit it, to reshape it. In a democratic civil body politic whose members see themselves as the source of the government's authority, this authority is always conditioned and alienated to a certain degree, and this alienation cannot be totally eliminated. Alienation may take on more or less refined forms. The government may appear more or less citizen-friendly. It may reduce or increase the oppressive friction between subjects and rule, softening or intensifying the fact of being governed and the feeling of being "ruled by an other." However, that feeling never really disappears. It is, in fact, an expression and a guarantee of the citizens' liberties vis-à-vis the power that rules them.

National habitus functions differently. The government is supposed to be the ultimate expression, driving force, and guardian of a national project that stems from a collective entity that both precedes this power and exceeds it. Ethno-national political habitus is about taking part in the nation, not the citizenry, and the ultimate way to do this is by taking part in the government that embodies it. Rising to the call of power, taking a position in government, serving in the military, violating basic human rights, or persecuting a national minority may all be perceived as ways of partaking in the national project. Hence, to the extent that democratic institutions introduce a certain sense of alienation with regard to the ruling power, they are perceived as obstacles to the national project and the functioning of the government, limiting the agenda of the Jewish nationalist forces in any Israeli government.

The British Mandate to rule Palestine ended in May 1948. The Jews celebrated as though they had single-handedly freed themselves of alien rule. For the Palestinians who survived the Nakba and were made Israeli citizens shortly thereafter,[6] the founding of the Jewish state was simply a transition from one alien rule to another. The integration of Arab citizens into the political community was limited and partial. They had the privilege of voting for the Knesset but were subject to martial law and close surveillance by the General Security

Services, which largely diminished their ability to organize, take political action, or participate in the discussion of the way they were governed. Their presence in the political sphere was perceived from the outset as a disturbance to be treated by nonpolitical means. Their concentration within reduced living areas and the restriction of their movement outside and among these areas removed them—at least for a while—from public space and made them subjects of governance by special state apparatuses (in the Ministry of Defense, the Military Government, the General Security Services, the Office of the Prime Minister's Adviser on Arab Matters, or the Ministry of Minorities).[7]

Until the mid-1990s, Arabs were never an explicit category in Israeli law. Their "treatment" was not a part of the government's overt policy; rather, it remained the business of the state's security system. Jewish citizens were expected to agree tacitly to this kind of treatment of their Arab fellow citizens. They were supposed to accept that a whole group of citizens posed a "security threat" and could therefore not be partner to the general public space, but had to be "treated" in supervised spaces, in a different manner than the rest of the state's citizens. This treatment was meted out covertly, behind the screen created by the military government, but its existence was an open secret. Even those not partaking in it were in the know. Knowledge of the "security" secret vested Jewish citizens with a sense of partaking in the government, as well as orientation in its clandestine affairs, even when they had no official position. This made it an effective tool for erasing the alienation of the government and its presentation as Jewish self-rule. An alliance was thus struck between Israel's government and its Jewish citizens in the context of the urgency and secrecy of "security matters." Jewish citizens became responsible for not forgetting that *other* citizens who were a potential danger lived among them. They were to stand guard, warn of danger, confront it, and, when necessary, act in the name of the government.

Since then, long after the dismantling of the military government in 1966, and even after the Palestinian citizens' civil status and economic condition largely improved, their alienation and exclusion from the ruling power have been basic aspects of it. This exclusion has been enacted time and again in the name of security, which has always been used to win the support or acquiescence of Jewish citizens and reduce their own alienation from the ruling power. The existence of their alliance with the government depends on distancing Israel's Arab citizens from "sensitive areas" and intensifying the government's alienation in their regard.

Taking part in "the security matter" or "the national matter" almost always means taking part in excluding Arabs—and vice versa. When it comes to Arabs, Jewish citizens soon enough see themselves as a part of the ruling power and stand in solidarity with one another; when they participate in the government's actions—in the army, public administration, or as appointed or voluntary representatives of Israel abroad—they are readily socialized to take part in this exclusion.[8] Nowhere is this more obvious than at points of "security inspections." It is obvious to one and all that Palestinians are the ones sought out, or Arabs, or Muslims; in any case, not Jews. Jews are not suspect. Everyone knows that it is permissible, and at times a must, to search for suspects everywhere. Until the Oslo Accords were implemented, as long as Palestinians living in the Territories could still move relatively freely within the Green Line, the ruling apparatus glided into Israel proper in their footsteps and attempted to supervise their movement. But this could not possibly suffice, because once in a while, Palestinians carried out deadly attacks in Israel's city streets, cafes, and cinemas. Security guards were therefore placed at public sites, as well as in private assemblies involving large audiences. When suicide bombings began, the number of security guards grew accordingly, and a huge security apparatus was set up within the Green Line. Suspect Palestinians are sought after, but the public at large has to be stopped, bags and trunks of cars opened, and personal effects x-rayed. Conversation has to be struck up to detect accents. As suspicion grows, IDs are demanded. When a Palestinian from the Occupied Territories is encountered, passage permits are demanded and a more meticulous inspection follows. Sometimes the waiting lines stretch long and everyone's time is consumed. And still, nearly always, nearly everyone cooperates.

The security apparatus created a new arena for the governing power to invade everyday life and endless opportunities for daily friction between Israeli citizens and the representatives of power. This friction is usually accepted with understanding on the part of most citizens, who have grown used to daily rites of passage at the entrance to any institution and public site. The body willingly concedes, the bag is opened and mechanically handed over to the guard, as its owner continues a cell-phone conversation or a chat with the neighbor in line, making the guard invisible. When things are calm, the threat is remote, but the governing power is always near.

People are not obedient participants in these rites because they believe in the government's idea of security. On the contrary: most believe because they have grown accustomed to reassure the guards at the gates—in gesture or

speech—that they are not Arabs, and that they have become used to the inevitable light search of their clothes and belongings. Any guard placed at a gate
creates a site displaying and reproducing separation. Every "security inspection" or simulation thereof is a small popular show in which citizens take part
in the act of separation. They agree to it and provide it with one side of the two
that must be separated. Clearly, Arab citizens cannot participate in this ritual
in the same manner, for they are always suspects, or at least potential suspects.
It makes no difference that Arab citizens might be injured by such an attack
(and already have been) just like Jews, and that Jews too committed violent attacks, and not only against Arabs. And yet Jews are not suspected of terrorism,
but perceived strictly as its victims.

The nationalized security apparatus thus deprives Israeli citizens of the right
to equal governance. Identifying the security issue with the national one is absolute. More than any other factor, this accounts for the identification of most
Jewish Israeli citizens with their ruling power—many of them behave as though
they own it, in fact—and for the almost complete lack of civil solidarity across
the national divide. It is in the interest of the government to keep identifying matters of security with the well-being of the Jewish nation, preserving the
principle of national separation and using it in order to undermine the very
possibility of a civil body politic. This separation has recently been re-created
under circumstances whereby certain political and legal differences between the
two groups are eroded, largely in response to the strengthening of the civil habitus of the Arab citizens, who are increasingly making political demands to reinforce their citizenship and implement their rights.

When military rule was dismantled in 1966, half a year prior to the occupation of the Territories, an opening had seemingly been made to reduce the
alienation of the Israeli government vis-à-vis its Arab citizens. Half a year later,
a new experiment began: maintaining a democratic regime to which about a
million noncitizen residents had been added, whom no one had the least intention of naturalizing as citizens. The appearance of this new, blatant form
of alienation only consolidated the alliance between Israel's ruling power and
its Jewish citizens, who were as always expected to participate in the exclusion
of "the Arabs"—henceforth above all Palestinians from the Occupied Territories—in the name of the religion of security and loyalty to the national cause.
Taking part in excluding "the Arabs" has been sweepingly legitimized by most
of the state's Jewish citizens; moreover, it became an acceptable way to partake
in the national cause, and through it—in the ruling power.

EMERGENCY REGULATIONS AND BRANCHES OF GOVERNMENT

Article 1A of chapter 1 of the State of Israel's Law and Administration Ordinance No. 1 of 1948 states:

> The Provisional Council of State consists of the persons whose names are set out in the Schedule to this Ordinance. Representatives of Arabs being residents of the State who recognize the State of Israel will be co-opted on the Provisional Council of State, as may be decided by the Council; their non-participation in the Council shall not derogate from its power.[9]

Formally, Arab citizens have been able to take part in both the legislative and the executive branches of the State of Israel ever since its founding. The law did not limit Arab participation in governance, but the same breath that permitted their participation established that their nonparticipation—the fact that they were not represented, although constituting about 13 percent of the state's population when it was founded[10]—did not detract from the legitimacy of the governing power. When the political habitus is a Jewish nationalized one, the government is not required to represent the citizens; rather, Jewish citizens volunteer to represent their government state and do so in every dimension of coexistence within the state.[11] This legal twisting and turning, the government's shirking of its duty to represent Israel's *entire* citizenry, has become the norm. The basic distinction between Jews and non-Jews is manifested in the distinction between the formal right to partake in political life and the essential weight of this participation and actual access to the various governing authorities. Governing power held by one ethnic nation and the national discourse of citizenship have produced differentiation and hierarchy among Jewish and Palestinian citizens in various realms of action. Formal civil equality has not done away with this, in spite of all the efforts made to expand it into areas where it is not assured and to manifest it in areas where it has been merely a dead letter of the law. The ethnic-national differentiation of citizenship is no passing evil, a distortion to be corrected, but rather a permanent aspect of the regime in Israel, to whose stabilization it contributes. It also organizes the relations among the various arms of the regime and enables its replication through democratic election procedures and regulated changes of power. This distortion cannot be changed without actually changing the regime.

The perpetuation of the state of emergency that has been maintained in Israel ever since the founding of the state is a characteristic expression of the structural difficulty of changing the hierarchical relationship of Jewish and Arab citizens. The state of emergency is one of the main instruments for producing differential citizenship and naturalizing national differences. It also contributes decisively to institutionalizing the Occupation as a regime and for its misrecognition as an appendage attached to the "Jewish and democratic state" from the outside as a project. The state of emergency was first declared immediately following the declaration of the State of Israel, under the Law and Administration Ordinance. This declaration was the first piece of legislation by the new state's temporary council, which became the Knesset (the Israeli parliament). Since then, the state of emergency has been regularly renewed every half-year by a Knesset ruling, usually almost automatically.[12] The declaration of a state of emergency grants the government nearly unlimited authority.[13] Its emergency powers are usually not employed, however, and the Jewish public hardly ever senses them. When emergency powers have been used, their objects have almost invariably been Arab citizens. The real possibility of their use always hovers over any confrontation between Palestinian citizens and the governing power, and any case where hostile activity is suspected.[14] The fact that the state of emergency has not been lifted enables the system to leave intact laws in various areas that if examined today from a constitutional standpoint would not pass the "High Court of Justice test"— among other reasons, because they embody discrimination against Arab citizens. The state of emergency, an exceptional situation that could be invoked as the rule in all circumstances because by default and in principle it is always already in force, was the seedbed for many laws and regulations that diminished civil and human rights, permitted undemocratic regulations, and reduced the transparency of Israel's ruling system.

The permanent state of emergency is not a consequence of a specific reality indicated by the sovereign power—after all, it is renewed almost automatically, a kind of parliamentary instinct that makes no reference to reality, invoking the formula of "the security situation" and its "existential threats" as a kind of incantation. Since the excuse for the state of emergency is always a security issue (rather than a political, economic, or ecological one), there is always ample justification for reinforcing national separation. As the state of "security emergency" is renewed regularly every six months, it has become part of the conditions of governing activity and a permanent constraint on civil relations and activities—in fact, part of the structure of Israel's regime. And since the excuse is always security, and "security" is always conceived of in terms of the "Jewish-Arab conflict," state-of-emergency regulations affect Jews and Palestinians differently.

The differentiation here is twofold. *First*, the mere use of emergency regulations is a call or excuse to silence public discussion, suspend the democratic game, dismantle binational civil partnerships, and recruit Jewish citizens to the ethnic-national cause as defined by the ruling power. Orchestrated Jewish participation in imposing military rule on non-Jewish citizens until 1966, and Israeli Jews' subsequent tacit consent to taking part in the implementation of emergency regulations in the "Arab sector," illustrate the way in which the interest of the government and the ruling hegemony and "the interest of the people"—that is, Jewish Israeli citizens—have been made to coincide through "security considerations." The state of emergency is also one of the major tools for managing the permanent distancing of non-Jews from power in Israel. The participation of so many Jewish citizens in the ruling apparatus in the Occupied Territories and the perpetuating of the Occupation regime, often against their private interests, constantly reiterates and often exacerbates the principle of differential citizenship and "the security effect" that accompanies it wherever it is applied.

Second, restrictions under the emergency regulations are implemented and enforced differently upon Jews and Arabs. Even if they are not, the regulations affect Palestinian citizens more than Jews, since they bestow more power upon the executive branch, in which Palestinians hardly take any part, at the expense of the legislative and judiciary branches, where they do have some say. A more general phenomenon can be discerned here as regards the balance between the three branches of government. Generally speaking, the strengthening of the High Court of Justice and of professional institutions such as the Israel Bank and State Comptroller's office, where experts preserve their professional autonomy to some extent, has benefited Palestinian citizens, whereas the weakening and loss of independence of these institutions since 2000 has injured them. The chronic weakness of the Knesset also diminishes the main political arena Palestinians share with Jewish citizens, while the strengthening of the executive branch enhances the influence of the latter and erodes the civil protection that Palestinian citizens are supposed to enjoy.

The picture is more complex than this, however. There is actually a kind of division of labor among the various governing authorities, which quickly comes into play whenever the principle of national separation is compromised by legislation, judicial rulings, NGO activity, or (more rarely) governmental regulations. For example, when the High Court of Justice insists on civil equality in matters like the right to buy property or choose one's neighborhood, the Knesset hastens to pass new ethno-nationalist laws. The government in turn stalls implementation of the court's rulings by budgetary and administrative means. When a new law of citizenship and of entry into the country was enacted, it was formulated in vague universalist language but gave the minister of the interior—traditionally a post occupied by one of the nationalist religious parties—authority on a scale nearly unprecedented in democratic governments to exercise judgment in granting, revoking, or denying citizenship.[15] Anticipating future compromises of the principle of national separation, the 2002 Law Ensuring Rejection of the Right of Return, which prohibits Palestinian refugees from returning to the Occupied Territories unless it is approved by an absolute majority in the Knesset, ties the hands of any future Israeli government on what has been construed as a "sensitive issue." This law was presented by its advocates as "nonpartisan, Zionist, Jewish, Israeli, moral, and historically just." However, behind the fear of acknowledgment of the Palestinians' right of return we may perhaps discern a deeper fear that someday political circumstances, whether internal or external, will cause a government in Israel to doubt the synonymy of the above adjectives, however obvious their equivalence may seem to its proponents at present. The deeper fear is here related to the possibility of an a-national understanding of universality and the clear logical aporia that such an understanding implies. It is not universal logic that is at stake here but the separatist logic of the regime, for which ethnic national separation is constitutive.

Even if the three branches of governance have differing interests in specific cases, even if a different aspect of the political order is at stake, the issue that repeatedly comes up, whether as cause or as effect, is the preservation of the ethnic-national character of Israeli citizenship in general and of Jewish supremacy in particular. Binding legislation by which the Knesset forces the hand of the executive branch has always been directed against civil-democratic trends that seem to jeopardize the national or religious "Jewish interest." The government in turn counters the Knesset and the Supreme Court by using emergency regulations, and these are always implemented in the name of "state security" and threats to "Jewishness" (which often causes the legislator to act like a mechanical puppet, and the Supreme Court to bury its head in the sand).

The Occupation regime is supposedly subordinate to the Israeli government as a whole, but in fact it answers only to an exclusive ministerial committee. In 1967, "primary legislative authority" in the Occupied Territories was vested in the "regional commander" of the West Bank and Gaza Strip, who in turn authorized local commanders to promulgate "secondary laws" regarding military-criminal matters, and staff officers to draw up civil and administrative laws. These officers thus in effect constituted a legislative power independent of the Knesset.[16] In practice, the "legislation" they engage in is an exclusively military affair that produces decrees, not laws. It is performed secretly, and even its products, the new regulations themselves, are not always made public, for it is up to the military commander to decide when and how to publicize them.[17] Moreover, military judges tend to ratify military edicts and accept them the way courts in Israel accept Knesset legislation, and they are rarely impressed by violations of the Geneva Convention.[18] Regulations and edicts change constantly and accumulate indefinitely. It is sometimes claimed that there is a "culture of illegalism" in Israel proper, but in the Territories, there is "overlegislation," owing to the enormous number of decrees and the number of those with legislative authority.

If in Israel itself the regulations replicate and intensify differential citizenship and structural discrimination among Jews and Arabs, in the Occupied Territories they directly impact the situation of Palestinians, exposing them to various types of violence, disrupting their ability to maintain social institutions and political lives, to work and create. Inevitably, they largely reduce their capacity to resist the ruling power. In Israel, emergency regulations restrict Palestinians' access to political space, but they by no means close it down completely. In the Territories, such space does not even exist, and the regulations generate countless state-induced injuries, which only rarely make their way to the Supreme Court or to political space in Israel, and are very rarely redressed by the court or become a stake in a political struggle that concerns Israeli citizens.

Like other civil branches of the Israeli government involved in ruling the Territories, whose formal role is to supervise the Occupation regime's military side, set its goals, and establish its budget, the High Court of Justice is too often manipulated by the military authorities. The former rely on data and analyses supplied by the latter, much of which is subject to censorship and cannot be made public. Alternative sources of information and analyses provided by a few investigating journalists and human rights and humanitarian organizations are considered biased and unreliable and usually rejected on sight. When there is discussion of such information and analysis, it remains an internal issue of the governing power. Usually disputes between various arms of the ruling apparatus do not become a matter of public discussion, nor are Israeli citizens—

let alone Palestinian noncitizens—party to them. The entire ruling apparatus "hangs" from the democratic regime of Israel itself as from a small hook. The military commander is legislator, executor, and judge. All authority is channeled to him from the apex of Israel's ruling power—the Ministry of Defense and the Prime Minister's Office.

Judicial supervision and civil resistance are too feeble to hamper this unification of authority in the Territories, and the pressure of international activists and public opinion actually solidify it even further. In spite of the multiplicity of its heads and emissaries, control of the Occupied Territories is unitary. If there is division and conflict among the various arms of the Occupation regime, the Palestinians have no part in it. Unlike Palestinian citizens of Israel, they cannot take advantage of such divisions. They are not present in the space where these gaps appear and unfold. They have no practical way of taking part in government, entering into negotiations with it (except those it holds itself, usually on its own terms, with those of their leaders who have been recognized as worthy partners), nor of opposing it within any accepted rules of the game. Their alienation from the governing power to which they are subjugated is absolute. They can either surrender or rebel. When they surrender, most Jewish Israelis see this as a normal state of affairs, in which "law and order" (of the Occupation regime, of course) are maintained, and the national project sails ahead on calm waters. When they rebel, most Jewish Israelis flock to the flag, and even if they do not take active part in suppressing rebellion, they vest full authority to do so in the ruling apparatus and its men—all neighbors, relatives, and friends.

THIS REGIME THAT IS NOT ONE

The Israeli regime was not doubled overnight. In the early days after the war of 1967, Occupation was simply a temporary state of deploying the armed forces in territories occupied in war and controlling the local population. However, control of the population and territory had to address the surge of nationalist sentiment among the Jewish public, the colonial ambitions of significant groups within it, and the broad political agreement among Israeli Jews that following a peace treaty, at least some of the Occupied Territory should remain in Israeli hands. Soon the administration of the situation became a project with its own inner logic, necessitating budgets and resources to promote it "in the best possible way." A lively debate took place among the Jewish public over "the future of the Occupied Territories": whether and what to give back or annex. Little attention was paid at the time to the question of how to control the Territories and their population until the eventual signing of a peace treaty. Reports on control of the Territories published in Israel before the outbreak of the First Intifada were relatively few and far between. Only a handful of people knew much about Palestinian resistance prior to the First Intifada and its violent suppression. Of the many aspects of the Occupation project, only one really penetrated the Israeli public sphere: the question of whether—and where—to build Jewish colonies in the Occupied Territories. This became the focus of an ongoing political dispute—exclusively among Jews, needless to say—that was always stormy, but in fact lagged behind the expansion of the colonies and the emergence of a new map of Jewish presence in the Territories. Other aspects of the project, such as moving army bases into the Territories, opening the borders, making the labor market accessible to Palestinians, civil modes of action by the military government, and the military measures taken to suppress Palestinian resistance, aroused very little public attention. They were discussed in closed government circles or simply "taken care of" without being discussed at all.

Even when the colonizing project burgeoned and began to demand enormous resources, however, no public or governing clarification took place in Israel as to its nature and purpose, its giant investments and oppressed population. The project grew and an institutionalized ruling apparatus was consolidated within a stable ruling format that set a space of possible action, creating some opportunities and closing off others. By the late 1970s or early 1980s, it was already possible to speak of a separate Occupation regime and of a ruling apparatus that systematically (albeit partially and differentially) erased borders between Israel and the Occupied Territories, enabled the mixing of the two populations, and at the same time constantly produced their separation, subjugated them, and ensured its own separation from the regime inside Israel itself.

Neither this separate regime nor the way it is attached to the democratic regime inside Israel itself were created by an explicit or conscious, regulated governmental or parliamentary decision to the making of which the governed were privy. Many explicit and conscious decisions relating to occupation as a project contributed to the emergence of the Occupation as a separate regime, but one cannot attribute the intention of establishing such a regime to them. One day, this simply came about and became the mold in which most important governmental decisions in Israel are cast.

Some of the governmental and military instruments serving this regime in its early years were created during the years of Israeli military government of Arab citizens in the Galilee and the "Triangle area" along the Jordanian border northeast of Tel Aviv in the 1950s and 1960s. The civil-national habitus that was shaped at the time was imprinted by the military government and naturalized the separate and special mode of governing Arab citizens. Hence there had been nothing unusual about the fact that the "new" Palestinians in the Occupied Territories were bereft of any political status and stateless—as if these were their congenital characteristics, which came along with their cheap labor power and the suspicion that they might be terrorists. Even years later, their political rights did not become an issue. Within this habitus, the governmental decision not to discuss and decide on the question of annexation of the Territories and naturalization of their residents has never been questioned. Citizens taking some part or other in the Occupation could thus imagine it as not harming the democratic nature of their regime and not subverting their good citizenship; quite the contrary: active participation in this project was proof of civic virtue.

As a project, the Occupation was perceived first of all nearly exclusively in terms of security and settlements. Control of the Palestinian population was conceived of as some kind of inevitable burden that Israel had to bear, the unwilled by-product of a war imposed on it (not by Palestinians—but this fact was hardly mentioned). In the meantime, until some deus ex machina arrangement was found, it seemed possible to gain from administering this control correctly, to benefit from Palestinian labor and improve Israel's security situation, as well as its standing in future political negotiations.

The economic integration of Israel and the Occupied Territories forced tens of thousands of Palestinians to work in Israel, where they were systematically exploited but also regularly exposed to different facets of Israeli society. They became external witnesses of a relatively developed economy, a divided yet mobile society, and a lively, vivid democratic game, in which they, the most harshly impacted victims of injury in every respect hallowed in Israeli political space (claim to land, ownership rights, freedom of expression and organization, the right to life) played no part, not even when it came to their own lives and future. Friendly contacts at the workplace between Jews and Palestinians could not change the basic conditions of Palestinian existence much. During work hours, they were no more than laborers—any other dimensions of their own universe were erased; and "after hours," their very presence was erased, and they were obliged either to go back to the tin shanties and basements they lived in or return to their homes in the Occupied Territories. They had no way of taking part in the power that governed them, and being governed nevertheless, if they sought for ways to improve their lot, they were left no choice but to resist.

The First Intifada brought this resistance to public awareness in Israel. Only then did the Palestinians succeed in turning their oppression and deprivation of rights into an issue addressed by Israeli political discourse. At this point, the Palestinian resistance organizations had already managed to persuade numerous Palestinians to reduce their contacts with the Israeli ruling apparatus, primarily through mass resignation from their posts in the civil administration. Although the civil administration collapsed, the effect of this step was smaller than anticipated, because the administration of Palestinian life in the Occupied Territories was already in the hands of the security system, and this resignation—like the commoner occasional traders' strikes—immediately became a "security" matter. Indeed the ruling apparatus in the Territories, which already functioned as a separate system of government, presented the Palestinian popular struggle entirely as a security problem and erased most of its civil facets.

The splitting of the Israeli ruling apparatus was gradual, and separation of the two halves was not fully institutionalized until the early 1980s, when the Israeli army assumed control of Palestinians' civil affairs. With the creation of the civil administration in the Occupied Territories as an office in the Ministry of Defense, they became a closed market both administratively and legally. Most governance questions dealing with the Palestinians in the Territories were decided upon and "solved" between the civil administration, the army, and the General Security Services, involving a small circle of officials in the Ministry of Defense and the Prime Minister's Office. This circle was—and still is—the bottleneck through which public discourse, political struggle, and legal and political decisions flow from Israel's political space to the Territories. This is also the bottleneck through which the political space and legal system of Israel proper are fed with "authorized" information about happenings in the Territories. Naturally, in an era of open globalized mass media, with the humanitarian crisis always already an international issue, information also flows through many other channels. It is not the actual information that is blocked, however, but rather its interpretation, processing, and translation into relevant political decisions. The general picture of ruling the Territories disappears into a series of cases, and the tally of casualties, demolished houses, and arrests, and questions about the "proportionality" of particular measures are substituted for any serious attempt to question the overall structure of the ruling apparatus and the regime it embodies.[19]

Even the High Court of Justice cannot bridge the gap between the two systems of government. When the court reviews petitions concerning government

actions and policies in the Territories, it limits itself to issues of the valid authorization and proportionality of isolated acts, without referring to any long-
standing, structural feature of the Occupation regime. The High Court of
Justice hardly ever questions the information provided by the Occupation authorities, lets them keep their sources confidential, and is very cautious about
overturning the military commander's edicts, even when they blatantly contradict Israeli law, international law, or natural justice.[20] In monitoring mostly
soldiers, commanders, and security agents, who are supposedly under its judicial supervision, the court assumes that "every Israeli soldier carries with him,
in his backpack, the rules of customary international public law concerning the
laws of war and the fundamental principles of Israeli administrative law" anywhere in the Occupied Territories."[21] In fact, however, this sententious maxim
is a perverted description of the true systemic bond between the High Court of
Justice and state violence in the Occupied Territories: the High Court is a device
employed by the ruling apparatus, an extension of the military, not a protector
of the governed population.

The High Court of Justice has no access whatsoever to the residents of the
Territories. It reaches them only because it is dragged there after the soldiers,
and only when their actions entail petitions that it is willing to review. This
willingness was its contribution to the Occupation project from the outset, but
soon became its duty under the Occupation regime. Like the few government
ministers in charge of administering control of the Occupied Territories and
the senior officials who assist them, the High Court functions at one and the
same time as a part of the closed governmental economy of the Occupation regime, and as a conduit connecting the two regimes, introducing a whiff of democracy into the Occupied territories and traces of military dictatorship into
the halls of justice of Israeli democracy. When the petitions from the Territories reach the High Court of Justice, it becomes clear time and again that the
supreme judges can be the defenders of democracy only in the civil regime of
Israel proper. When they intervene in Occupation matters, and even in the rare
cases when they rule in favor of Palestinians, they are revealed as the defenders
of the military regime of inclusive separation.

Inside Israel, administration of the Occupation as a project took on the
nature of an ongoing military operation. As is commonly the case in such operations, the government's military leading edge runs things and may conduct
a considerable part of its activity in secret, without any prior public discussion, and often even without regular accountability or the possibility of ex-

ternal criticism. When especially blatant assaults on human rights—targeted assassinations, house demolitions, and the erection of the separation wall, for example—are subject to public and legal debate, they enjoy much more support among the Israeli Jewish public than the government does in other matters. The reason is obvious: the issue is presented in terms of national security, overruling legal and moral considerations. Palestinian grievances are all too quickly addressed as issues of the abuse of power, whose legitimacy, in itself, is not questioned. Israeli soldiers following orders, facing violent resistance, and acting under pressure are counterposed to victimized Palestinians. Such rhetoric makes it nearly impossible to ask what project is served by such measures and what kind of regime thus enables the abandonment of some of its subjects for the sake of the security of others.

Occasional debates over specific actions and policies do not threaten the Occupation regime, because they revolve around the Occupation as a military project. When the struggle of Jewish citizens is perceived as more threatening, as is the case with movements that cross the national divide (Sheikh Jarakh Solidarity or the Anarchists Against the Wall in Bil'in), the ruling apparatus act violently and, aided by mainstream Israeli media, seek to marginalize the activists. Jewish citizens are required to take an active part in the ruling apparatus and legitimize it, because its action is a function of legally and democratically constituted governmental authority. Recruitment to the Occupation as to some military project makes it possible to see it as a necessity, a lesser evil, whose temporariness is its mode of existence. It seems then as though there is no choice but to continue maintaining it as the present condition of Jewish and Israeli existence.

Once every few years, the Israeli public is called upon to take part in elections, where political parties propose different "solutions" to "the Palestinian problem," but never address the mode of ruling the Palestinian people, and end up playing their roles in the ruling apparatus, which no one dreams of dismantling. The democratic game and a change of power are always possible—their regularity assures the stability of the regime—and, indeed, parties with different answers to questions about the Territories do rise to power. They do not—indeed, cannot—differ regarding regime questions, however, because they all presuppose a differential and split regime and believe in separating the governed populations, and for most of them, only Jewish political parties are authorized to decide regime and security issues.

Regular changes of power preserve the stability of both regimes, but in a different manner. In Israel proper, they ensure the realization of the prime democratic principle that government does not belong to anyone in particular—as Claude Lefort expressed it, "the seat of power is empty."[22] Anyone may seize it, as long as it is done by the book. But since this is "an ethnic democracy," "anyone" can only be a Jewish citizen. In the Territories regular changes of power in *Israel* contribute to the stability of the Occupation regime precisely because they leave the ruling apparatuses intact and ensure the separation of the ruling apparatus in the Territories from Israel's political space.

The two separate regimes that constitute the Israeli regime, then, are relatively stable. The main significant regime change in Israel's history took place with the institutionalizing of the Occupation project, when the Israeli regime was doubled and split into two adjacent parts, creating two relatively "clean" forms of regime: on the one hand, the rule of law, democratic rules of the game, and limited ethnic discrimination; on the other hand, military dictatorship and spatial-ethnic separation mechanisms. This split enables the forces that preserve the regime form on both sides to act without disturbing each other. Thus, for example, liberalization of the economy and judicial system in Israel proper might leak into the Occupation regime to some extent. But there it will soon enough be blocked by recurring emergency situations, new edicts, and ignored court rulings. By the same token, the new mode of violence that has made its appearance in the Occupied Territories—the increasing disengagement of eruptive violence from withheld violence and the law, allowing the ruling apparatus to exert violence upon its subjects with no due legal process—increasingly seeps into Israel proper. So far, however, these processes have been more or less balanced by various branches of government, a still functioning system of law enforcement, and a certain measure of respect for human and civil rights. Israeli democratic institutions *keep* the Occupation regime *out*, temporarily, of course, and the military institutions of the Occupation regime *preserve* the civil regime in Israel proper *from the outside*. The inverse is also true: the Occupation *keeps* Israeli democratic institutions *out*, while these very institutions *preserve* the Occupation *from the outside*.

CONCLUSION
Toward a New Regime

GUIDED IMAGINATION

Imagine a state whose residents have learned to speak "civil" (language) to one another. Imagine a regime that does not tag populations by their race, religion, gender, and ethnic nationality. Imagine a regime that has obliterated such categories as "refugees," "stateless," "illegal aliens," and "foreign workers" from its political lexicon, or at least neutralized their toxic import. Imagine a regime that sees the rapid naturalization of people who had been hitherto defined by such categories as necessary for maintaining a political space open to and shared by all the governed. Imagine citizenship that is not just a resource allotted to the governed by the government to protect them from its long arms, but also, and primarily, a form of belonging and partnership, and the condition for living together that is both fair and significant.

In order to imagine such a regime, three main features of the commonly accepted conception of modern democracy must be given up: the idea that the state is a closed, given entity that dictates the borders of the political system and maintains relations with similar closed entities in the international arena; the idea that national sovereignty is tested by the state's military might and its willingness to exert it occasionally; the acceptance as inevitable of a "state backyard" that accommodates noncitizens and flawed citizens, allowing them to be governed differently. Ridding oneself of these ideas, one can imagine the state not as a given, a priori framework of power relations and political struggles, but rather as their ever-changing product. Then one can also acknowledge the necessity of the use of force and the government's duty to regulate this use without placing sovereignty outside and above power relations among the governed or as a possible objective for the use of military force. In short, imagine a regime in which the government is, in every sense, of and for all its citizens, never against them, and participation in political space presupposes a concern for their shared world. Imagine a regime whose primary questions are always: who are entitled to benefit from the state, and how should the state care for them?

Under such a regime, ethnicity—like religion—is separate from the state, in a way that enables it to remain unadulterated and not become a vehicle of power, an engine for atrocious acts of state. Imagine a regime under which multiple ethnicities and religious communities enjoy equal status, shelter, and protection. Under such a regime, the nation would serve as a resource and space of civil culture and morality. It would offer depth of heritage and tradition, meanings and rituals, and extends family ties, but not be allowed to monopolize the state apparatus. Imagine a situation whereby civil solidarity harnesses the forces of the market, not just nationalism and fundamentalism, and grants the poor and weak a security net, a decent living, and opportunities to extricate themselves from their misery. Imagine a state where people are neither impoverished nor abandoned, and do not resort to crime as an outcome of their deprived origins or places of residence.

Imagine a state where gender, race, and color have nothing to do with differences of status and well-being, and minorities' achievements in the struggle for equality are no longer doubted or repeatedly stolen. Imagine a regime where historical injustice done to minorities of all kinds is now showcased in museums as an object of research and study. Imagine a state whose school curricula are written by the oppressed of the past, and the past is reassessed and recounted with the requisite urgency. Imagine a place where people rediscover their common past in order to imagine a future for themselves in which regression to a regime that made them enemies would be impossible.

Imagine a democracy in the Middle East not based on denying the Middle East, one that is equally open to the Mizrahi (Jewish Israeli of "eastern"—Arab—background), the Arab, the Muslim, and the Christian, creating a truly common safe haven, rid of atomic weapons and chemical missiles, nationalist aggression and mobilization orders, a habitus where memories of annihilation of the Jews do not turn into a palpable, immediate threat. Imagine a government that feels uneasy about military might and seeks partners for disarmament. Imagine a government that cares for the world, its natural resources, environmental equilibrium, and its future. Imagine a regime where equal partnership in government is a common denominator that dictates the way all other differences are maintained and cherished. Imagine a government that assures its citizens of a fair income and leisure time so as to enable them to take part in public life and shape it; a government that actually feels threatened when the governed feel alienated from it and do not partake in decisions concerning their common existence and the future of the regime. Imagine a ruling power whose citizens do not regard it as a lesser evil, a nuisance, or an annoying burden, but always as a medium confirming life, partnership, creation, and uncompromising struggle against malevolence.

This is utterly naïve, say many. It shows no understanding whatsoever of realpolitik, power relations, human passions, and man's innately evil nature. In Israel, they would say, this vision is both futile and dangerous: futile, because of the heritage of Jewish self-segregation and because of the economic and political interests of numerous Israelis of various classes deeply invested in the perpetuation of the Occupation regime; dangerous, inasmuch as Arab nationalism and Islamic fundamentalism are determined to annihilate Israel not because it is undemocratic but because it is Jewish.

But the real answer to fundamentalism, be it Jewish nationalist, Islamic, or any other kind, cannot be the sort of "security fundamentalism" hailed by the Occupation regime, based on and nurturing Jewish self-segregation. The real answer lies in a nonfundamentalist society that will not turn any demand for self-segregation into a deadlock against others. It is a society that offers people hope for a decent living, without dispossessing or abandoning them, without either abusing their traditions or forcing others to sanctify their principles. Upon the scorched earth that modern democracy has left behind in many parts of the world, in isolated enclaves such as Israel-Palestine more than elsewhere, criticism and opposition do not suffice. In this political wasteland, a new utopian horizon must be drawn.

A new utopian horizon is necessary for coping with a discourse of realpolitik, bred by disaster and leading from one catastrophe to another. Utopian imagination is not related to revolutionary change but to the possibility of decency and hope in the midst of the disaster zone. Utopian discourse cannot be measured in terms of its applicability, as if the world could be shaped by political programs. It represents an opening to possibilities, of the future as well as of a new past yet to come, a past that has so far been perceived as frozen, fossilized, irreversible, but is in fact replete both with possibilities that have been thought and not realized and with others that have been experienced and extinguished. Such possibilities are restorable, they may enrich the imagination, expand the horizon of thinking about the future. Their restoration and processing are the condition for a new understanding of the present and for the possibility that a different future will grow out of it, a future that will not exclude any of those who share it.

We pose a single condition for any thought of another regime. In its light we wish to read the past, restore that which has been trampled on and imagine a different future: a call to consider all those governed and not only those whom the government has recognized and counted; not to examine the past or visualize the future without taking them into account, not to accept the way in which the government makes them transparent, erases them, or inscribes them in its invisible ink. The shared world where people of different status are governed cannot be understood from the perspective of such division; a division into separate entities must be self-evident, and its contribution to creating the shared world must receive its proper weight. For us, this is the condition necessary for sober assessment of the past and for any decent regime in the future.

VIOLENT REGIME CHANGE

The constitution of the Occupation regime as a part of the Israeli regime and the Siamese twin of Israeli democracy, separate but attached to and dependent on it, was nothing less than a coup d'état. But this coup went unnoticed. "The Occupation" has been perceived by most Israelis as a project; as a regime, it remains invisible to this day, not only to most researchers but to most citizens, to the governed, which is more important. Jewish Israelis have preferred to imagine the Occupation in a way that enabled them to deny its cruelty and live with it in peace. For most Palestinians, it has dictated a single mode of resistance: ending the Occupation and removing the Jewish colonies. For the noncitizens who are subjugated by it, the Occupation has been and remains illegitimate; but the citizens who partake in the Occupation regime, too, have never legitimized it as such. They have never faced the question of whether or not to accept it as a structural element of the Israeli state. The Occupation's impact upon the democratic structure of Israel proper has been denied. When it is discussed, it is presented as negligible, or as a threat that would materialize in some undefined future in the absence of any peace treaty.

Constituted alongside the ethnic democratic regime in Israel as the result of fateful daily decisions by the ruling power, and based upon the active participation of so many Israeli citizens, the Occupation regime has totally changed the meaning of Israeli democracy itself. If, up until 1967 Israeli citizens were required to forget the expelled Palestinians of the first years of the state, they have since 1967 had to forget the noncitizens governed alongside them. If citizenship means being governed equally, and enjoying equal opportunities to partake in governance, then since 1967, in order to tell themselves that they themselves are citizens, the citizens of the State of Israel have had to ignore those with whom they share their everyday lives and their government, and to define their citizenship in relation to the noncitizenship of the "uncounted."

Decades of ruling over millions of noncitizens has made them come to seem external, negligible, and inconsequential to the civil and political status of Israeli citizens. The Occupation has been seen as temporary, the Occupied Territories as something borrowed, and their inhabitants as a population that Israel had best rid itself of at the first opportunity. The colonization process that has integrated the Territories into Israel has been gradual, and its borders have never been defined. There was no consensus about this process, which settled in slowly till it became quasi "natural." The ritual of dispute between the Right and the Left in Israel about the future of the Territories is out of touch with the changes that have already taken place on the ground. Moreover, placing more territories and a million noncitizens under Israeli rule seems to have no effect upon the relations between Israeli citizens and their ruling power. The fact that this was the beginning of a regime change escaped them: after all, the citizens did not violently topple an old regime in order to instate a new one, and the ruling power did not violently dismantle the institutions of the old regime.

Still, we wish to argue that the process whereby Palestinians became subjects of the Israeli regime without becoming its citizens was a violent regime change brought about by the Israeli government and army. The Israeli regime had to exert constant violent force in order to govern the Palestinians in the Occupied Territories and quench their resistance, integrate them into the labor market but exclude them from public space. Israel's treatment of its new subjects faced faint objection—if any—on the Jewish side. The use of force, the dismantling of most political institutions that had been a part of the Palestinians' old regime, the prohibition on establishing new political organizations, and the exclusion of Palestinians from the Israeli political sphere were all perceived as lesser necessary evils. The forced coexistence of citizens and noncitizens has come to seem a law of nature. It has reshaped Israeli citizenship, because it has made citizenship the status and privilege of less than two-thirds of Israel-Palestine's adult population. Since the regime change went unnoticed among Israeli Jews, Palestinian resistance to this change could be conceived of and portrayed as violence coming from the "outside," and its much more violent quenching was presented as a defensive war of sorts. Palestinians who had taken no part in the war in 1967 were quickly tagged as enemies, and the struggle against them was seen as yet another phase of the Jewish people's revival in its homeland.

In fact, ignoring the Occupation as a regime is the other face of ignoring the non-Jews governed within the political space of Israel proper. The combination of these two blind spots enables the famous conjunctive formula "a Jewish and democratic state" in terms of which Israeli Jews are invited to see their country. This formula is promulgated by leading legal and liberal arts scholars and disseminated by all Israeli state media. Clearly, however, in order to say that the State of Israel is Jewish, one must not count the five million non-Jews ruled by the Israeli state, or the hundreds of thousands who were expelled from the country in order to enable, *not the founding of the state, but the creation of its regime*, who with their descendants by now number further millions. And in order to claim that the State of Israel is democratic, one must ignore the Occupation as a structural and constitutive element of the Israeli regime itself.

A regime founded in violence that has not ceased since generates and feeds the violent struggle that seeks to dismantle it. Violent upheaval is a real possibility as long as the horizon is closed to a nonnational conception of the conflict, as long as only the Palestinians and their relatively weak or uncommitted allies recognize the violence that constitutes this regime and oppose it, only Palestinians are seen as victims of this violence, and Jews continue to deny the violence in which they are complicit, and the fact that they too are its victims. One cannot rule out the possibility that one day, under historic and political circumstances that are not difficult to envisage—through an alliance with others that have material and ideological interests in entering this arena and are able to engage Israeli military power—those upon whom this regime has been violently forced will manage to free themselves of it by equally violent means.

The urgent need for an end to the imposition of a separatist Jewish national vision on a binational demographic reality—a regime in which Jewish citizens are accomplices, either voluntarily or because they are obliged to be— cannot remain the business of Palestinians alone. The struggle against this regime must become the civil duty of all those it rules. A common recognition of the regime's horrors both by those it violently oppresses and those it recruits to violently oppress others might be the basis for a different civil partnership that limits the power of familiar differences of religion, ethnic nationality, race, and gender. Such a partnership would not enable anyone to create a permanent hierarchy of power. It would not enable anyone to regard the disaster befalling citizens of a certain type as a "disaster for and of others." It will not enable one group in the population to suffer regime crimes perpetrated in the defense of another group.

A shared recognition of the fact that regime-made disaster can never remain limited merely to the population for which it is intended can both halt the present disaster along national lines of separation and prevent the next one. As long as reality is shaped by national demarcation lines, as long as regime violence is represented as a life-or-death struggle between two nationalities, a struggle in which one side will have to surrender in order to survive, the end of the present regime will not be a civil revolution but rather the creation of another dark regime in which nationality is the major active force. Nothing in human history allows one to foretell how such struggles end, and much of human history indicates that national victory in such struggles is in fact civil defeat, whereby many years are needed for the rehabilitation of both losers and winners—the former of their defeat, loss, and humiliation, and the latter of their corruption and the debt that their crimes incur. Insistence on maintaining the Occupation regime promotes a struggle to the death of this kind.

Even if the threat of such struggle for survival or elimination of the Occupation regime does not materialize, the Occupation has already subjected the Jewish people to the worst disaster since the destruction of European Jewry. It is horrific, first of all, because of the image of the new Jew that it tended in the Land of Israel. This new Jew is recruited for Jewish sovereignty based upon a unique regime of Jewish separation. This regime has distorted Jewish existence, not only in Israel, but nearly everywhere in the world: Jews worldwide are called upon to identify with the violent, heartless, and mindless displacement of the principle of Jewish separateness—from the Diaspora communities observing Halachic law to a partly secularized society of immigrants and colonizers who maintain and impose self-segregation by means of the apparatus of a sovereign nation-state. Those who have not identified with Israel's actions have for years been hard put to make their stand public, and when they do so their communities and congregations threaten to disown them. Israel has become that which Jews outside are called upon to defend at any price and to avoid criticizing regardless of circumstances.

The Jewish principle of self-segregation is now inscribed in the space lying between the Mediterranean Sea and the Jordan River by means of apartheid roads, checkpoints and walls, travel and work permits. Jews of the world learn not to see the new forms of separation, but to understand them as a welcome continuation of their own struggle for self-segregation and survival in the Diaspora. Organized Jewry the world over is fed the lies disseminated by the Israeli state about the nature of its regime in general and the Occupation in particular. In order to justify these lies, shows of anti-Semitism are magnified out of all proportion, legitimate criticism of Israel is confounded with anti-Semitism, anti-Semitic motifs flourishing in radical Islam or found among the European Left are dragged to the fore, and the long positive history of coexistence shared by Jews and Arabs in various countries, including Palestine until the end of the British Mandate, is played down. Muslims everywhere are presented, at least potentially, as the Palestinians' emissaries, deliberately out to annihilate Israel. The Palestinians are presented as the cutting edge in a worldwide war being waged against the West by fundamentalist Islam. The lie covering the Occupation has been woven into every fabric of cultural and social life. It requires a continual warping of reality and an inherent blindness handed on from one generation to the next. Today's lie is the plowshare that prepares the soil out of which future Occupation horrors will sprout. In order for the lying to stop, the Occupation regime must be eradicated. In order to eradicate the Occupation regime, the Israeli regime must be changed. In order to change the Israeli regime, the lying must stop—first and foremost.

THE BACKYARD

The Occupation regime might be described as an extreme development of a structural feature familiar to democratic regimes: the existence of a large "backyard" that consists of a governed population forsaken by the government, which does not partake in its affairs and is excluded from the common shaping of public life. Nearly every known democratic regime contains a rift between the governed population and the community of citizens considered equals and taking part in shaping the government. This gap between the demos partaking of power and the governed many who have no part in the demos has been known since ancient Athens, through the tradition of the social contract, down to the established democracies of our own time, where immigrants from formerly colonized lands, who are often impaired citizens or noncitizens, live alongside citizens.

Democratic regimes are distinct from one another in the way they administer gradations of citizenship and stabilize the gap between citizens and noncitizens; enable the governed to become equal citizens; limit those deprived of civil

status or whose civil status allows no access to governance and common public space; protect them when necessary—or abandon them. Even in the best of
them, a certain backyard remains for those who are not taken in consideration,
unaccounted for, and may easily become disposable. In every democratic regime, there is a struggle over the relations between that backyard and the joint
civil front. The backyard of modern democracies has been populated by Jews,
women, blacks, refugees, ethnic-national minorities, and immigrants from past
colonies. Today, the backyards of the United States and European states, for example, consist of Latino American, African, and Asian migrant workers whose
labor is vital to local economies and whose presence escalates the erection of
new national barriers but also requires citizens to rethink the demarcation lines
of their own nationality.

People living in the backyard of even a well-functioning democracy are a
residue of governed subjects, subordinated to and unprotected from the government, people whose consent and authorization are not necessary to its legitimacy. These people are vulnerable to harm and wrongdoing by the authorities
as well as by their neighbors, relatively protected citizens who rarely even need
justify such wrongs and harm in terms of some collective interest. In the backyard are men and women who can be exploited as laborers, whose property,
bodies, and blood can be abandoned for the sake of general interests of a partnership in which they have no part, as well as in the private interests of common citizens.

Ruling the backyard requires the use of force, because many who dwell in it
resist their lot. This use of force leaves its mark upon citizens recruited for the
task. They tend to describe the violence they witness or in which they take part
as a necessary response to the resisting subjects. When it comes to the backyard, they tend to justify or be oblivious of deeds that in other contexts they
themselves would condemn, and whose perpetrators they would wish to punish. A continuum of possible situations of vulnerability can be described here.
The total abandonment of the governed by the government—e.g., slaves in the
American South before the abolition of slavery; Bosnian Muslim women under
Serbian rule during the Balkan War—lies at one end of this continuum; the
protection that a liberal-democratic regime respectful of human and political
rights provides its citizens lies at the other. Between these two extremes stand
citizens whose protection and privileges are conditioned, in fact, by not contesting the denial of such protection and privilege to their fellow governed. Democratic regimes differ in their tolerance of harm, humiliation, and exploitation in

their backyards, the rhetoric and principles that justify this tolerance, the rigidity of the line separating the backyard from the civil front space, and the way in which the backyard is reflected in the citizens' conception of their regime.

Can we, then, understand the Occupied Territories as the relatively large backyard of Israeli democracy? As we have shown, under the conditions created by the Occupation regime, spatial separation of the backyard cannot be total. Civil separation cannot take place without preserving the relationship of subjection through mechanisms whose operation requires the continual interruption of spatial separation. This backyard, then, has been defined in identity-territorial terms: it is enforced first and foremost upon non-Jews living outside the Green Line;[1] the border separating it from the shared political space is rigid; the threshold of bearable harm to those populating the backyard is subject to certain legal and political limitations, but these are flexible and incessantly diminishing. Since the creation of this backyard, it has been populated by over one-third of the governed population, and still its existence is not recognized as part of the democratic household. No democratic regime in the world today has such a large backyard in proportion to the size of its citizenry, enclosed within such rigid boundaries, and represented to such a degree of bad faith.

Under such conditions, the main ideological effort of the ruling elite does not aim to ensure the preservation of a democratic political body whose citizens participate in governance, to regulate passage between the backyard and the common space, nor to justify the harm it causes Palestinian noncitizens. Its main ideological effort is to preserve the representation of the backyard as "exterior" without giving up its place as a backyard, a part of the common household that can at any moment be entered, used, destroyed, and rebuilt, abandoning the noncitizens who live in it. Failure of such an effort would expose this "exterior" as being an inseparable part of the "interior." During elections and in times of crisis, at moments when the legitimacy and authority of the government are at stake, that which is revalidated is the separate regime of which the Occupation is not considered a part, while matters concerning the control of the Occupied Territories usually appear as security issues of a strategic or tactical nature, having to do with the proper administration of the project. Israeli citizens participate in democratic procedures of replacing government, but if they are not Jews, they cannot become true partners in power itself, and if they are not settlers or members of a small group of military and government officials in control of the Occupied Territories, their access to rule of the occupied backyard is greatly limited. Election rituals, on the one hand,

and the administration of the Occupation regime rooted in the idea of a state of emergency, on the other, continue to hide the Janus face of the Israeli regime, in which each part assures the existence of the other. Only the state's self-bestowed qualifier "Jewish and democratic" may betray the truth, like a symptomatic signifier with its inherent ambiguity, its dividing/binding conjunction that seeks to negate the exclusive "either-or" in order to conceal the constative neither-nor: neither democratic nor Jewish, because it is only half-democratic and half-Jewish.

Nationalism, appearing in the nineteenth century as an ideology of national liberation, has in fact (and most typically since the end of World War II) become an ideology serving the regulation of relations between the public sphere shared by free citizens and its backyard. In other words, it is responsible for distancing some of the governed from sharing in rule, and for justifying this distancing. What began as a struggle of liberation from tyranny and aspirations of self-determination by a collective that wished to constitute itself as a political one has emerged time and again as a struggle in which one national group recruits state apparatuses in order to oppress other national groups. Wherever the surge of nationalism in the nation-state has not been curbed by strong civil institutions and rooted civil tradition, it has destroyed the universal component of the state. It has often turned the state itself into a disaster-wreaking power that was quick to deprive members of the subjugated national group of many or all of their political rights. Indeed, the modern state has generated more wars and political catastrophes after becoming the monopoly of one national group.

This disastrous fusion of nationalism and the nation-state has a political, physical, and psychological price as well, paid by the citizens belonging to the hegemonic national group. It is a subtle price, accumulating slowly and touching upon the nature of the political association that they can maintain. It poses a permanent threat to the most basic characteristics of a democratic regime, such as civil equality, openness, transparency of state mechanisms, freedom of association and expression, and so on. It erodes apparatuses meant to monitor the government and distorts the political agenda and the economic or cultural scale of priorities. It perpetuates the willingness of countless parents to prepare their children for conscription, control, oppression, and sacrifice from early childhood on and hand them over to the state without demanding to know what exactly goes on in the places where they are posted, and without asking whether all of this is truly unavoidable.

Nationalism that infiltrates state apparatuses and is recruited by them in return erodes the universal dimension of *democratic institutions and turns citizenship from an infrastructure of solidarity and liberty into a mechanism of segregation and hatred*, producing other governed groups as aliens. Nationalism that functions from within the state and in its name creates the need for self-segregation that it is supposed to fulfill and endangers different forms of social relations and human mixtures. It recruits people for struggles across cities, religions, and sometimes even families in the name of an impossible purist ideal. It takes over state mechanisms in order to damage some of the state's citizens. It infects everyone, rulers as well as ruled, because it imposes models of belonging and rituals of identification upon them that force them to keep their distance from, disown, dismiss, dispossess, and exploit people who under different circumstances would have been their partners, friends, or simply neighbors. Finally, nationalism nurtures the illusion that state apparatuses are safer if entrusted to members of the same nationality, the one ruling the state, thus infringing upon the justness of equal distribution of state power and contradicting the democratic checks and balances that would never let one group rule another indefinitely. It is this nationalism that, more than any other factor, is responsible for the creation of Israel's occupied backyard and must be strictly separated from the state in any future political accord and reconciliation between Jews and Palestinians.

NONVIOLENT REGIME CHANGE

Ending the Occupation, in any scenario, cannot be exhausted by a mere series of acts such as a withdrawal of the forces, apparatuses, and institutions engendered by the Occupation regime. Ending the Occupation must necessarily lead to a regime change within Israel, a change that would transform not only the situation of Palestinians now living under the Occupation, but also of Israelis who perceive it as external to their lives. Suggested "solutions" such as "disengagement," "withdrawal," "dismantling outposts," or "territorial exchange while retaining the settlement blocs" continue to regard the Occupation as a project and undo civil-political discussion of the question of the new regime to be constituted. In such a discussion, the crucial questions are not where the border will be drawn or how many settlers will be evacuated, but rather who will live under what regime, who will determine its nature, whether civil discourse can replace the military-security rationale, what form the participation of the governed in the new regime will take, and what the rules for joining it will be.

All the common formulas for envisaging the end of the Occupation take the security threat for granted and offer an answer of the same "security" school. Since the founding of the State of Israel, its idea of peace has been a slave to "security" logic. The single solution package envisaged to date has never broken out of the limited dichotomy that poses two political solutions as mutually exclusive opposites: two states versus one state. The former solution is presented as highly dangerous but the only possible one, and whoever accepts it on principle usually adds various reservations regarding the settlements, the partition of Jerusalem, and demilitarizing the Palestinian state, which sterilize it and make it unacceptable by Palestinian leaders and basically inapplicable. On the other hand, the one-state solution is presented as a mirage; whoever dares mention it is automatically suspected of treason and a desire to destroy the State of Israel. However, civil thinking about ending the Occupation as a regime must not search for answers to security or demographic questions but rather replace them with political questions pertaining to the structure of the regime, and understand "security threats" as a consequence of political relations and the resulting construct of political-economic relations. Alongside this limited idea of security, we propose to reject its close ally, the reductive, antagonistic conception of the nation that needs an existential threat against itself in order to stabilize nationality as a recruiting identity. More important, we propose reexamination of the assumption that the two solutions—one state or partition into two states—are mutually exclusive. We seek creative ways to emphasize a variety of identities that are not reducible to national identity and to invent new channels of cooperation, interrelations, and alliances.

The First Solution:

Ending the Occupation by Repartitioning Space Between the Mediterranean Sea and the Jordan River into Two Nation-States

This solution, for many years the only one considered feasible, would change Israel's demographics, but does not suffice to change its democratic structure and rehabilitate its civil life. Presumably it is based upon the right of any nation to self-determination, to be fulfilled without denying other nations the same right. National separation is necessary in order to grant sovereignty to the ethnic nation and let it monopolize the state apparatus. But why would the ethnic nation need sovereignty that requires its political separation from other ethnic nations? If one refuses to attribute imaginary metaphysical characteristics to the nation, one is left with only the security consideration: only a sovereign nation-state can defend the nation against the threat embodied by other nations. This conception suppresses the role played by the nation-state itself in creating national hostility and nationalizing the enemy and its threats. It seeks to solve the problem by its very cause.

All "peace negotiations" held to date have accepted the "two-state" principle—either implicitly or explicitly—as the only possible solution and interpreted the principle of self-determination solely through the military-security prism. Neither Israeli and Palestinian thinking about "peace" nor the Israeli approach to "negotiations" in their various metamorphoses have ever envisaged a civil project seeking a new form of partnership between Israelis and Palestinians sharing the same space. The explanation of why the only feasible solution has not been reached for over forty years is nearly always given in strategic terms. For the Israelis, no substitute—of the security kind, naturally—has been found for "strategic depth" to be given up along with the Occupied Territories. Meanwhile, the Palestinians have not accepted Israel's conception of security. They insist on the evacuation of all the Jewish colonies, full withdrawal, and return to the 1949 armistice lines, even in Jerusalem. Moreover, they refuse to demilitarize their territory and insist on including the refugees in a peace treaty. The Palestinian position is presented time and again as evidence that "there is no partner for peace," as if Israel's insistence upon continuing and escalating its colonial project, its refusal to return to the 1949 lines, and its obstinate opposition to the refugees' return were not proof that *the Palestinians* are the ones who have "no partner for peace."

In both cases, each of the issues presented as an obstacle to a peace treaty assumes the continuation of the conflict and the persistence of its military framing. Israel is willing to end the conflict only if the Palestinians give up whatever has been taken from them; the Palestinians are willing to end the conflict only if the Israelis give back everything they have taken since 1967 (the PLO) or 1948 (Hamas). Both would like to add to any agreement something that would somehow guarantee, miraculously, that the other side will never turn aggressive again.

Since the Oslo Accords, all Israeli governments have had a common interest with the Palestinian Authority: to conduct and present the "peace talks" as taking place between two equal partners, two national entities, that have to agree on how to repartition the land and its resources. We do not reject the principle of partition itself—but we do reject its national framing. Partition, or perhaps a series of partitions, might be a useful way to envisage and organize new forms of sharing, partnership, and association between Israelis and Palestinians. The condition for ending the Occupation regime—and, along with this, ridding the Israeli civil regime of its backyard and its security cult—is a formulation of the principle of partition and a "two-state solution" as a form of partnership. Territorial division, state apparatuses, and the different resources between two nation-states must take into account both a past of oppression and dispossession and a future open to collaboration in all realms of life. They must ensure that the Occupation will not be pursued in other ways, that neither Palestinian inferiority in matters of land possession, economy, and education nor Jewish self-segregation behind walls and the fear of Palestinian violence will be replicated or perpetuated, and that the security question will become a matter of mutual concern for both governments as well as a civil issue: concern for the personal, environmental, economic, social, and cultural security of *all* citizens, Palestinians and Jews alike.

The Second Solution:
Ending the Occupation by Granting Equal Citizenship to Jews
and Palestinians in a State of All Its Citizens

This solution will not change Israel's demographics but will change the representation that the demographic composition of the population receives in government, political space, and the democratic game. Granting Jews and Palestinians equal civil status in Israel-Palestine will not only correct the injustice suffered by Palestinians over the years of being governed as helpless humans deprived of their rights. Equal citizenship for Jews and Palestinians will encourage—perhaps even oblige—both the government in the transformed regime and its citizens to go beyond a conception of citizenship as an asset of privileged individuals and of a government authorized to grant and deny it. Such equality will enable the state to free itself of the logic of ethnic-nationalism and open the door for developing citizenship as a framework for a constantly *renewed distribution* among equals, shaping new mechanisms and models of civil empowerment.

In accepting the principle of a "state of all its citizens" in the entire space between the Mediterranean Sea and the Jordan River, we do not ignore the national question, differences of tradition and custom, aspirations and fears, traumatic memories and residues of hostility and hatred, anger and vengefulness shaped as a national problem that can only be settled in national terms. We believe that these should be dealt with by organizations of civil society alongside state mechanisms that bear an equal responsibility to both nations, destined to live together, and with sufficient means to address the separate national matters and the contradictions they embody. The separation of nation and state, conceived of along lines not dissimilar to the separation of church and state will allow the flourishing and coexistence of multiple nationalities. National communities will differentiate themselves from one another within the framework of a single state, not unlike religious communities. State mechanisms providing such differentiation within civil partnership should be envisaged and developed. In a state of all its citizens, civil partnership could be stabilized only if ways and means are found to respect and express the principles of national division. And just as political partition does not require the dismantling of civil, economic, cultural, and religious partnerships and associations shared by people living between the sea and the river, so too the one state in which all are equal citizens does not require the blurring of national differences of whoever wishes to maintain them as such.

In other words, the contrast between the two familiar solutions—"two states for two peoples" and "a binational state" of all its citizens—is real only when the solution is considered from a nationalist point of view, or its derivative "demographic" one, and as a matter of security and state strategy. From a civil point of view, the differences fade out. Either one speaks of partition through partnership, or of partnership that contains principles of multiple divisions and partial partition. In any case, neither of these solutions is possible if the state apparatus is monopolized by one nation and the absolute equality of the rights of Jews and Arabs is not recognized. Minimizing differences between the two solutions leads, almost automatically, to a third—the federative solution.

The Third Solution:
Ending the Occupation Through a Federation
of Separate Spatial or National Entities

This solution will require the creation of a new set of balances between democratic representation and the demographic composition of populations in separate, relatively autonomous units, bound together in a single federative framework and stabilizing the relations between them through the federative state. One should already begin to think of models of separation and federation that would take into account religious, geographic, and economic differences alongside national ones, as well as the variety of existing and possible interrelations.

Israelis and Palestinians have *shared a history* since the nineteenth century. Any attempt to split the joint history that involves people in common territory and present it as the history of two separate sides, as if what happened to "one side" was not a part of the history of "the other side," is bound to produce false, distorted narratives. The national point of view cannot erase their shared past and the variety of forms of being-together—including the more violent ones—of Jews and Arabs, shaped in Palestine / The Land of Israel. For decades, the idea of nation-state as the culmination of national aspirations and a condition for their realization has erased the mere possibility of envisaging national existence in other forms and ways, legitimizing attempts to maximize the concurrence of nation with the governed population in its entirety. Where such concurrence was lacking, as in Israel, the monopolizing of the state apparatus by the dominant nation and the marginalizing of the national minority were perceived as legitimate, necessary, and natural, precluding any other option.

Whoever rejects ideas of transfer, however, and is aware of the inevitable failure of any ethnic cleansing, must cope with the simple fact that no territorial division of the space between the sea and the river would produce total concurrence between the residents in national territory and the ethnic nation. Therefore, even the choice to identify the nation with the state would have to be made with reservations, granting full, decent civil existence for the national minority. Hence, any solution of the present situation requires thinking national separation from within the framework and perspective of a binational partnership and civil association, and understanding this solution as a form of this partnership and association.

These solutions, although they seem completely differentiated and mutually exclusive, appear to be three dimensions of a single possible solution: *distinct national belonging, full citizenship*, and the freedom to envisage and together shape a *form of partnership that would cross national boundaries and would not be limited by state apparatuses.*

CO-IMAGINING

Following the outbreak of the Second Intifada and the extensive use of violence by police forces in demonstrations organized by Palestinian citizens in October 2000, Palestinian citizens of Israel created several "vision documents" in which they sought to envisage a different civil future. These documents were never seriously discussed by the Jewish public in Israel, however. They were treated as a "security" issue. Instead of being regarded as a challenge or invitation to dialogue, the beginning of a civil discussion among partners, documents that would have to be rewritten time and again in order to reach an agreed-upon version, one that would be feasible, reasonable for one and all, the "vision documents" were taken to be "an existential threat" to the State of Israel. The fact that they contested the form of regime practiced in Israel was interpreted as a contestation of the actual right of the state to exist. The right of citizens to reshape the regime under which they live—self-evident when Jews wish to change the election system or write a "constitution for Israel"—is automatically denied the Palestinians, who are barred at the threshold of legitimacy. Although there was nothing illegal about their views, they were declared a "security threat" by politicians and officials of the security apparatus. In 2010, in response to "the vision documents," trying to criminalize their authors retroactively and prevent others from following them, the Knesset passed an amendment to the "Budget Foundation Law" that prohibits governmental allocation of money to any organization or institution that allows voices and activities challenging the Jewish monopoly of the state, thus limiting the democratic space open for citizens to reflect upon the principles of their regime and reshape it.[2]

Needless to say, the Palestinian citizens concerned did not contest the democratic characteristics of the Israeli regime, but only wished to reinforce them. They suggested a discourse that opens a civil horizon for the existence of the State of Israel, and envisages a future free of the security prism. Such a horizon is sought from different directions, in different contexts, by several groups of Jewish citizens as well.

Eitan Bronstein and Norma Musih of the Israeli NGO "Zochrot" have proposed various forms of return and absorption of Palestinian refugees. Eyal Weizman, Sandi Hilal, and Alessandro Petti, architects active in the Palestinian town of Beit Sahour, plan various forms of spatial decolonization of several settlements, whose dismantling they envisage, in a way that would avoid destruction and return some of the land to its owners, but also make renewed use of the space for the benefit of the Palestinian public. Yehuda Shenhav has proposed rethinking the common future of Jews and Arabs, abandoning the framework of the Green Line. In her video works, the artist Yael Bartana envisages the return of Jews to Poland as a model for the return of displaced persons to their countries of origin. Yael Bartana and the curator Galit Eilat have co-edited a "recipe book" containing essays, artworks, and architectural plans envisaging a postnational future. The artist-curator Joshua Simon has edited *Solution 196–213: United States of Palestine-Israel*, a book containing various proposals and formulas for a joint Israeli-Palestinian future. The annual project of exhibitions and symposia "Where To?" at the Israeli Center for Digital Art, a nonprofit organization supported by the city of Holon, examines "other visions of Zionism," and Eyal Sivan and Eric Hazan have reconstructed the history of the many attempts to establish a Jewish-Palestinian state.[3] At Bil'in, Ni'ilin, Nabi Salah, Ma'asara, Sheikh Jarrah, Ras al Amud, and several other sites, Jews and Palestinians demonstrate together regularly, developing various forms of civil nonviolent struggle against the Occupation authorities and gradually reducing the separation of the "treatment" accorded citizen and noncitizen demonstrators.

Examples abound, but they are still a tiny minority. Against the conflictive reality of life in which Jewish citizens find themselves and in view of their blooming imagination in other realms, the lack of discourse envisaging a different future manifests the ongoing oppression of civil imagination under the existing regime. This is the least familiar and seldom mentioned of all forms of Israeli oppression. It is easy to notice the oppression of Palestinians in the Occupied Territories or inside the State of Israel. It is harder, if not impossible, to acknowledge that the civil horizon of Israeli citizens of Jewish origin is simply blocked. Zionism pre-1947, before the emergence of the fatal combination of colonial, majoritarian, and destruction projects was an environment rich with political imagination that invented new possibilities for Jewish existence. The freedom to imagine—even to imagine the impossible—was cut down as the "statist" stream of Zionism took over and recruited all human and material resources to materialize the vision of a Jewish state in which the Arabs have little or no part.

For most Jews today, the presence of Palestinians not as enemies but as partners—including partners in the work of political imagination—requires a long stretch of the imagination. We assume that this is no less true for Palestinians trying to imagine Jews as their partners, not enemies. But when this is made possible, Jewish citizens will be able to break out of the shackles of their imagination.[4] If the Palestinians had been partners in governance and political agenda-setting, the Occupation might not have been institutionalized as a regime, the Territories could not have been constituted as Israel's backyard, and the Palestinians expelled from their land would not have been defined as "refugees" (a category that in the Israeli political discourse has lost its association with suffering and injustice and become the signifier of an existential threat that is easily replaced by the category "infiltrators"). Were the Arab citizens of the state full partners in governance, Jewish citizens would not suffer such extreme repression of their civil, political consciousness. They would see the division of political power among all of the governed as self-evident, and something that must be fought for when the government tries to deny it. They would essentially and unconditionally oppose the differential control of Jews and non-Jews and act to prevent the institutionalization of the regime monster that has grown up in Israel.

The covert assumption and half-denied practice that ensure the distinct yet inseparable existence of the two halves of the regime rests on naturalizing the Jewish monopoly of the state and the exclusion of Palestinian citizens from sharing in the government. Israel's Judeocracy is the condition for the coexistence of the civil and the military regimes, with their variously democratic and oppressive institutions. Judeocracy must be firmly protected to ensure the reproduction of the Janus-faced regime. In order to end the Occupation and generate regime change without violence and bloodshed, the Arab citizens must be made full partners in ruling, in construction commissions, and in the institutions of culture, finance, development, and especially security—first and foremost. They would help the Jewish citizens put a halt to the present fascist tidal wave and rescue them from the regime demonization that threatens the Jews, not because they have become victims of the regime, but rather because they have become a part of its body. In the present state of things, the participation of Palestinian citizens in power is a condition for Jewish citizens to start to restore the meaning of their citizenship.

No change of law is needed at the outset for gradual regime change. Most forms of distancing of the Arabs from rule do not derive from the cut-and-dried language of legislation; they are a result of the way in which the law is implemented by the government in its various spheres of action, with the tacit approval or silence of the Supreme Court. No legislative revolution or electoral miracle is needed to put a stop to such exclusion of Arabs. It suffices that a governing coalition be composed of the existing political parties—both Jewish and Arab—in such a way that positions of power in the government are distributed according to normal political party practice, without an a priori guarantee of exclusive regional Jewish control. In such a situation, the vision documents created by the Arab intellectuals would be translated into practical demands and presented for discussion within the current administration of government offices and Knesset legislation. At the same time, resources would be directed to committees charged with the gradual but determined civilizing of existing state mechanisms. Affirmative action would create new possibilities for Palestinian citizens to take key positions in state apparatuses. They would be able to lead a joint effort to cope with the past with commitment and responsibility, without

forfeiting concrete demands for restitution and rehabilitation, and without giving up the horizon of reconciliation and forgiveness.

Along with redefining its commitment to the Palestinians, the new regime
would have to redefine its commitment to the Jews. Such commitments would
naturally be of a different nature if an independent Palestinian state were to be
founded alongside the State of Israel, or if a federation were to be created. But
the principle would be the same: conceiving the state as a means in the hands of
all its citizens rather than of one national group, let alone as an end in itself. In
this conception, groups of citizens that form on a national, religious, language,
or gender basis would be entitled to demand that the state serve their collective
interests and not only the private interests of each and every individual in their
midst. The Jews would not be required to give up the state tools that protect
the Jewish collective, help Jews in the Diaspora, stand by to rescue persecuted
Jews, and promote Jewish culture, including Israeli national Jewish culture.
Such mechanisms or their like would also serve the Palestinian collective and
its Diaspora, created by the Nakba, under any solution that would be reached.

The Israeli regime has strong mechanisms of self-preservation, based on
strong interests, the support of politically and economically powerful groups in
Israel and abroad, recruiting ideologies, a sense of existential threat, and great
fear of change. The last time the government's policies were regarded as a threat
to this regime, a young nationalist assassinated Prime Minister Yitzhak Rabin.
Rabin's heirs of the political Zionist Left renewed the war in Lebanon, set out
to mend the "people torn asunder," lost the elections, and missed the sliver of
a chance embodied in the Oslo process. This is probably what the future holds
as well—anything that would appear to threaten the double regime in Israel
will face violent opposition. And still, one must envisage and think a different regime. Occupation will not end without a whole regime change, and such
change cannot take place without dismantling or reorganizing every one of the
projects that feed Israel's dual regime.

The first project that must go is the majoritarian one. Under the new regime, a Jewish majority would be meaningless. There will be no need of a
Jewish majority, nor will it be possible to ensure it. But forces nurturing the
proliferation of Jews and Jewishnesses, promoting cultural, religious, and national Jewish institutions would receive the support of the state in its federal or
republican form. Palestinian institutions would receive similar support. Alongside national promotion, resources would be invested in developing state institutions that promote the principles of the new regime and hone it. Second to

be dismantled would be the destruction project. Forces that have been invested in systematic destruction would be invested in preservation and restoration, and Palestinians would be promised conditions enabling legal construction in all their living areas.

A variety of models would be developed for the restoration and resuscitation of the life environment—both Palestinian and mixed—that had been destroyed, and the project of destruction would be replaced by one of accommodating new uses of parts of the Wall, the colonies, and most of the Jewish outposts where the land grab is still reversible and the land can be returned to its owners without resorting to mass eviction.

The liberal project would be free of the contradictions imposed by the need to protect universal rights in a nationalist society governed by the apparatuses of a nationalized state. At long last, other contradictions will have to be confronted—those created by a globalized market economy that threatens the very possibility of a political, public space and makes so many people not only so much poorer but ultimately disposable, almost irrespective of nation, gender, color, or religion.

The decolonization project, at the heart of which lies a reorganization of space, would not be abandoned altogether, but rather guided by new principles: refraining from mass displacement; political equality of opportunity, conditions, and rights; respecting the right of different groups to maintain distinct, separate life frameworks that preserve authentic customs; affirmative action in allotment of resources for planning and construction that would enable the Palestinians to revive some of the architectural, social, and housing diversity that characterized their life in the past; support of joint housing projects for Jews and Palestinians; creation of a restitution fund for Palestinians whose lands were stolen from them, supported by donations and taxation of real estate in Israel, that would make building sites available for returning Palestinian refugees, in the Territories as well as within the Green Line;[5] turning army bases in the Occupied Territories into public facilities for the benefit of all the residents in their vicinity.

Some of the Jewish settlers would have to evacuate their homes, while others will relocate of their own free will if they wish to avoid living in mixed localities. Yet others could go on living in the Territories, just as numerous Palestinians would be able to come back and live within the Green Line. Various models of mixed localities would be developed, and people willing to populate them would be offered various incentives. Similar incentives would be offered to partnerships of Jews and Palestinians in industry, trade, education, and culture. Mixed localities would be declared the new frontier of this new regime, a place of real pioneers. Mixed organizations in all other areas would be the anchors of the new regime. The ruling power of this new regime would have a genuine interest in promoting mixed organizations and rewarding their participants, who might then in turn support it.

Under such conditions, the return of refugees to Israel would not be regarded by Jews as an existential threat—the ultimate Palestinian demand that upends any agreement. Return arrangements (and restitution for refugees who choose not to return) would be shaped according to the general framework of the new regime and would differ depending on whether a single state, a federative framework, or an independent Palestinian state alongside a Jewish one is created. The Jews would be full partners in the return effort in any of these formations, while the geographic distribution of the returning refugees and their absorption would be part of the historic reconciliation between Jews and Arabs.

REFERENCE MATTER

NOTES

PROLOGUE: THE FIRST YEAR OF THE OCCUPATION

1. Halabi 1982, 33.
2. Meron Benvenisti 1976; Gazit 1985.
3. Halabi 1982, 35–36.
4. Efrat 2006, 76. On the eve of the war, about 900,000 people were living in the West Bank. About 250,000 of them were expelled and 14,000 allowed to return (Sanbar 1994, 80).
5. Morris 1999, 335–36.
6. Agabaria 2007; Matta and Abu Jabal 2006, 11; Meron Benvenisti 1987a; Davis and Mezvinsky 1975.
7. According to data held by the League for Human and Civil Rights, during the first three years of the Occupation, 5,554 houses were demolished, in addition to the 2,500 houses demolished in a concentrated operation at the Latroun villages and in the town of Qalqiliya (Davis and Mezvinsky 1975, 147).
8. Algazi 1974, 28.
9. Shehadeh and Kuttab 1980.
10. In 1970, 1,262 Palestinians were held as administrative detainees, 220 of whom were imprisoned for over a year, one hundred of them women (Hofnung 1996, 225–26; Jad 1990, 129).
11. Gazit 1985, 23–38; Eldar and Zertal 2007, 333–99; Teveth 1970, 29–34.
12. Ronen 1989, 17–20.
13. Ibid., 18.
14. Gazit 1985, 37–43.
15. Dayan rejected a proposal made by Joseph Hermelin, then chief of the GSS, to do just that (Black and Morris 1991, 239). Dayan failed, however, to avoid recruiting the professional cadre that had operated Israel's military government within the Green Line (Korn 1996, 44–45).
16. Korn 1996, 194–96; Benzimann and Mansour 1992.
17. Black and Morris 1991, 236–360; Ronen 1989.
18. Shehadeh and Kuttab 1980, 82–83.

19. Shlomo Gazit, the first coordinator of government activities in the Territories, published a book titled *The Carrot and the Stick* (Gazit 1985).

20. For a typical case, see Eilon 1971.

21. Shehadeh and Kuttab 1980, 103.

22. Ronen 1989.

23. Teveth 1970, 246–55.

24. Ibid., 263.

INTRODUCTION

1. This situation has changed since the Second Intifada. See, e.g., *Theory and Criticism*'s special volume [in Hebrew] on the Occupation (vol. 31, 2007); Weizman 2007; Kotef and Amir 2007, 2011; Azoulay 2008; Gordon 2008; Ophir et al. 2009; Hever 2010; Handel 2010a; Amir 2011.

2. Terms applied to both the Jewish people and its land by Zionist ideologues, like "return" and "redemption," which are used to justify the ruling of the Territories, but not to describe it, will not be addressed here at all.

3. In this study we could only delineate the place of the Palestinian Authority and the Hamas government within the overall structure of the Israeli ruling apparatus. A detailed account of the role these two Palestinian bodies play in the Israeli regime still awaits further research.

4. Except for residents in the areas annexed in Jerusalem and its environs, who could, for a short period after the annexation, apply for citizenship.

5. This applies to the Gaza Strip despite "the disengagement." See pt. 2, chap. 5 of this book.

6. Taking into account Kretzmer's differentiation of historical periods according to changes in the legal status and ideological perception of the Territories (Kretzmer 2002, 7–9), without sticking to it, and Gordon's elaborate differentiation according to changing power formations (Gordon 2008).

CHAPTER 1. THE FIRST DECADE

1. Gazit 1985, 23–28; Eldar and Zertal 2007, 333–99; Teveth 1970, 29–34; Shamgar 1967, 540–44.

2. Gordon 2008, introduction.

3. Teveth 1970, 31; Rubinstein 1988, 63–64.

4. This legal argument has been widely criticized. See, e.g., Eyal Benvenisti 1993, 109–14 and the sources cited there; Pacheco 2001; Kretzmer 2002, chaps. 2–3; Ben Naftali et al. 2009.

5. Kretzmer 2002, 40–42.

6. Rubinstein 1988, 68–72, 77–79; Rubinstein 1991, 104–7, 116–31; Felner and Rosen, 1994, 15–18; Eyal Benvenisti 1990, 3–31; Eldar and Zertal 2007, 371–80.

7. Shehadeh and Kuttab 1980, 24.

8. Ibid.

9. Shehadeh 1982, 23–27.

10. Rubinstein 1988, 68–69; Hofnung 1996, 229–32; Eyal Benvenisti 1990, 3–16.

11. Sason 2005, chap. 10; Eyal Benvenisti 1990, 3–31.

12. *Edicts Concerning the Authority of Governance and Legislation*, Israel, Legal Advisor 1975, article 2, June 7, 1967.

13. Admoni 1992, 20. The annexation was a rare case in which policy was executed through parliamentary legislation (amendment to *Edicts Concerning the Authority of Governance and Legislation*, article 11b, June 27, 1967), to which two government decrees were added later (Felner 1995, 20–21). In 1981, Israeli jurisdiction was also imposed on the Golan Heights.

14. The Hebrew *mukhzakim* (מוחזקים) is fruitfully ambiguous.

15. Israel, High Court of Justice 2005.

16. Stein 1997, 14–18.

17. Kretzmer 2002, chap. 6.

18. Ibid., 21–22.

19. Verdict was often given after years of procrastination, and 90 percent of the appeals have been turned down.

20. Kretzmer 2002, 39–40.

21. Ibid., 187; cf. Gross 2006, 2007.

22. Shehadeh and Kuttab 1980, 35–36.

23. Langer 1975.

24. Hajjar 2005, 96–131; Drori 1980, 41.

25. Holzmann 1968, 18–19.

26. Shehadeh and Kuttab 1980, 30–33.

27. Shamir 1990, 785–86.

28. Hajjar 2005, 4–29; Shehadeh 1982, 10–18.

29. Gazit 1985, 186, 203–4; Ronen 1989, 34.

30. Gordon 2008, introduction, chap. 2.

31. Efrat 2006, 23–25; Gazit 2003, 67.

32. Gordon 2008, chap. 1.

33. Meron Benvenisti 1984, 8–18; Kleiman 1993, 305–33.

34. Meron Benvenisti 1987b, 202–3.

35. Ibid., 91.

36. Pappe 2003.

37. Gazit 1985, 94–95.

38. Ibid., 65.

39. Guillou and Stagh 1975.

40. Leaflet published by Israeli League for Human and Civil Rights 1978, 16; Yosef Algazi's personal archive.

41. Teveth 1970, 71–90; Drori 1980, 43–58.

42. Gazit 1985, 153.

43. Halabi 1982, 64–65.

44. The image of the collaborator, the representation of Palestinians as collaborators, and the patterns of collaborators' recruitment and operation go back to the early days of the Zionist project. See Cohen 2008, 2010; Azoulay 2008, chap. 9.

45. Teveth 1970, 143–51.

46. Gazit 1985, 212.

47. Shalev 1990, 24; Sarna 2007, 121–28 and n. 189.

48. Gazit 1985, 207.

49. Ibid.; Algazi 1974; Ronen 1989.

50. Thus forcing Palestinian workers to pay the daily cost of transportation (Portugali 1993, 12–13).

51. Yanov 1975.

52. Kleiman 1993, 305–33; Meron Benvenisti 1984, 8–18; Portugali 1993; Peled and Shafir 2002, 185–90; Schiff and Ya'ari 1990b, 79–93; Shalev 1990, 24–25; Tamari 1992, 7–28; Swirski 2005, 12–42; Arnon et al. 1997; Farsakh 2005.

53. Exploitation of women and children was the harshest. Roy 1986; Jad 1990.

54. Swirski 2005, 16–42.

55. Gazit 2003; Israel, Ministry of Defense 1982; id., Civil Administration 1983.

56. Hofnung 1996, 101–123; Kedar 1998.

57. "Order Concerning Abandoned Properties (Private Property) (Judea and Samaria) (No. 58), 1967" (in Hebrew), in Israel, Legal Advisor 1975, 158. www.aka.idf.il/SIP_STORAGE/FILES/0/60630.pdf (accessed May 12, 2012). Extracts in English in Dinstein 1971, 419–64.

58. Hofnung 1996, 249–50; Shehadeh and Kuttab 1980, 61–62.

59. Article 10(A) in "Order Concerning Abandoned Properties (Private Property) (Judea and Samaria) (No. 58), 1967" (in Hebrew), in Israel, Legal Advisor 1975, 158. www.aka.idf.il/SIP_STORAGE/FILES/0/60630.pdf (accessed May 12, 2012). Extracts in English in Dinstein 1971, 419–64.

60. Lein 2002, 48–63.

61. State Comptroller's annual report, no. 37 (Jerusalem 1987), 1189.

62. Meron Benvenisti 1987b, 112–13; Eldar and Zertal 2007, 367–68.

63. Meron Benvenisti 1987b, 116–20; Gazit 2003, 318–19, 278–85; Eldar and Zertal 2007, 333–61.

64. Sa'abana 1994.

65. Eldar and Zertal 2007, chap. 1.

66. Ibid.

67. Sanbar 1994, 75–79; Shalev 1990, 65–71.

68. Ronen 1989.

69. Ibid., 42.

70. Halabi 1982, 77–79.

71. Amos Eilon, *Ha'aretz*, February 5, 1971.

72. Leaflet published by Israeli League for Human and Civil Rights, August 3, 1971, Yosef Algazi's personal archive; Langer 1975, 108–17.

73. Algazi 1974, 61–72, 69.

74. Halabi 1982, 56–57.

75. Guttman and Levi 1976.

76. See, e.g., Raja Shehadeh's perceptive description of a Palestinian clerk at the military court (Shehadeh 1982, 14–16).

77. Teveth 1970, 334.

78. Gazit 1985, 203.

79. Edict concerning Village Management Act No. 5, 1954 (edict 191), in Israel, Legal Advisor 1975, 1: 327.

80. Shlaim 2000, chaps. 5–7.

81. Gordon 2008, chap. 4.

82. Jad 1990; Kuttab 1992.

83. Drori 1980, 87.

84. Ibid., 88.

85. Jamal 2005b, 39–42.

86. Drori 1980, 203–4.

87. Shehadeh 1982, 24–26; Portugali 1993, 93–112; Meron Benvenisti 1987b, 176; Schiff and Ya'ari 1990b, 50–55.

88. Jamal 2005b, 39–54.

89. Ma'oz 1984, 133–39; Jad 1990.

90. Ma'oz 1984, 162–65.

91. Algazi 1974; Gazit 1985, 307–20.

CHAPTER 2. THE SECOND DECADE

1. Hofnung 1996, 238–53; Eldar and Zertal 2007, 364–71; Lein 2002, 51–57.

2. Kretzmer 2002, 90–94.

3. Gazit 2003, 278–81; Lein 2002, 62–63.

4. Hofnung 1996, 253–57; Etkes and Ofran 2006; Meron Benvenisti 1987b, 139.

5. Eldar and Zertal 2007, 99.

6. Meron Benvenisti 1988, 40.

7. Swirski 2005, 57; Meron Benvenisti 1984, 52–63; Meron Benvenisti 1987b, 111; Peled and Shafir 2002, 172–80.

8. Segal and Weizman 2003, chaps. 5–6; Gordon 2008, chap. 5.

9. Eldar and Zertal 2007, 56–58; 139–42. The unity government was based on a coalition of the Labor and Likud parties.

10. Ibid., 58–61; 98–100.

11. Israel, Ministry of Agriculture and Settlement Division of the World Zionist Organization, *Master Plan for Settlement for Judea and Samaria: A Plan for the Development of the Region, for the Years 1983–1986* (in Hebrew) (Jerusalem, 1983).

12. Eldar and Zertal 2007, 98; Meron Benvenisti 1987b, 115, 120–21.

13. Meron Benvenisti 1984, 10.

14. Hofnung 1996, 231–32; Yakobson and Rubinstein 2009, 103–4.

15. Gordon 2008, introduction.

16. Ibid., chap. 3.

17. Lein 1998.

18. Gordon 2008, chap. 3; Hamed and Shaban 1993.

19. Portugali 1993, 6–19, 75–92.

20. Salim Tamari argues, however, that Israeli control had a distorting effect on the Palestinian economy from the very beginning (Tamari 1992, 10–14).

21. Etkes and Ofran 2006.

22. Schiff and Ya'ari 1990b, 79–93.

23. Ma'oz 1984, 198–203.

24. Yakobson and Rubinstein 2009, 103–4; Gazit 2003, 210–17.

25. Hofnung 1996, 223–24.

26. Meron Benvenisti 1984, 45–46.

27. Gordon 2008, chap. 6.

28. Ma'oz 1984, 163–64.

29. Kimmerling 2003.

30. Ron 2003, 171–81.

31. Gazit 2003, 45ff.

32. E.g., Shehadeh 1982, 175–76n290.

33. Meron Benvenisti 1986, 63.

34. Hajjar 2005, 44, relying on reports in the *Jerusalem Post*, February 20, 1987.

35. Sarna 2007, 36–68.

36. Leibowitz 1986; Benvenisti and Richardson 1982; Aloni 1997, 83–85; Talmon 1980; Shahak 1988; Algazi 1988.

37. Shamir 1990, 786–89.

38. Kretzmer 2002, 79–84.

39. Ibid., 99.

40. Saragusti 1986.

41. Hofnung 1996, 256–57; Felner and Rosen, 1994.

42. Dudai 2001b, 22–23, 31–51.

43. Lein 2001; Lein and Cohen-Lifshitz 2005.

CHAPTER 3. UPRISINGS, SEPARATIONS, AND SUBJUGATIONS

1. An increase in the number of cases classified as "public disorder," as well as stabbings, had been recorded since the mid-1980s. Meron Benvenisti 1986, 63–69; 1987a, 40–50; Shalev 1990, 44–45.

2. See, e.g., Kuttab 1992, 125.

3. Yahya 1990, 95.

4. Jad 1990, 134.

5. Shalev 1990, 36.

6. Jad 1990, 133–34; Schiff and Ya'ari 1990b, chap. 9.

7. Schiff and Ya'ari 1990b, chap. 6.

8. Shalev 1990, 147–48; Jarbawi 1990, 300–301.

9. Schiff and Ya'ari 1990a, 343.

10. Hanafi and Tabar 2005.

11. Ron 2003, 148–52.

12. Schiff and Ya'ari 1990b, 139–43.

13. Daphna Golan 1992, 7; Hajjar 2005, 3; Golan and Cohen 1991.

14. Shalev 1990, 123–26; Gideon Levy 2004, 216–17; Ezrahi 1997, chap. 9.

15. Carmi 1999, 11–14; Ginbar 1997, 18–19.

16. Ron 2003, chaps. 7–8; Andoni 2001.

17. Cf. Hajjar 2005, 27.

18. Hofnung 1996, 285–87.

19. Ibid., 331.

20. Kretzmer 2002, 149–55.

21. The League of Human Rights was established in 1936. Its first report on the Occupied Territories was issued in 1971.

22. Kretzmer 2002, 187–98.

23. Lein 1999, 17-18.

24. Segal and Weizman 2003, 79–143; Eldar and Zertal 2007, 112–13.

25. Gutwein 2005, 291–92. For critiques of this position and alternative economic explanations, see Kleiman 2005 and Hever 2005.

26. Peled and Shafir 2002, 188–90.

27. Ashrawi 1996; Said 2000; Shehadeh 1997; Greenberg 2007.

28. Area A was later extended to contain 18 percent of the Occupied Territories, area B was reduced to about 22 percent, and C to 60 percent. A regional council controls a block of several settlements and a relatively large area surrounding them dedicated to future Jewish expansion.

29. The Hebron accord was signed by Prime Minister Netanyahu in January 1997 and was the last agreement reached—but never fully implemented—within the framework of the Oslo Accords. The city was divided into area H-1, under direct Palestinian control, and area H-2, where security was in the hands of Israel and the administrative

charge of Palestinian everyday life was assigned to the Palestinian Authority. The Jewish neighborhoods were under full Israeli control.

30. Jamal 2005b.

31. Hamami and Tamari in Beinin and Stein 2006, 269; Gordon 2008, chap. 7.

32. For a detailed analysis of the simulative nature of the political sphere in that period, see Azoulay and Ophir 2002, 89–98.

33. Jamal 2005b.

34. Morris 1999, 628–29; Carmi 1999; B'Tselem and Palestinian Human Rights Monitoring Group 1996.

35. Gordon 2008, chap. 7.

36. A. B. Yehoshua in *Yediot Aharonot*, March 1, 1996, quoted in Shiftan 1999, 58.

37. Yehoshua called for the creation of the separation system along the Green Line, but on this point there has never been a consensus.

38. Shiftan 1999, 12–13.

39. Ibid., 220.

40. Lein 2001.

41. Ibid.; Hass 2003.

42. Gideon Levy 2003.

43. Said 2000; Halper 2005a; Hass 2004.

44. Almog 2004, xi.

45. Lein 1999, 18; Halper 2000; Handel 2010a.

46. Handel 2008, 2009.

47. Meron Benvenisti 1998.

48. OCHA 2006.

49. Said 2001; Rabbani 2001; Rubinstein 2004; Handel 2010b.

50. Lein 2002, 15–18, 42–43; Swirski et al. 2002, 13–14.

51. Sason 2005, chaps. 6–10.

52. Ibid.; Harel 2003.

53. Efrat 2006, 93–101.

54. And yet the government asked for special satellite services to document the exact spread of settlement throughout the West Bank (Schiff 2004).

55. Azoulay and Ophir 2002, 98–112.

56. Ibid., chap. 6.

57. Azoulay and Ophir 2005, 190–93.

58. Hofnung 1996, 284–88.

59. Bishara 2003.

60. Petti 2007.

61. Gordon 2008, chap. 7, describes this as a form of "outsourcing."

62. Kemp and Reichman 2003, 2–3.

63. Golan and Shaul 2004.

CHAPTER 4. THE ORDER OF VIOLENCE

1. Gordon 2009. See B'Tselem n.d. for data on the First Intifada and B'Tselem 2011 and GSS 2009 for data on the Second Intifada.

2. Lein 2005, introduction. According to statistics provided by several Israeli and international organizations, Israeli deaths from Palestinian violence have steadily decreased: from 230 in 2002 to 139 in 2003, 29 in 2005, 15 in 2006, and 3 in 2007.

3. The term "demarcation" denotes a written order or oral instruction forbidding the entry of Palestinians into certain areas, mostly Jews-only roads (including strips of terrain of varying breadth alongside them) and areas surrounding colonies, outposts, and army posts. These areas and their dimensions are often changed (Lein 2004; Akiva Eldar 2005). "Fragmentation" is a military term for forbidding Palestinians movement from one area to another (Akiva Eldar 2005; Amira Hass, 2005, 2006).

4. This sentence appears in the original Hebrew edition of this book, published in 2008; it is still true today in the summer of 2012.

5. Gisha 2006.

6. For the military view of these changes, see www.nrg.co.il/online/1/ART/772/991 .html (in Hebrew); an English abbreviated version is available at www.freerepublic.com/ focus/f-news/1093305/posts (both accessed May 12, 2012).

7. See, e.g., Gideon Levy 2004; Hammami 2004; Lein 1998; Goldschmit 2004.

8. Foucault 2000, 340.

9. Benjamin 1999, 277.

10. E.g., Mann 1986, 22–28.

11. Marin 1987, introduction.

12. Agamben 1998, pt. 1, chap. 3; Agamben 1999, chap. 11.

13. Althusser 1971.

14. Jamal 2005b.

15. A case in point is the army's not opening Shuhada Street in Hebron in spite of an explicit court order to do so (Feuerstein 2007). Another is the army's shirking its instructions to dismantle a 41-kilometer-long low concrete wall built along a main road in the South Hebron hills (Harel 2007).

16. See, e.g., Arendt 1979, pt. 2, 243–50.

17. E.g., Suissa 2004.

18. Ben-Naftali et al. 2009.

19. Our debt to Agamben's analysis of suspension of the law and abandonment of life in *Homo Sacer* (Agamben 1998) is clear, but we are careful not to project it blindly on the phenomena we are describing.

20. Hajjar 2005, 207–10.

21. Balibar 1991, 40–44.

22. Weizman 2007, chap. 7.

23. Before Operation Cast Lead in 2009, the most extensive destruction was car-

ried out in 2004 next to the border at Rafah, where 116 houses were demolished during Operation Rainbow, and 1,160 people had to evacuate the area. During this activity, 55 Palestinians were killed. This ratio—55 dead versus 1,160 people who were made refugees and forced to relocate—clearly expresses the relation between the means—violence—and the end, evacuating territory and transferring population.

24. The numbers cited are combined from the B'Tselem web sites www.btselem.org /english/statistics/casualties.asp and http://old.btselem.org/statistics/english/Casualties .asp?sD=19&sM=01&sY=2009&filterby=event&oferet_stat=after (both accessed May 12, 2012), and from the Palestinian Authority's Bureau of Statistics, www.pcbs.gov.ps/Portals/ _pcbs/intifada/2095d332-40f8-4b1e-9cb1-422bcdef6a01.htm (accessed April 18, 2012). It is hard to obtain definitive data on casualties in both sides, and there are always discrepancies between Palestinian and Israeli sources, as well as between governmental and nongovernmental sources. Since the ratio of the two populations is about 1:2, the real ratio of Israeli and Palestinian casualties is about 1:8 and 1:20 respectively.

25. The Palestinians' refusal to distinguish between Israeli military and civil apparatuses has changed in the past few years, because the Palestinian Authority hoped to resume effective negotiations and appeal to the United Nations has seemed a promising route of diplomatic action.

26. Small groups of colonists regularly assault Palestinians living and working in their vicinity, refuting the Israeli ruling power's assumed monopoly on violence in the Occupied Territories. It is hard to tell whether this widespread phenomenon stems from helplessness on the part of law-enforcement authorities or from a tacit division of labor among the security forces and the colonists' undeclared militias (cf. Ron 2003, chap. 8).

27. Shamir 2005, 197–217; Padan and Hartman 2006.

28. Benjamin 1999, 284.

29. Ibid., 286.

30. Stein 1997.

31. Rubinstein 1988, 67–68, Hofnung 1996, 229–37.

32. Gazit 2003, 17.

33. Kretzmer 2002, 20.

34. Stein 2001.

35. Kotef and Amir 2007; Mansbach 2007.

36. We are borrowing Deleuze's term here and use it according to his conception of singularity. See Deleuze 1990, 52ff., 113–115.

37. Kimmerling 2003, chap. 10.

38. See, e.g., Harel 2005; Shavit 2005; Ben 2005.

39. This situation has only slowly and partly been reversed with the complete renunciation of resistance in the West Bank and the growing cleavage and enmity between the Hamas government in Gaza and Salam Fayyad's new Palestinian Authority government in the West Bank.

CHAPTER 5. ABANDONING GAZA

1. Tobi 2001.

2. The estimated number is 200,000, mostly from the southern coastal plain, including 3,000 who were transferred from Maj'dal in a special operation in 1950 after the end of the war.

3. Hass 2000.

4. Shlomi Eldar 2005, 125.

5. Ibid., 116.

6. Roy 1995.

7. Gisha 2006.

8. Roy 2007.

9. Gisha 2007.

10. Israel, High Court of Justice 2007a, 2007b.

11. Agamben 1998, introduction, pt. 2, chap. 5, and part 3, chaps. 1, 2, and 7.

12. Derek Gregory (2004) has already proposed a systematic use of Agamben's notions of sovereignty, exception, and abandonment for analyzing control of the Occupied Territories since the outbreak of the Second Intifada, and others have followed him (e.g., Lentin 2004; Tawil-Suri 2011; Hanafi 2010; Azoulay and Ophir 2004). The series of observations on the situation in the Gaza Strip that follows makes use of Agamben's conceptual grid but goes beyond it in dealing with the complexity of this quite unusual, ongoing case of colonization in which pushing the colonized to the brink of catastrophe has become more than a means of governance; it has become the mode in which they are ruled.

13. Israel has used nonviolent funerals and memorial ceremonies as a pretext for arrests and interrogations ever since the outset of the Occupation (see Algazi 1974).

14. Agamben 1998, 133.

15. Weizman 2007, 238–39.

16. Until its final closure in June 2007, the Rafah crossing operated under an agreement stipulating the presence of EU and PA inspectors (who could reach Rafah only through the Kerem Shalom crossing, which is under full Israeli control). "Control room" allowed Israel to prevent the opening of the crossing (Gisha 2007).

17. B'Tselem 2007b.

18. Eldar 2007.

19. United Nations, Economic and Social Council 2004, 3–4.

20. See, e.g., Bertini 2002; Dugard 2004; United Kingdom 2004.

21. Colonel Orli Malka and Lieutenant Colonel Itzik Gorevitch, interviewed by Ariella Azoulay in her documentary film *The Food Chain* (Azoulay 2002).

22. UNRWA General Director Richard Cook, interviewed by Ariella Azoulay, ibid.

23. Malka, ibid.

24. Malka, ibid.

25. Harel and Ravid 2007.

26. Harel and Yissakharof 2007.

27. Mizrahi 2007.

28. Kaspit 2007.

29. Trucks loaded with goods arriving from Israel and empty trucks that will carry those goods in Palestinian territory are parked back-to-back in parking lots at border crossings and checkpoints in the heart of the West Bank, and the goods are transferred from one vehicle to the other under close military scrutiny. Only goods delivered in this manner may legally enter the West Bank. See Azoulay 2002.

30. Feldman 2010.

31. Gisha 2010.

32. Ibid.

33. Shlomi Eldar 2005, 123.

34. Data and analyses from Shlomi Eldar 2005, chaps. 5–6; Lein 2005; Gisha 2007; B'Tselem 2007a, 2007b; OCHA 2005–6, 2007b.

35. Already in 2006, prior to the establishment of the Hamas government, income per capita in the Gaza Strip was U.S. $2.10 a day. Nearly two-thirds of the population depended on food handouts. During the first month of Hamas in power, even before the occurrence of any violent clashes, over 1,300 containers with imports on their way to the Strip were held in storerooms in Israel. The general loss as a result of suspending delivery of these goods has been estimated at $16 million (Coordinating Council 2008). On disaster conditions in the Gaza Strip, see, e.g., periodic situation reports by the UN Office for the Coordination of Humanitarian Affairs (OCHA) and the periodic reports by Oxfam (e.g., 2008, 2009, 2010). On the implications of the economic boycott on the humanitarian situation in the Gaza Strip, see Roy 2009, 2010; Oxfam 2007, 2010; OCHA 2010, 2011.

36. Ophir 2010.

37. Lein 2005.

38. OCHA 2007a.

39. According to B'Tselem, Israeli security forces killed 1,387 Palestinians in the course of the three-week operation. Of these, 773 did not take part in the hostilities, including 320 minors, 109 women over the age of eighteen, and 248 Palestinian police officers, most of whom were killed in aerial bombings of police stations on the operation's first day (B'Tselem 2009). According to Al-Haq 2009, 1,409 people were killed and 11,154 housing units, 211 industrial premises, 703 shops, and 700 public buildings were completely destroyed or severely damaged.

40. See a collection of reports by Israeli human rights groups at http://gazaeng.blogspot.com (accessed March 20, 2012) and B'Tselem 2009.

41. The statement was recorded at the meeting by Adi Ophir. On the Goldstone report, see www.goldstonereport.org (accessed March 11, 2012).

42. Agamben 2005, 31.

CHAPTER 6. THE CONCEPTUAL SCHEME

1. Bishara 1995.

2. Skinner 1997; Spruyt 1994.

3. Mann 1986, chaps. 13–14; Tilly 1990.

4. This imaginary dimension characterizes any social institution, the state first and foremost. See Runciman 2003.

5. The notion of a strategy without an author is Michel Foucault's. See e.g., Foucault 1990, 94–95; 99–100.

6. Schmitt 1985 [1922].

7. Stoler 2006.

8. See Hannah Arendt's definition of political space in *The Human Condition* (Arendt 1958), chap. 5.

CHAPTER 7. STRUCTURAL DIVISIONS AND STATE PROJECTS

1. See Bishara 2001, 143. The discrimination of Palestinian citizens was exacerbated after the Citizenship Law was amended in 2006.

2. With one exception, a minister of science and culture who served about two years in the government of Prime Minister Ehud Olmert.

3. In order to protect themselves from this Jewish majority, the Arabs need to recruit the support of no fewer than fifty Jewish members of the Knesset.

4. "In any cabinet presided over by a Jewish Prime Minister, there will be an Arab deputy Prime Minister, and vice-versa," Ze'ev Jabotinsky asserted (Jabotinsky 1942, 215, quoted in Yakobson and Rubinstein 2009, 120).

5. On "ethnic democracy," see Smooha 1997; Gavison 1999.

6. Yiftachel 2006, pt. 3.

7. Hamadeh et al. 2006; Adalah 1998; Rouhana 1997, chaps. 3–4.

8. Meron Benvenisti 1987c.

9. See, e.g., the eviction and destruction of Shaykh Muwannis, Khirbat al-Manshiyya, and many other villages and neighborhoods (Pappe 1994, 76–82; 2006, 55–61, 103–14; Morris 2004, chap. 3).

10. See Masalha 1992; Morris 2004, chaps. 2–3; Pappe 2006, chaps. 3–4.

11. Gardi 2011.

12. In and around Jerusalem, along the seam line, and in the hills south of Bethlehem known as Gush Etzion.

13. We could not find documents that would enable a more accurate estimate of the number of houses demolished before 1967.

14. Israeli Committee Against House Demolitions 2010.

15. Maoz 2009; Daniel Levy 2008; Buckin 2008.

16. Klein 2007a; 2007b, chap. 21.

CHAPTER 8. CIVIL RECRUITMENT

1. See, e.g., Rapoport 2007.

2. Bourdieu 1980, chap. 3.

3. Ben Eliezer 2003; Gur 2005.

4. Cohen 2004.

5. Arendt 1979, vol. 2, chap. 5.

6. Israel's joining the United Nations as a member state was conditional on its naturalizing the Palestinians remaining within its borders. They were granted Israeli citizenship in January 1949.

7. Rouhana 1997, 27.

8. Ibid.

9. www.knesset.gov.il/review/data/eng/law/knso_govt-justice_eng.pdf (accessed March 17, 2012). The same principle of Arab representation is expressed in Article 2A concerning the provisional government (ibid.).

10. Stendhal 1992, 70.

11. There are, of course, differences in the recruitment of various sectors in the Jewish population of the State of Israel, but we do not address them here, because they are dwarfed by the nationally determined difference.

12. Legally, the Knesset has sovereign authority to declare a state of emergency and it does so annually as a matter of routine. The government may declare a state of emergency only if the Knesset is unable to convene immediately, and then merely for a period of seven days.

13. Article 39 of Israel's Basic Law: The Government states: "During a state of emergency the Government may make emergency regulations for the defense of the State, public security and the maintenance of supplies and essential services; emergency regulations will be submitted to the Foreign Affairs and Security Committee at the earliest possible date after their enactment."

14. Hofnung 1996, chap. 2; Adalah 2003; Korn 2004.

15. See the Citizenship and Entry into Israel Law (temporary provision) 5763–2003 of August 6, 2003, amended on March 28, 2007, www.knesset.gov.il/laws/special/eng/citizenship_law.htm (accessed March 20, 2012).

16. Drori 1975; Holzmann 1968.

17. "A bulletin, edict or announcement on my [military commander's] behalf will be made public in any way that I find proper" (Drori 1975, 97).

18. "Violation of the convention is a matter for the military commander and whoever appointed him. . . . We, the judges, and for that matter the subjects in the Occupied Territories . . . like us—have only what the commander-legislator issues us as orders—and the only law valid as to publicizing and enforcement is in fact the instructions and edicts issued by the regional commander" (Drori 1975, 69).

19. The concept of "proportionality" became popular in the late 1990s. Previously, similar use was made of the term "reasonableness." See Gross 2007; Shamir 1994.

20. Kretzmer 2002, 187.

21. High Court of Justice, HCJ 393/82 (December 28, 1983), # 33, English translation, www.hamoked.org/items/160_eng.pdf (accessed May 12, 2012).

22. Lefort 1988, introduction.

CONCLUSION: TOWARD A NEW REGIME

1. Foreign migrant workers and refugees, whose number has grown greatly in recent years, are also part of Israel's backyard, but their number is still much smaller than that of the Palestinian noncitizens. Their residence status is temporary and they can easily be expelled.

2. For the official version of the amendment, see http://oknesset.org/vote/3335 (in Hebrew); an unofficial English translation can be found at www.acri.org.il/en/wp-con tent/uploads/2011/10/Nakba-Law-ENG.pdf (both accessed March 20, 2012).

3. Musih and Bronstein 2010; Petti 2007; Bartana 2011; Shenhav 2012; Bartana, Cichocki, et al. 2011; Simon 2011; "Where To," www.digitalartlab.org.il/ExhibitionPage.asp ?id=577&path=level_1 (accessed March 19, 2012); Sivan and Hazan 2012.

4. The intellectual and artistic work of Jews from Arab countries who insist on speaking their mother tongue and refuse to deny the Arabic culture they have inherited may be a beginning. See, e.g., Shohat 2006, Shenhav 2006, and the 2011 event "Beginning—התחלה بدايـة" organized in Tel Aviv by Noam Segal, where Jews spoke in and about Arabic and Palestinians translated what they said into Hebrew.

5. Musih and Bronstein 2010; Hilal et al. 2009.

REFERENCES

Adalah [The Legal Center for Arab Minority Rights in Israel]. 1998. *Legal Violations of Arab Minorities in Israel—A Report on Israel's Implementation of the International Convention on the Elimination of All Forms of Racial Discrimination.* www.adalah .org/eng/publications/violations.htm (accessed February 29, 2012).

———. 2003. "UN Human Rights Committee—Information Sheet # 1: State of Emergency, 22 July 2003" (78th sess., July). www.adalah.org/eng/intladvocacy/unhrc_03_ emergency.pdf (accessed February 29, 2012).

Admoni, Yehiel. 1992. *Decade of Discretion: Settlement Policy in the Territories, 1967–1977* [in Hebrew]. Tel Aviv: ha-Kibuts ha-me'uhad.

Agabaria, Omar, ed. 2007. *Remembering Imwas, Yalu, and Bayt Nuba* [in Hebrew and Arabic]. Tel Aviv: Zochrot Association. www.zochrot.org/sites/default/files/latrun_ booklet_web2.pdf (accessed February 29, 2012).

Agamben, Giorgio. 1998. *Homo Sacer: Sovereign Power and Bare Life.* Translated by Daniel Heller-Roazen. Stanford: Stanford University Press.

———. 1999. *Potentialities: Collected Essays in Philosophy.* Translated by Daniel Heller-Roazen. Stanford: Stanford University Press.

———. 2005. *State of Exception.* Translated by Kevin Attell. Chicago: University of Chicago Press.

Algazi, Yosef. 1974. *Dad, What Did You Do When They Demolished Nadder's House?— 1967–1974: What I Saw and Heard in the Occupied Territories: A Collection of News Reports* [in Hebrew]. Tel Aviv: the author.

———. 1988. "The June 1967 War: The Root of All Evil. 21 Years of Occupation, 6 Months of Uprising" [in Hebrew]. *Zu Haderech*, June 1, 1988. www.defeatist-diary .com/index.asp?p=memories_new10581&period=2/8/2010-25/9/2011 (accessed February 28, 2012).

Al-Haq [independent Palestinian human rights organization]. 2009. *Operation Cast Lead: A Statistical Analysis.* www.alhaq.org/attachments/article/252/gaza-operation -cast-Lead-statistical-analysis%20.pdf (accessed April 18, 2012).

Almog, Doron. 2004. "The West Bank Fence: A Vital Component in Israel's Strategy of Defense." *Washington Institute Policy Focus: Research Memorandum*, March 2004. Washington, DC: Washington Institute for Near East Policy (WINEP).

Aloni, Shulamit. 1997. *Can't Do Otherwise: A Political Biography* [in Hebrew]. Tel Aviv: Hed Artzi.

Althusser, Louis. 1971. "Ideology and Ideological State Apparatuses." In id., *Lenin and Philosophy*, 127–77. New York: Monthly Review Press.

Amir, Merav. 2011. "Borders Beyond Territory: Population Management Through Border-Making and the Borders of Israel." PhD diss., Tel Aviv University.

Andoni, Ghassam. 2001. "A Comparative Study of Intifada 1987 and Intifada 2000." In *The New Intifada: Resisting Israel's Apartheid*, ed. Roane Carey, 209–20. London: Verso.

Arendt, Hannah. 1958. *The Human Condition*. Chicago: University of Chicago Press.

———. 1979. *The Origins of Totalitarianism*. San Diego: Harcourt Brace Jovanovich.

Arnon, Arie, Israel Luski, Avia Spivak, and Jimmy Weinblatt. 1997. *The Palestinian Economy: Between Imposed Integration and Voluntary Separation*. Leiden: Brill.

Ashrawi, Hannan. 1996. *This Side of Peace: A Personal Account*. New York: Touchstone.

Association for Civil Rights in Israel. 1989. *Restraints on the Freedom of Movement Right in the Held Territories* [in Hebrew]. Jerusalem: Association for Civil Rights in Israel.

Azoulay, Ariela. 2002. *The Food Chain*. Documentary film. 17 minutes. http://cargocol lective.com/AriellaAzoulay/filter/Films#1164266/The-Food-Chain (accessed February 29, 2012).

———. 2005. *I Also Dwell Among Your Own People—Conversations with Azmi Bishara*. Film. 50 minutes. Alma Productions.

———. 2008. *The Civil Contract of Photography*. New York: Zone Books.

———. 2012. *Civil Contracts: Palestine, 1947–1948*. Documentary film. 48 minutes.

Azoulay, Ariela, and Adi Ophir. 2002. *Bad Days* [in Hebrew]. Tel Aviv: Resling.

———. 2004. "The Israeli Ruling Apparatus in the Palestinian Occupied Territories." Paper presented at conference on The Politics of Humanitarianism in the Occupied Territories at the Van Leer Jerusalem Institute, April 20–21.

———. 2005. "La paix qui n'a pas eu lieu." In *Israël et l'autre*, ed. William Ossipow, 139–93. Geneva: Labor et Fides.

———. 2012. "Abandoning Gaza." In *Agamben and Colonialism*, ed. Marcelo Svirsky and Simone Bignall. Edinburgh: Edinburgh University Press.

Balibar, Étienne. 1991. "Citizen Subject." In *Who Comes After the Subject?* ed. Eduardo Cadava, Peter Connor, and Jean-Luc Nancy, 33–57. New York: Routledge.

Barghouthi, Mustafa, Ibrahim Diabes, et al. 1996. *Infrastructure and Health Services in the Gaza Strip: The Gaza Strip Primary Health Care Survey*. Ramallah, West Bank: Health Development Information Project in cooperation with the World Health Organization (WHO).

Bartana, Yael. 2011. . . . *and Europe will be stunned*. Film trilogy presented at the Polish Pavilion in the 54th Venice Biennale of Art.

Bartana, Yael, Sebastian Cichocki, et al., eds. 2011. *A Cookbook for Political Imagination*. Berlin: Sternberg Press; Warsaw: Zacheta National Gallery of Art.

Bash, Tami, Yuval Ginbar, and Eitan Felner. 1993. "Deportation of Palestinians from the Occupied Territories and the Mass Deportation of December 1992," B'Tselem report. www.btselem.org/sites/default/files2/deportation_of_palestinians_from_the_ occupied_territories_and_the_mass_deportation_of_december_1992.pdf (accessed April 18, 2012).

Beinin, Joel, and Rebecca Stein. 2006. *The Struggle for Sovereignty: Palestine and Israel, 1993–2005*. Stanford: Stanford University Press.

Ben, Aluf. 2005. "The Second Qassam Test" [in Hebrew]. *Ha'aretz*, September 9, 2005. www.haaretz.co.il/misc/1.1042980 (accessed April 18, 2012).

Ben Eliezer, Uri. 2003. "Civil Society and Military Society in Israel: Neo-militarism and Anti-militarism in the Post-hegemonic Era." In *In the Name of Security: Sociology of Peace and War in Israel in Changing Times* [in Hebrew], ed. Majid Al-Haj and Uri Ben Eliezer, 29–76. Haifa: University of Haifa Press and Pardes Publishing.

Benjamin, Walter. 1999. "Critique of Violence." In id., *Selected Writings*, 1: 277–300. Cambridge, MA: Belknap Press.

Ben-Naftali, Orna, Aeyal M. Gross, and Keren Michaeli. 2009. "The Illegality of the Occupation Regime: The Fabric of Law in the Occupied Palestinian Territory." In *The Power of Inclusive Exclusion: Anatomy of Israeli Rule in the Occupied Palestinian Territories*, ed. Michal Givoni, Sari Hanafi, and Adi Ophir. New York: Zone Books.

Benvenisti, Eyal. 1990. *Legal Dualism: The Absorption of the Occupied Territories into Israel*. West Bank Data Base Project Report. Boulder, CO: Westview Press.

———. 1993. *The International Law of Occupation*. Princeton, NJ: Princeton University Press.

Benvenisti, Meron. 1976. *Jerusalem, the Torn City*. Minneapolis: University of Minnesota Press.

———. 1984. *The West Bank Data Project: A Survey of Israel's Policies*. West Bank Data Base Project Report, Washington, DC: American Enterprise Institute for Public Policy Research.

———. 1986. *Demographic, Economic, Legal, Social and Political Development in the West Bank*. West Bank Data Base Project Report. Jerusalem: Jerusalem Post.

———. 1987a. *Demographic, Economic, Legal, Social and Political Developments in the West Bank*. West Bank Data Base Project Report. Jerusalem: Jerusalem Post.

———. 1987b. *The West Bank Handbook*. Jerusalem: West Bank Data Project and the Jerusalem Post.

———. 1987c. "The Second Republic." *Journal of Palestine Studies* 16, no. 3: 197–201.

———. 1988. *The Slingshot and the Bat: Territories, Jews and Arabs* [in Hebrew]. Jerusalem: Keter.

———. 1996. *City of Stone: The Hidden History of Jerusalem.* Berkeley: University of California Press.

———. 1998. "A Feat of Engineering" [in Hebrew]. *Plastica* 2: 59–61.

Benvenisti, Meron, and David Richardson. 1982. "Annexation and Colonization." *Jerusalem Post*, September 10. Reprinted in *Journal of Palestine Studies* 12, no. 2 (Winter 1983): 182–87.

Benzimann, Uzi, and Attalah Mansour. 1992. *Secondary Tenants: Israeli Arabs, Their Status, and the Policy Toward Them* [in Hebrew]. Jerusalem: Keter.

Bertini, Catherine [personal humanitarian envoy of the UN secretary-general]. 2002. "Mission Report, 11–19 August, 2002," http://domino.un.org/bertini_rpt.htm (accessed February 29, 2012).

Bishara, Azmi, 1995. "Between Nation and Nationality: Reflections on Nationalism" [in Hebrew]. *Theory and Criticism* 6: 19–43.

———. 2001. "The Palestinians of Israel." Anonymous interview. In *The New Intifada: Resisting Israel's Apartheid*, ed. Roane Carey, 139–59. London: Verso.

———. 2003. "On the Intifada, Sharon's Aims, 48 Palestinians and NDA/Tajamu' Strategy." *Between the Lines* 3, nos. 23–24: 3–16.

Black, Ian, and Benny Morris. 1991. *Israel's Secret Wars: A History of Israel's Intelligence Services.* New York: Grove Weidenfeld.

Bourdieu, Pierre. 1980. *The Logic of Practice.* Translated by Richard Nice. Stanford: Stanford University Press. Originally published as *Le sens pratique* (Paris: Éditions de Minuit, 1980).

B'Tselem [Israeli Information Center for Human Rights in the Occupied Territories]. 2007a. "Gaza Strip After the Disengagement," www.btselem.org/gaza_strip (accessed April 18, 2012).

———. 2007b. "The Gaza Strip: One Big Prison," www.btselem.org/sites/default/files/publication/200705_gaza_insert_eng.pdf (accessed February 29, 2012).

———. 2011. "Rafah Crossing," www.btselem.org/gaza_strip/rafah_crossing (accessed April 30 2012).

———. 2009. Press releases, September. www.btselem.org/english/press_releases/2009 0909.asp (accessed April 19, 2012).

———. 2011. "Statistics: Fatalities" (September 29, 2000-December 31, 2011). http://old .btselem.org/statistics/english/casualties.asp (accessed February 28, 2012).

———. N.d. "Statistics: Fatalities in the First Intifada," www.btselem.org/statistics/first_ intifada_tables (accessed February 28, 2012).

B'Tselem and the Palestinian Human Rights Monitoring Group. 1996. "Human Rights in the Occupied Territories Since the Oslo Accords," www.btselem.org/sites/default/

files/download/human_rights_in_the_occupied_territories_since_the_oslo_accords
.pdf (accessed February 28, 2012).

Buckin, Tobias. 2008. "Israeli Shift to Private Security Draws Fire." *Financial Times*, June 3,
2008. www.ft.com/cms/s/0/d7f193c2-318e-11dd-b77c-0000779fd2ac.html#axzz1sOM
pnL4B (accessed April 18, 2012).

Carmi, Na'ama. 1999. "Oslo: Before and After: The Status of Human Rights in the Occupied Territories." B'Tselem report. www.btselem.org/sites/default/files2/oslo_befor_
and_after.pdf (accessed April 19, 2012).

Cohen, Hillel. 2004. "The Archive Law, the GSS Law and Public Discourse in Israel."
Adalah's Review 4: 45–46.

———. 2008. *Army of Shadows: Palestinian Collaboration with Zionism, 1917–1948.*
Translated by Haim Watzman. Berkeley: University of California Press.

———. 2010. *Good Arabs: The Israeli Security Agencies and the Israeli Arabs, 1948–1967.*
Translated by Haim Watzman. Berkeley: University of California Press.

Coordinating Council of the Palestinian Private Sector [cited as PSCC]. 2008. Report.
www.paltrade.org/en/publications/EN_Private_Sector_Perspective_to_Cope_with_
the_Current_Economic_Crisis_in_the_Gaza_Strip.pdf (accessed February 29, 2012).

Davis, Uri, and Norton Mezvinsky, eds. 1975. *Documents from Israel, 1967–1973.* London:
Ithaca Press.

Decolonizing Architecture/Art Residency. www.decolonizing.ps/site/about (accessed
February 28, 2012).

Deleuze, Gilles. 1990. *The Logic of Sense.* Translated by Mark Lester with Charles Stivale.
New York: Columbia University Press.

Dinstein, Yoram, ed. 1971. *Israel Yearbook on Human Rights.* Vol. 1. Tel Aviv: Published
under the auspices of the Faculty of Law, Tel Aviv University.

Drori, Moshe. 1975. *The Legislation in the Area of Judea and Samaria* [in Hebrew]. Jerusalem: Harry Sacher Institute for Legislative Research and Comparative Law, Hebrew
University, Faculty of Law.

———. 1980. *Local Authority, Democracy and Elections in Judea and Samaria* [in He-
brew]. Tel Aviv: Bar Ilan University Press.

Dudai, Ron. 2001a. *Free Rein: Vigilante Settlers and Israel's Non-enforcement of the Law.*
B'tselem report. www.btselem.org/sites/default/files/publication/200110_free_rein_
eng.pdf (accessed April 18, 2012).

———. 2001b. *Tacit Consent: Israeli Policy on Law Enforcement Toward Settlers in the Occupied Territories.* B'tselem report. www.btselem.org/sites/default/files/publication
/200103_tacit_consent_eng.doc (accessed April 18, 2012).

———. 2002. *Trigger Happy: Unjustified Shooting and Violation of the Open-Fire Regulations During the al-Aqsa Intifada.* B'tselem report. www.btselem.org/sites/default/
files/publication/200203_trigger_happy_eng.pdf (accessed April 18, 2012).

Dugard, John. 2004. "Statement by Mr. John Dugard, Special Rapporteur on the Situation of Human Rights in the Palestinian Territories Occupied by Israel Since 1967." Submitted to the General Assembly of the United Nations, New York, 28 October 2004. www.cjpme.ca/documents/Dugard-Statement-2004.pdf (accessed April 18, 2012).

Efrat, Elisha. 2006. *The West Bank and Gaza Strip: A Geography of Occupation and Disengagement.* New York: Routledge.

Eid, Bassem, and Eitan Felner. 1995. *Neither Law nor Justice: Extrajuridical Punishment, Abduction, Unlawful Arrest, Torture of Palestinian Residents of the West Bank by the Palestinian Preventive Security Service.* Jerusalem: B'Tselem.

Eilon, Amos. 1971. "A Strong Hand in Gaza" [in Hebrew]. *Ha'aretz,* February 5, 1971.

Eldar, Akiva. 2005. "Deprived Muslim Minority, Revolting: Sounds Familiar" [in Hebrew]. *Ha'aretz,* October 11, 2005. http://news.walla.co.il/?w=/21/806988 (accessed March 27, 2012).

———. 2007. "40% of Gazans' Requests to Get Medical Treatment in Israel Have Been Declined" [in Hebrew]. *Ha'aretz,* September 7, 2007. http://news.walla.co.il/?w=/9/1166279/@@/item/printer (accessed March 27, 2012).

Eldar, Akiva, and Idith Zertal. 2007. *Lords of the Land: The War over Israel's Settlements in the Occupied Territories, 1967–2007.* Translated by Vivian Eden. New York: Nation Books.

Eldar, Shlomi. 2005. *Eyeless in Gaza* [in Hebrew]. Tel Aviv: Yediot Aharonot.

Etkes, Dror, and Hagit Ofran. 2006. *One Violation Leads to Another: Israeli Settlement Building on Private Palestinian Property.* A Report of Peace Now's Settlement Watch Team. http://peacenow.org.il/eng/sites/default/files/Breaking_The_Law_in_WB_nov06Eng.pdf (accessed April 18, 2012).

Ezrahi, Yaron. 1997. *Rubber Bullets: Power and Conscience in Modern Israel.* New York: Farrar, Straus & Giroux.

———. 2001. "Introduction." In *Israel Toward a Constitutional Democracy* [in Hebrew], ed. Yaron Ezrahi and Mordechai Kremnitzer. Jerusalem: Israel Democracy Institute. www.idi.org.il/PublicationsCatalog/Documents/BOOK_600ישראללקראתדמוקרטיהחוקתית/1.pdf (accessed February 28, 2012).

Farsakh, Leila. 2005. *Palestinian Labour Migration to Israel: Labour, Land and Occupation.* New York: Routledge.

Feldman, Yotam. 2010. "Red Lines: Rationing Food to Besieged Gaza" [in Hebrew]. *Mitaam* 22: 132–43.

Felner, Eitan. 1995. *A Policy of Discrimination: Land Expropriation, Planning and Building in East Jerusalem.* B'Tselem report. www.btselem.org/sites/default/files2/a_policy_of_discrimination.pdf (accessed May 12, 2012).

Felner, Eitan, and Rolly Rosen. 1994. *Law Enforcement vis-à-vis Israeli Civilians in the Occupied Territories.* B'Tselem report. www.btselem.org/sites/default/files2/law_enforcement_vis_a_vis_israeli_civilians_in_the_occupied_territories.pdf (accessed February 29, 2012).

Feuerstein, Ofir. 2007. "Ghost Town: Israel's Separation Policy and Forced Eviction of Palestinians from the Center of Hebron." B'Tselem and Association for Civil Rights in Israel. www.btselem.org/download/200705_hebron_eng.pdf (accessed April 18, 2012).

Foucault, Michel. 1978. "Qu'est-ce que la critique?" *Bulletin de la Société française de philosophie* 84, no. 2: 35–63.

———. 1990. *The History of Sexuality: An Introduction.* Vol. 1. Translated by Robert Hurley. New York: Vintage Books.

———. 2000. "The Subject and Power." In *Power: The Essential Works of Foucault, 1954–1984,* vol. 3, ed. James D. Faubion, 326–48. New York: New Press.

———. 2007. *Security, Territory, Population: Lectures at the College de France 1977–1978.* Edited by Michel Senellart. Translated by Graham Burchell. New York: Palgrave Macmillan.

Gardi, Tomer, 2011. *Paper, Stone.* Tel Aviv: Hakibutz Hameuchad.

Gavison, Ruth. 1999. "Jewish and Democratic? A Rejoinder to the 'Ethnic Democracy' Debate." *Israel Studies* 4, no. 1: 44–72.

Gazit, Shlomo. 1985. *The Carrot and the Stick: Israel's Government in Judea and Samaria* [in Hebrew]. Tel Aviv: Zmora-Bitan.

———. 1995. *The Carrot and the Stick: Israel's Policy in Judaea and Samaria, 1967–68.* Translated from the Hebrew by Reuvik Danielli. Washington, DC: B'nai B'rith Books.

———. 2003. *Trapped Fools: Thirty Years of Israeli Policy in the Territories.* Translated by Shoshana Sappir. London: Frank Cass.

Ginbar, Yuval. 1997. "Demolishing Peace: Israel's Policy of Mass Demolition of Palestinian Houses in the West Bank." B'Tselem information sheet. www.btselem.org/sites/default/files/publication/199709_demolishing_peace_eng.rtf (accessed April 19, 2012).

Gisha [Center for the Legal Protection of Freedom of Movement]. 2006. *Disengagement Danger: Israeli Attempts to Separate Gaza from the West Bank.* www.gisha.org/User Files/File/publications_english/Publications%20and%20Reports_English/Disengage ment%20Danger%20feb%2006.doc (accessed February 28, 2012).

———. 2007. *Disengaged Occupiers: The Legal Status of Gaza.* Report. www.gisha.org/UserFiles/File/publications_english/Publications%20and%20Reports_English/Exec utiveSummary.pdf (accessed April 19, 2012).

———. 2010. "Due to Gisha's Petition: Israel Reveals Documents Related to the Gaza Closure Policy." www.gisha.org/item.asp?lang_id=en&p_id=517 (accessed February 29, 2012).

Golan, Daphna. 1992. *Detained Without Trial: Administrative Detention in the Occupied Territories Since the Beginning of the Intifada.* B'Tselem report. www.btselem.org/sites/default/files2/detained_without_trial.pdf (accessed April 18, 2012).

Golan, Daphna, and Stanley Cohen. 1991. *Interrogation of Palestinians During the Intifada. Ill-Treatment, "Moderate Physical Pressure" or Torture?* B'Tselem report: www.btselem

.org/sites/default/files2/the_interrogations_of_palestinians_during_the_intefada_ill_
treatment_moderate_physical_pressure_or_torture_march_1991.pdf (accessed April
18, 2012).

Golan, Hagai, and Shay Shaul, eds. 2004. *The Limited Conflict* [in Hebrew]. Tel Aviv:
Ma'arachot and the Ministry of Defense.

Goldschmit, Tamar. 2004. *Qalandiya Report*. Documentary film. www.mahsanmilim.
com/qalandiyareportHE.htm (accessed April 18, 2012).

Golomb, Naftali. N.d. *Two Orders of Court Rulings* [שני סדרי פסיקה] [in Hebrew]. Published by the author.

Gordon, Neve. 2008. *Israel's Occupation: Sovereignty, Discipline and Control*. Berkeley:
University of California Press.

———. 2009. "From Colonization to Separation: Exploring the Structure of Israel's Occupation." In *The Power of Inclusive Exclusion: Anatomy of Israeli Rule in the Occupied Palestinian Territories*, ed. Michal Givoni, Sari Hanafi, and Adi Ophir. New York:
Zone Books.

Greenberg, Lev. 2007. *Imaginary Peace, War Discourse: The Failure of the Leadership, the
Politics and the Democracy in Israel, 1992–2006* [in Hebrew]. Tel Aviv: Resling.

Gregory, Derek. 2004. *The Colonial Present: Afghanistan, Palestine, Iraq*. Malden, MA:
Blackwell.

Gross, Eyal M. 2006. "The Construction of a Wall Between The Hague and Jerusalem:
The Enforcement and Limits of Humanitarian Law and the Structure of Occupation." *Leiden Journal of International Law* 19, no. 2: 393–440.

———. 2007. "Human Proportions: Are Human Rights the Emperor's New Clothes of
the International Law of Occupation?" *European Journal of International Law* 18, no.
1: 1–35.

GSS. *See* Israel. General Security Service.

Guillou, Jan, and Marina Stagh. 1975. "There Is a Factory Behind the Barbed Wire Fence."
In *Documents from Israel, 1967–1973*, ed. Uri Davis and Norton Mezvinsky, 160–62.
London: Ithaca Press.

Gur, Hagit. 2005. *Militarism in Education* [in Hebrew]. Tel Aviv: Babel.

Guttman, Emanuel, and Ya'acov Levi, eds. 1976. *The Regime of the State of Israel: Source
Book* [in Hebrew]. Jerusalem: Kaplan School of Economics and Social Sciences, Hebrew University.

Gutwein, Daniel. 2005. "On Economy and Prejudice" [in Hebrew]. *Theory and Criticism* 26: 286–94.

Hajjar, Lisa. 2005. *Courting Conflict: The Israeli Military Court System in the West Bank
and Gaza*. Berkeley: University of California Press.

Halabi, Rafik. 1982. *The West Bank Story*. Translated by Ina Friedman. New York: Harcourt Brace Jovanovich.

Halper, Jeff. 2000. "Matrix of Control." *Middle East Report* 216 (Fall).

———. 2005a. *Obstacles to Peace: A Critical Reframing of the Israeli-Palestinian Conflict.* Jerusalem: Israeli Committee Against House Demolitions (ICAHD), PalMap (Palestine Mapping Centre).

———. 2005b. "The End of a Viable Palestinian State." *CounterPunch*, March 31. www .counterpunch.org/2005/03/31/the-end-of-a-viable-palestinian-state (accessed February 29, 2012).

Hamadeh, Sharif, Hana Hamdan, and Suhad Bishara. 2006. "Four Cases of Segregated Spaces." *Makan: Adalah's Journal for Land, Planning and Justice* 1: 54–68. www.adalah .org/eng/publications/makan/segspaces.pdf (accessed March 1, 2012).

Hamed, Osama A., and Radwan A. Shaban. 1993. "One-Sided Customs and Monetary Union: The Case of the West Bank and Gaza Strip Under Israeli Occupation." In *The Economics of the Middle East: Views from the Region*, ed. Stanley Fischer, Dani Rodrik, and Elias Tuma, 117–47. Cambridge, MA: MIT Press.

Hammami, Rema. 2004. "On the Importance of Thugs: The Moral Economy of a Checkpoint." *Middle East Report* 231 (Summer).

Hanafi, Sari. 2010. "Governance, Governmentality, and the State of Exception in the Palestinian Refugee Camps in Lebanon." *Journal of Refugee Studies* 23, no. 2: 134–59.

Hanafi, Sari, and Linda Tabar. 2005. *The Emergence of a Globalized Palestinian Elite: Donors, International Organizations and Local NGOs*. Jerusalem: Institute of Jerusalem Studies and Muwatin.

Handel, Ariel. 2008. "Controlling the Space Through the Space: Uncertainty as Control Technology" [in Hebrew]. *Theory and Criticism* 31.

———. 2009. "Where, Whereto and When in the Occupied Territories: An Introduction to Geography of Disaster." In *The Power of Inclusive Exclusion: Anatomy of Israeli Rule in the Occupied Palestinian Territories*, ed. Adi Ophir, Michal Givoni, and Sari Hanafi. New York: Zone Books.

———. 2010a. "The Movement Regime in the West Bank and Gaza Strip: Historical, Technological and Social Aspects" [in Hebrew]. PhD diss.

———. 2010b. "Gated/Gating Community: The Settlements Array in the West Bank." In *Gated Communities*, ed. Amnon Lehavi. Tel Aviv: Buchman Law Faculty, Tel Aviv University.

Harel, Amos. 2003."The IDF in the Service of the Settlers." *Ha'aretz*, September 23, www .haaretz.co.il/misc/1.912539 (accessed April 16, 2012).

———. 2005. "Preparations for the Third Round Have Begun" [in Hebrew]. *Ha'aretz*, April 29.

———. 2007. "Beinisch: IDF Is Delaying Execution of High Court of Justice Instructions" [in Hebrew]. *Ha'aretz*, July 24. www.haaretz.co.il/misc/1.1428368 (accessed April 18, 2012).

Harel, Amos, and Avi Yissakharof. 2007. "Toward the Big Blackout" [in Hebrew]. *Ha'aretz*, October 25. www.haaretz.co.il/misc/1.1452823 (accessed April 18, 2012).

Harel, Amos, and Barak Ravid. 2007. "Barak: The IDF is Coming Closer to a Wide-Scale Ground Operation in Gaza" [in Hebrew]. *Ha'aretz*, September 6. www.haaretz.co.il/misc/1.1440289 (accessed April 18, 2012).

Hass, Amira. 2000. *Drinking the Sea of Gaza: Days and Nights in a Land Under Siege.* Translated by Elana Wesley and Maxine Kaufman-Lacusta. New York: Holt.

———. 2003. "The Israeli Army Is More Dangerous Than the Iraqi Missiles" [in Hebrew]. *Ha'aretz*, March 19, 2003. www.haaretz.co.il/misc/1.869893 (accessed February 28, 2012).

———. 2004. "Colonialism Under the Cover of the Peace Process" [in Hebrew]. *Theory and Criticism* 24: 191–202.

———. 2005. "For Israel, Gazans Staying in the West Bank Are Illegal Aliens" [in Hebrew]. *Ha'aretz*, October 7, 2005. www.haaretz.co.il/misc/1.1049086 (accessed June 18, 2012).

———. 2006. "The IDF Disconnected the Northern West Bank" [in Hebrew]. *Ha'aretz*, January 13, 2006. www.haaretz.co.il/misc/1.1074508 (accessed June 18, 2012).

Hever, Shir. 2005. "Economics and Politics: The Poverty Policy in Israel and the Territories." *Theory and Criticism* 26: 295–301.

———. 2010. *The Political Economy of Israel's Occupation: Repression Beyond Exploitation.* London: Pluto Press.

Hilal, Sandi, Alessandro Petti, and Eyal Weizman. 2009. "Decolonizing Architecture: The Future Archaeology of Israel's Colonization." *Roulotte* 05: 94–125. www.roulottemagazine.com/?p=234 (accessed May 12, 2012).

Hofnung, Menachem. 1991. *Israel—Security Needs vs. the Rule of Law, 1948–1991* [in Hebrew]. Jerusalem: Nevo Publishing House, 1991.

———. 1996. *Democracy, Law, and National Security in Israel.* Aldershot, UK: Dartmouth.

Holzmann, Haim. 1968. *Security Legislation in the Held Territories* [in Hebrew]. Giv'at Chaviva: Center for Arab and Afro-Asian Studies.

Ignatieff, Michel. 2004. *The Lesser Evil: Political Ethics in the Age of Terror.* Princeton, NJ: Princeton University Press.

Israel. Civil Administration of the Area of Judea and Samaria. 1983. "Report: The Sixteenth Year of the Administration, Unclassified, April 1981–March 1983" [in Hebrew].

Israel. General Security Service [cited as GSS]. 2009. Annual Summary: Data and Trends in Palestinian Terrorism. www.shabak.gov.il/SiteCollectionImages/english/TerrorInfo/reports/terrorreport2009_en.pdf (accessed February 28, 2012).

Israel. High Court of Justice. 2005. *Regional Committee of Gaza Shore vs. Israeli Parliament* [in Hebrew].1661/05.

———. 2007a. *Association for Civil Rights in Israel vs. Ministry of Defense* [in Hebrew]. 5841/06.

———. 2007b. *Hamdan vs. Southern Commander General* [in Hebrew]. 11120/05.

Israel. Legal Advisor. 1975. *The Legal Advisor of the Judea and Samaria Regional Head-*

quarters. A collection of proclamations, edicts, and appointments, Judea and Samaria region (up-to-date version) [in Hebrew].

Israel. Ministry of Defense. 1982. *Fourteen Years of Civil Administration in the Areas of Judea and Samaria, Gaza and Sinai, and the Golan Heights* [in Hebrew].

Israel. Ministry of Foreign Affairs. 2005. "Summary of the Opinion Concerning Unauthorized Outposts—Talya Sason, Adv." www.mfa.gov.il/MFA/Government/Law/Legal+Issues+and+Rulings/Summary+of+Opinion+Concerning+Unauthorized+Outposts+-+Talya+Sason+Adv.htm (accessed February 28, 2012).

Israeli Committee Against House Demolitions. 2010. "Statistics on House Demolitions (1967–2010)." www.icahd.org/?page_id=5508 (accessed February 28, 2012).

Israeli League for Human and Civil Rights. 1978. "The Market for Arab Children in Israel" [in Hebrew]. Tel Aviv.

Jabotinsky, Vladimir [Ze'ev]. 1942. *The War and the Jew.* New York: Dial Press.

Jad, Islah. 1990. "From Salons to the Popular Committees: Palestinian Women, 1919–1989." In *Intifada: Palestine at the Crossroads*, ed. Jamal Nassar and Roger Heacock, 125–42. New York: Praeger.

Jamal, Amal. 2005a. "The Palestinian IDPs in Israel and the Predicament of Return: Between Imagining the Impossible and Enabling the Imaginative." In *Exile and Return: Predicaments of Palestinians and Jews*, ed. Ann Mosely Lesch and Ian S. Lustick, 133–60. Philadelphia: University of Pennsylvania Press.

———. 2005b. *The Palestinian National Movement: Politics of Contention, 1967–2005.* Bloomington: Indiana University Press.

Jarbawi, Ali. 1990. "Palestinian Elites in the Occupied Territories: Stability and Change Through the Intifada." In *Intifada: Palestine at the Crossroads*, ed. Jamal Nassar and Roger Heacock, 287–305. New York: Praeger.

Kafka, Franz. 1992. *The Trial.* Translated by Willa and Edwin Muir. New York: Schocken Books.

Kaspit, Ben. 2007. "Mazuz Approved: Israel Will Black Out the Gaza Strip" [in Hebrew]. *Maariv nrg*, November 15, 2007. www.nrg.co.il/online/1/ART1/659/418.html (accessed March 11, 2012).

Kedar, Sandy. 1998. "Majority Time, Minority Time, Land Nation, and the Law of Adverse Possession in Israel" [in Hebrew]. *Law Review* 21 (1998): 665–746.

Kemp, Adriana, and Rivka Reichman. 2003. *"Foreign Workers" in Israel* [in Hebrew]. Information on Equality, 13. Tel Aviv: Adva Center. www.adva.org/UPLOADED/ovdim%20zarim%20kamp.pdf (accessed April 18, 2012).

Kimmerling, Baruch. 2003. *Politicide: Ariel Sharon's Wars Against the Palestinians.* London: Verso.

Kleiman, Ephraim. 1993. "Some Basic Problems of the Economic Relationship Between Israel, the West Bank and Gaza." In *The Economics of the Middle East Peace: Views from the Region*, ed. Stanley Fischer, Dani Rodrik, and Elias Tuma, 305–33. Cambridge, MA: MIT Press.

———. 2005. "Theory Without Criticism" [in Hebrew]. *Theory and Criticism* 26: 275–85.

Klein, Naomi. 2007a. "Laboratory for a Fortressed World." *The Nation*, July 2, 2007. www.thenation.com/article/laboratory-fortressed-world (accessed February 29, 2012).

———. 2007b. *The Shock Doctrine: The Rise of Disaster Capitalism*. New York: Metropolitan Books/Henry Holt.

Korn, Alina. 1996. "Crime and Law Enforcement in the Israeli Arab Population Under the Military Government." PhD diss., Hebrew University, Jerusalem.

———. 2004. "Political Control and Crime: The Use of Defense (Emergency) Regulations During the Military Government." *Adalah's Review* 4: 23–32.

Kotef, Hagar, and Merav Amir. 2007. "(En)Gendering Checkpoints: Checkpoint Watch and the Repercussions of Intervention." *Signs: Journal of Women in Culture and Society* 32, no. 4: 973–96.

———. 2011. "Between Imaginary Lines: Violence and Its Justifications at the Military Checkpoints in Occupied Palestine." *Theory, Culture & Society* 28, no. 1: 55–80.

Kretzmer, David. 2002. *The Occupation of Justice: The Supreme Court of Israel and the Occupied Territories*. Albany: State University of New York Press.

Kuttab, Eileen. 1992. "The Palestinian Woman's Participation in the Intifada: An Essential Element of the National Liberation Movement." In *Intifada: A Look from the Inside* [in Hebrew], ed. Shlomo Swirski and Ilan Pappe, 125–40. Tel Aviv: Mifras.

Langer, Felicia. 1975. *With My Own Eyes: Israel and the Occupied Territories, 1967-1973*. London: Ithaca Press.

Lefort, Claude. 1988. *Democracy and Political Theory*. Translated by David Macey. Minneapolis: University of Minnesota Press.

Leibowitz, Yeshayahu. 1986. "Liberating Israel from the Occupied Territories." *Journal of Palestine Studies* 15, no. 2 (Winter): 102–8.

Lein, Yehezkiel. 1998. *Disputed Waters: Israel's Responsibility for the Water Shortage in the Occupied Territories*. B'Tselem report. www.btselem.org/download/199809_disputed_waters_eng.doc (accessed April 18, 2012).

———. 1999. *Builders of Zion: Human Rights Violations of Palestinians from the Occupied Territories Working in Israel and the Settlements*. B'Tselem report. www.btselem.org/sites/default/files2/builders_of_zion.pdf (accessed April 17, 2012).

———. 2001. *Civilians Under Siege: Restrictions on Freedom of Movement as Collective Punishment*. B'Tselem report. www.btselem.org/download/200101_civilians_under_siege_eng.doc (accessed April 18, 2012).

———. 2002. *Land Grab: Israel's Settlement Policy in the West Bank*. B'Tselem report. www.btselem.org/publications/summaries/200205_land_grab (accessed April 18, 2012).

———. 2004. *Forbidden Roads: The Discriminatory West Bank Road Regime*. B'Tselem report. www.btselem.org/download/200408_forbidden_roads_eng.doc (accessed April 18, 2012).

———. 2005. *One Big Prison: Freedom of Movement to and from the Gaza Strip on the Eve of the Disengagement Plan.* B'Tselem and the Center for the Defense of the Individual report. www.btselem.org/download/200503_gaza_prison_english.doc (accessed April 18, 2012).

Lein, Yehezkiel, and Alon Cohen-Lifshitz. 2005. *Under the Guise of Security: Routing the Separation Barrier to Enable the Expansion of Israeli Settlements in the West Bank.* B'Tselem and Bimkom [Planners for Planning Rights] report. www.btselem.org/download/200512_under_the_guise_of_security_eng.doc (accessed April 18, 2012).

Lentin, Ronit. 2004. "'No Woman's Law Will Rot This State': The Israeli Racial State and Feminist Resistance." *Sociological Research Online* 9, no. 3. www.socresonline.org.uk/9/3/lentin.html (accessed April 18, 2012).

Levy, Daniel. 2008. "A More Private Occupation." *Ha'aretz*, April 11, 2008. www.haaretz.com/print-edition/opinion/a-more-private-occupation-1.243793 (accessed April 18, 2012).

Levy, Gideon. 2003. "Un million de personnes sous couvre-feu." In *À contre-choeur: Les voix dissidentes en Israël*, ed. Michel Warschawski and Michèle Sibony. Paris: Textuel.

———. 2004. *Twilight Zone—Life and Death Under the Israeli Occupation, 1988–2003* [in Hebrew]. Tel Aviv: Babylon Printing.

Mann, Michael. 1986. *The Sources of Social Power.* Vol. 1. Cambridge: Cambridge University Press.

Mansbach, Daniella. 2007. "Protest on the Border: The Power of Duality in the Protest Practices of Machsom Watch" [in Hebrew]. *Theoria ve-Bikoret* 31.

Maoz, Eilat. 2009. "The Privatization of the Checkpoints and the Late Occupation." www.whoprofits.org/content/privatization-checkpoints-and-late-occupation-eilat-maoz%EF%BB%BF (accessed April 18, 2012).

Ma'oz, Moshe. 1984. *Palestinian Leadership on the West Bank: The Changing Role of the Arab Mayors Under Jordan and Israel.* London: Frank Cass.

Marin, Louis. 1987. *Portrait of the King.* Translated by Martha M. Houle. Minneapolis: University of Minnesota Press.

Masalha, Nur. 1992. *Expulsion of the Palestinians: The Concept of "Transfer" in Zionist Political Thought, 1882–1948.* Washington, DC: Institute for Palestine Studies.

Matta, Nada, and Salim Abu Jabal, eds. 2006. *Remembering al-Golan.* Booklet. www.zochrot.org/en/content/remembering-al-golan (accessed February 29, 2012). Tel Aviv: Zochrot Association.

Mizrahi, Shani. 2007. "Mazuz: For the Moment Gaza Cannot Be Blacked Out" [in Hebrew]. *Maariv nrg*, October 29, 2007. www.nrg.co.il/online/1/ART1/652/552 (accessed February 29, 2012).

Morris, Benny. 1999. *Righteous Victims: A History of the Arab-Zionist Conflict, 1882–1999*. New York: Knopf.

———. 2004. *The Birth of the Palestinian Refugee Problem Revisited*. Cambridge: Cambridge University Press.

Musih, Norma, and Eitan Bronstein. 2010. "Thinking Practically About the Return of the Palestinian Refugees." *Sedek: A Journal on the Ongoing Nakba*, special translated issue, 8–32. http://arenaofspeculation.org/wp-content/uploads/2011/05/Sedek-eng -final.pdf (accessed February 29, 2012).

OCHA. *See* United Nations. Office for the Coordination of Humanitarian Affairs, Occupied Palestinian Territories.

Ophir, Adi. 2010. "The Politics of Catastrophization." In *Contemporary States of Emergency: The Politics of Military and Humanitarian Intervention*, ed. Didier Fassin and Mariella Pandolfi, 59–88. New York: Zone Books.

Ophir, Adi, Michal Givoni, and Sari Hanafi, eds. 2009. *The Power of Inclusive Exclusion: Anatomy of Israeli Rule in the Occupied Palestinian Territories*. New York: Zone Books.

Oxfam. 2007. "Poverty in Palestine: The Human Cost of the Financial Boycott." Briefing note. http://policy-practice.oxfam.org.uk/publications/poverty-in-palestine-the-human -cost-of-the-financial-boycott-114566 (accessed February 29, 2012).

———. 2008. "The Gaza Strip: A Humanitarian Implosion." Research report. www .oxfam.org.uk/resources/policy/conflict_disasters/gaza_implosion.html (accessed February 29, 2012).

———. 2009. "Gaza Humanitarian Crisis," www.oxfam.org.uk/oxfam_in_action/emer gencies/gaza_crisis.html (accessed February 29, 2012).

———. 2010. *Dashed Hopes: Continuation of the Gaza Blockade*. www.oxfam.org.uk/ resources/policy/conflict_disasters/downloads/dashed-hopes-continuation-gaza -blockade-301110-en.pdf (accessed February 29, 2012).

Pacheco, Allegra. 2001. "Flouting Convention: The Oslo Agreements." In *The New Intifada: Resisting Israel's Apartheid*, ed. Roane Carey, 181–209. London: Verso.

Padan, Yael, and Shuli Hartman. 2006. *Fences, Walls, and Environmental Justice* [in Hebrew]. *Bimkom* [Planners for Planning Rights] report. www.bimkom.org/dynCon tent/articles/walls,%20fences,%20justice.pdf (accessed March 1, 2012).

Pappe, Ilan. 1994. *The Making of the Arab-Israeli Conflict*. London: I. B. Tauris.

———. 1999. "Were They Expelled? The History, Historiography and Relevance of the Palestinian Refugee Problem." In *The Palestinian Exodus, 1948–1998*, ed. Ghada Carmi and Eugene Cotran. London: Ithaca Press.

———. 2003. "Démons de la Nakbah." In *À contre-choeur: Les voix dissidentes en Israël*, ed. Michel Warschawski and Michèle Sibony, 134–40. Paris: Textuel.

———. 2006. *The Ethnic Cleansing of Palestine*. Oxford: Oneworld.

Peled, Yoav, and Yagil Levy. 1993. "The Break That Never Was: Israeli Sociology Reflected Through the Six-Day War" [in Hebrew]. *Theory and Criticism* 3: 115–28.

Peled, Yoav, and Gershon Shafir. 2002. *Being Israeli: The Dynamics of Multiple Citizenship*. Cambridge: Cambridge University Press.

Petti, Alessandro. 2007. *Arcipelaghi e enclave. Architettura dell'ordinamento spaziale contemporaneo*. Milan: Bruno Mondadori.

Portugali, Juval. 1993. *Implicate Relations: Society and Space in the Israeli-Palestinian Conflict*. Dordrecht: Kluwer Academic Publishers.

Rabbani, Mouin. 2001. "Smorgasbord of Failure: Oslo and the Al-Aqsa Intifada." In *The New Intifada: Resisting Israel's Apartheid*, ed. Roane Carey, 69–90. London: Verso.

Rapoport, Meron. 2007. "Outsourcing the Checkpoints." *Ha'aretz*, October 2, 2007. www.haaretz.com/weekend/week-s-end/outsourcing-the-checkpoints-1.230416 (accessed March 20, 2012).

Ron, James. 2003. *Frontiers and Ghettos: State Violence in Serbia and Israel*. Berkeley: University of California Press.

Ronen, David. 1989. *The GSS Year* [in Hebrew]. Tel Aviv: Ministry of Defense.

Rouhana, Nadim. 1997. *The Palestinian Citizens in an Ethnic Jewish State: Identities in Conflict*. New Haven, CT: Yale University Press.

Roy, Sara. 1986. *The Gaza Strip: A Demographic, Economic, Social and Legal Survey*. West Bank Database Project. Boulder, CO: Westview Press.

———. 1995. *The Gaza Strip: The Political Economy of De-Development*. Washington, DC: Institute for Palestine Studies.

———. 2007. *Failing Peace: Gaza and the Palestinian-Israeli Conflict*. London: Pluto Press.

———. 2009. "If Gaza Falls . . . ." *London Review of Books* 31, no. 1:26.

———. 2010. "Treading on Shards." *Jewish Peace News*, February 24, 2010. jewishpeacenews.blogspot.co.il/2010/02/sara-roy-gaza-treading-on-shards-nation.html (accessed April 21, 2012).

Rubinstein, Amnon. 1988. "The Changing Status of the Territories: From Escrow to Legal Mongrel." *Tel Aviv University Studies in Law* 8: 59–79.

———. 1991. *The Constitutional Law of the State of Israel* [in Hebrew]. Jerusalem: Schoken.

Rubinstein, Danny. 2004. "On the Ruins of the Peace Plans" [in Hebrew]. *Ha'aretz*, January 19, 2004. www.haaretz.com/print-edition/opinion/on-the-ruins-of-the-peace-plans-1.111425 (accessed May 12, 2012).

Runciman, David. 2003. "The Concept of the State: The Sovereignty of a Fiction." In *States and Citizens: History, Theory, Prospects*, ed. Quentin Skinner and Bo Strath. Cambridge: Cambridge University Press.

Sa'abana, Salach. 1994. "'Permanent Resident' Status in Israel." Palestinians' Residency in Eastern Jerusalem Seminar. Jerusalem: HaMoked—Center for the Defence of the Individual. www.hamoked.org.il/items/10900.pdf (accessed April 18, 2012).

Said, Edward W. 1979. *The Question of Palestine*. New York: Times Books.

———. 2000. *The End of the Peace Process: Oslo and After*. New York: Pantheon Books.

———. 2001. "Palestinians Under Siege." In *The New Intifada: Resisting Israel's Apartheid*, ed. Roane Carey, 27–44. London: Verso.

Sanbar, Elias. 1994. *Les Palestiniens dans le siècle*. Paris: Gallimard.

Saragusti, Anat. 1986. "Robbers" [in Hebrew]. *Ha'olam Haze*, January 8, 1986.

Sarna, Igal. 2007. *State Witness* [in Hebrew]. Tel Aviv: Xargol and Am Oved.

Sason, Talya. 2005. *Opinion Concerning Unauthorized Outposts: A Report Handed to the Israeli Government* [in Hebrew]. www.pmo.gov.il/NR/rdonlyres/0A0FBE3C-C741 -46A6-8CB5-F6CDC042465D/0/sason2.pdf (accessed April 18, 2012).

Schiff, Ze'ev. 2004. "Israel Mulls Using Satellite to Document Settlement Borders." *Ha'aretz*, September 6. www.haaretz.com/print-edition/news/israel-mulls-using -satellite-to-document-settlement-borders-1.133928 (accessed April 17, 2012).

Schiff, Ze'ev, and Ehud Ya'ari. 1984. *Israel's Lebanon War*. Edited and translated by Ina Friedman. New York: Simon & Schuster.

———. 1990a. *Intifada* [in Hebrew]. Jerusalem: Schoken.

———. 1990b. *Intifada: The Palestinian Uprising—Israel's Third Front*. Edited and translated by Ina Friedman. New York: Simon & Schuster.

Schmitt, Carl. 1985 [1922]. *Political Theology: Four Chapters on the Concept of Sovereignty*. Translated by George Schwab. Cambridge, MA: MIT Press. Originally published as *Politische Theologie. Vier Kapitel zur Lehre von der Souveränität* (Munich: Duncker & Humblot, 1922).

Segal, Rafi, and Eyal Weizman, eds. 2003. *A Civilian Occupation: The Politics of Israeli Architecture*. Tel Aviv: Babel; London: Verso.

Shahak, Israel. 1988. "Israeli Apartheid and the Intifada." *Race and Class* 30, no. 1: 1–13.

Shalev, Arie. 1990. *The Intifada: Causes, Attributes and Effects* [in Hebrew]. Tel Aviv: Papirus and Jaffe Center for Strategic Studies.

Shamgar, Meir. 1967. "The Law in the Areas Held by the Israel Defense Forces" [in Hebrew]. *Hapraklit* 23: 540–44.

Shamir, Ronen. 1990. "'Landmark Cases' and the Reproduction of Legitimacy: The Case of Israel's High Court of Justice." *Law and Society Review* 24, no. 3: 781–806.

———. 1994. "The Politics of Reasonableness" [in Hebrew]. *Theory and Criticism* 5: 7–23.

———. 2005. "Without Borders? Notes on Globalization as a Mobility Regime." *Sociological Theory* 23, no. 2: 197–217.

Shavit, Ari. 2005. "After the Disengagement, a Second War of Terror Is to Be Expected" [in Hebrew]. *Ha'aretz*, January 1, 2005. www.haaretz.co.il/misc/1.1015704 (accessed April 18, 2012).

Shehadeh, Raja. 1982. *The Third Way: A Journal of Life in the West Bank*. London and New York: Quartet Books.

———. 1997. *From Occupation to Interim Accords: Israel and the Palestinian Territories*. Boston: Kluwer Law International.

———. 2002. *Strangers in the House: Coming of Age in Occupied Palestine*. South Royalton, VT: Steerforth Press.

———. 2003. *When the Birds Stopped Singing: Life in Ramallah Under Siege*. South Royalton, VT: Steerforth Press.

Shehadeh, Raja, and Jonathan Kuttab. 1980. *The West Bank and the Rule of Law*. Geneva: International Commission of Jurists.

Shenhav, Yehuda. 2006. *The Arab Jews: A Postcolonial Reading of Nationalism, Religion, and Ethnicity*. Stanford: Stanford University Press.

———. 2012. *Beyond the Two States Solution: A Jewish Political Essay*. London: Polity Press.

Shiftan, Dan. 1999. *Disengagement: Israel and the Palestinian Entity* [in Hebrew]. Haifa: Haifa University and Zmora Bitan.

Shlaim, Avi. 2000. *The Iron Wall: Israel and the Arab World*. London: Allen Lane, Penguin Press.

Shohat, Ella. 2006. *Taboo Memories, Diasporic Voices*. Durham, NC: Duke University Press.

Simon, Joshua, ed. 2011. *Solution 196–213: United States of Palestine-Israel*. Berlin: Sternberg Press.

Sivan, Eyal, and Eric Hazan. 2012. *Un État commun entre le Jourdain et la mer*. Paris: La Fabrique éditions.

Skinner, Quentin. 1997. "The State." In *A Companion to Contemporary Political Philosophy*, ed. Robert E. Goodin and Philip Pettit. Oxford: Blackwell.

Smooha, Sammy. 1997. "Ethnic Democracy: Israel as an Archetype." *Israel Studies* 2, no. 2: 198–241.

Spruyt, Hendrik. 1994. *The Sovereign State and Its Competitors: An Analysis of Systems Change*. Princeton, NJ: Princeton University Press.

Stein, Yael. 1997. *The Quiet Deportation: Revocation of Residency of East Jerusalem Palestinians*. B'Tselem and HaMoked [Center for the Defence of the Individual] report. www.btselem.org/sites/default/files/publication/199704_quiet_deportation_eng.doc (accessed April 18, 2012).

———. 2001. "Standard Routine: Beatings and Abuse of Palestinians by Israeli Security Forces During the Al-Aqsa Intifada." B'Tselem report. www.btselem.org/sites/default/files/publication/200105_standard_routine_eng.doc (accessed April 18, 2012).

Stendhal, Uri. 1992. *Israeli Arabs: Between the Hammer and the Anvil* [in Hebrew]. Jerusalem: Academon.

Stoler, Ann Laura. 2006. "On Degrees of Imperial Sovereignty." *Public Culture* 18, no. 1: 125–46.

Suissa, Shlomi. 2004. *Not All It Seems: Preventing Palestinians Access to Their Lands West of*

the Separation Barrier in the Tulkarm-Qalqiliya Area. B'Tselem report. www.btselem
.org/sites/default/files/publication/200406_qalqiliya_tulkarm_barrier_eng.pdf (accessed May 12, 2012).

Swirski, Shlomo. 2005. *The Price of Vanity: The Price Israel Pays (1967–2005)* [in Hebrew].
Tel Aviv: ADVA Center, MAPA Publishers. 2008 updated version in English, *The Burden of Occupation: The Cost of the Occupation to Israeli Society, Polity and Economy.*
http://israeli-occupation.org/docs/shlomo-swirski_the-burden-of%20occupation
_200811.pdf (accessed March 1, 2012).

Swirski, Shlomo, Etty Konor-Attias, and Alon Etkin. 2002. *Government Funding of the Israeli Settlements in the West Bank, Gaza Strip and Golan Heights in the 1990s of Local
Governments, Home Construction, and Road Building.* Tel Aviv: Adva Center. English
summary, www.adva.org/uploaded/Government%20Funding%20of%20the%20Israeli
%20Settlements%202002.pdf; Hebrew, www.adva.org/UPLOADED/mimun%20mem
shalti%20be%20esha%20&%20golan.pdf (both accessed May 12, 2012).

Swirski, Shlomo, and Ilan Pappe, eds. 1992. *Intifada: A Look from the Inside* [in Hebrew].
Tel Aviv: Mifras.

Talmon, Jacob. 1980. "An Open Letter to the Historian Menachem Begin from the Historian Jacob Talmon" [in Hebrew]. *Ha'aretz,* March 31, 1980.

Tamari, Salim. 1992. "The Palestinians in the West Bank and Gaza: Sociology of Dependence." In *Intifada: A Look from the Inside,* ed. Shlomo Swirski and Ilan Pappe, 7–28.
Tel Aviv: Mifras.

———. 1996. *Palestinian Refugee Negotiations: From Madrid to Oslo II (Final Status Issues).* Washington, DC: Institute for Palestinian Studies.

———. 2001. *Reinterpreting the Historical Records: The Uses of Palestinian Refugee Archives for Social Science Research and Policy Analysis.* Jerusalem: Institute for Palestine Studies.

Tawil-Suri, Helga. 2011. "Kalandia Checkpoint as Place and Non-Place." *Space and Culture* 14, no. 1: 4–26.

Teveth, Shabtai. 1970. *The Cursed Blessing: The Story of Israel's Occupation of the West
Bank.* Translated by Myra Bank. London: Weidenfeld & Nicolson.

Tilly, Charles. 1990. *Coercion, Capital, and European States, AD 990–1990.* Oxford:
Blackwell.

Tobi, Y. 2001. "Israel's Policy with Respect to the Gaza Strip and Its Refugees, November
1956–March 1957." *Jama'a* 7: 9–53.

United Kingdom. House of Commons. International Development Committee. 2004.
Development, Assistance, and the Occupied Palestinian Territories. www.publications
.parliament.uk/pa/cm200304/cmselect/cmintdev/230/230.pdf (accessed February
28, 2012).

United Nations. Economic and Social Council. Commission on Human Rights. 2004.
"Economic, Social and Cultural Rights: The Right to Food." Report by Special Rap-

porteur Jean Ziegler. www.righttofood.org/new/PDF/ECN4200410.pdf (accessed February 28, 2012).

United Nations. Office for the Coordination of Humanitarian Affairs, Occupied Palestinian Territories [cited as OCHA]. 2005–6. "Access and Movement (Barrier and Checkpoints." Periodical reports. www.ochaopt.org/reports.aspx?id=105&page=4 (accessed February 28, 2012).

———. 2006. *West Bank Closure Count and Analysis.* http://unispal.un.org/pdfs/WB 0106.pdf (accessed April 18, 2012).

———. 2007a. "The Closure of the Gaza Strip: The Economic and Humanitarian Consequences." www.ochaopt.org/documents/Gaza_Special_Focus_December_2007.pdf (accessed April 18, 2012).

———. 2007b. "Access and Movement." Periodical reports. www.ochaopt.org/reports .aspx?id=105&page=3 (accessed April 18, 2012).

———. 2008. *Gaza Strip Inter-Agency Humanitarian Fact Sheet.* www.ochaopt.org/doc uments/Gaza_Interagency_Factsheet_2008_May.pdf (accessed April 18, 2012).

———. 2009 (January). *Gaza Humanitarian Situation Report.* www.ochaopt.org/doc uments/ocha_opt_gaza_humanitarian_situation_report_2009_01_07_english.pdf (accessed April 18, 2012).

———. 2010. *The Humanitarian Impact of Israeli-Imposed Restrictions on Access to Land and Sea in the Gaza Strip.* www.ochaopt.org/documents/ocha_opt_special_ focus_2010_08_19_english.pdf (accessed April 18, 2012).

———. 2011. *Easing the Blockade: Assessing the Humanitarian Impact on the Population of the Gaza Strip.* www.ochaopt.org/documents/ocha_opt_special_easing_the_ blockade_2011_03_english.pdf (accessed April 18, 2012).

———. 2012. *Humanitarian Monitor.* Monthly. www.ochaopt.org/reports.aspx?id=118 &page=1 (accessed February 28, 2012).

United Nations. Relief and Work Agency for Palestinian Refugees in the Near East [cited as UNRWA]. 2007. "Emergency Appeal." unispal.un.org/UNISPAL.NSF/0/CBAFB54 B8CB98886852574720048B002w (accessed April 30, 2012).

Weizman, Eyal. 2007. *Hollow Land: Israel's Architecture of Occupation.* London: Verso.

———. 2009. "Lawfare in Gaza: Legislative Attack." *Open Democracy*, March 1, 2009. www.opendemocracy.net/article/legislative-attack (accessed April 18, 2012).

Yahya, Adil. 1990. "The Role of the Refugee Camps." In *Intifada: Palestine at the Crossroads*, ed. Roger Heacock and Jamal R. Nassar, 91–106. New York: Praeger.

Yakobson, Alexander, and Amnon Rubinstein. 2009. *Israel and the Family of Nations: The Jewish Nation-State and Human Rights.* New York: Routledge.

Yanov, Ezra. 1975. "The Gaza Strip: A Reservoir of Cheap Labour." In *Documents from Israel, 1967–1973*, ed. Uri Davis and Norton Mezvinsky, 55–59. London: Ithaca Press.

Yiftachel, Oren. 2006. *Ethnocracy: Land and Identity Politics in Israel/Palestine.* Philadelphia: University of Pennsylvania Press.

INDEX